How to Cook Gluten-Free

How to Cook Gluten-Free

Over 150 Recipes That Really Work

Elizabeth Barbone

Photography by Tina Rupp

LAKE ISLE PRESS NEW YORK

Published by:
Lake Isle Press, Inc.
2095 Broadway, Suite 301
New York, NY 10023
(212) 273-0796
E-mail: lakeisle@earthlink.net

Distributed to the trade by:
National Book Network, Inc.
4501 Forbes Boulevard, Suite 200
Lanham, MD 20706
1(800) 462-6420
www.nbnbooks.com

Library of Congress Control Number: 2011941417

ISBN-13: 978-1-891105-51-7
ISBN-10: 1-891105-51-5

Book and cover design: Liz Trovato

Editors: Stephanie White
        Jennifer Sit

This book is available at special sales discounts for bulk purchases as premiums or special editions,
 including customized covers. For more information, contact the publisher at
(212) 273-0796 or by e-mail, lakeisle@earthlink.net.

First edition
Printed in China

10 9 8 7 6 5 4 3 2 1

*To my mom and dad, Chris and Ralph
Barbone, for teaching me about love, life,
and good food.*

*To my husband, Greg Meuer, for making life
a delicious adventure. I love you.*

Acknowledgments

More than ten years ago I decided I wanted to teach people how to cook gluten-free. Back then the response to "gluten-free" was "what's that?" How things have changed! What hasn't changed is that my life is still filled with the love and support of amazing and tenderhearted people. I can't think of beginning this list of thank yous without first thanking you, my readers and students. Every lesson and recipe in this book is for you. Thanks for always encouraging me and cooking along with me each step of the way.

Four years ago, Hiroko Kiiffner took a chance on me when she decided to publish my first book, *Easy Gluten-Free Baking*. Her support, from our very first conversation, has never wavered. She's a champion most authors only dream of having. My deepest thanks to Hiroko for believing in this book and bringing *How to Cook Gluten-Free* to life in such a beautiful and meaningful way.

Some writers dread hearing from their editorial team, not me! I owe Stephanie White and Jennifer Sit a huge (huge!) thanks for the way they wrangled my manuscript into the book it has become. They're organized, thoughtful, detail-oriented, and, best of all, an absolute delight to work with! Thank you, ladies, for everything you've done.

When Tina Rupp and food stylist Toni Brogan agreed to create photographs for my book, I was thrilled. (They were the force behind the photos in *Easy Gluten-Free Baking*.) Working with them again was a dream come true. Joining them was prop stylist Leslie Siegel. Together, Tina, Toni, and Leslie worked seamlessly to produce photos that I fell in love with at first glance.

Liz Trovato must have a magic wand tucked away somewhere in her studio! Somehow she took my pile of words, lessons, and photographs, and, from that jumble, created a book that's a joy to the eye.

Working with Maureen Murphy and Gail Failing at Price Chopper Supermarkets has never, even after five years, felt like work. Maureen and Gail organize fabulous gluten-free events and listen—really listen—to the needs of the gluten-free community. Thank you, ladies, for caring about the gluten-free community so deeply.

The team at WNYT helps me spread the word about gluten-free eating. Thank you especially to Ben Gorenstein, Tim Drawbridge, and Dan Bazile. Cooking with you guys in three minutes (on live TV!) is way more fun than it has any right to be!

A little over a year ago, I wandered into Stuyvesant Photo thinking about making the leap from my tiny (safe) point and shoot camera to the big (scary-to-me) world of DSL, aka "grown-up cameras." Peter Harris held my hand during the leap. Without his guidance, I never would have taken the photos that make up the how-to's in this book. Thanks, Peter, for sharing your love of photography with a newbie like me.

Not only did I not own a "grown-up" camera before this project began, I had no idea how the "computer side" of photography worked. (I am a cook; not a tech person!) Enter Nick. Through our classes at the Apple Store, of all places, Nick taught me everything I needed to know from saving my pictures safely to basic photo editing. His gentle guidance turned a once overwhelming project into a joyful artistic endeavor.

A true friend is someone who shows up when your kitchen is a mess and doesn't bat an eye. Rachel Heintz is that friend! While I tested recipes, Rachel would often stop by when my kitchen was, well, let's just say it wasn't neat. Not once did she exclaim, "Look at this mess!" Instead, she'd ask how things were going, cheering me up on rough days and rejoicing with me when things went right. The fact that she and her husband, Harry, are two of my favorite people to share a meal with is just the icing on a very sweet cake.

I can't believe it's been fourteen years since I ran into Michele Giglio-Uy at culinary school in a beautiful act of kismet. Since then, our friendship has blossomed into one of the joys of my life. Michele and I chat about everything, from our love of food to the most personal moments of life. Thanks to Michele for always believing in me and my work.

One source of unwavering support in my life is Rita Brenenstuhl, whom I lovingly call my "Aunt Rita." She has supported this project in numerous ways, including lending me the lens that I used to take photos for the book. Thank you, Rita, for believing in me from the very beginning.

Much of this book came together at Jessica Brearton's kitchen table. From a vague idea to the final piece, Jessica has supported me all along the way. She also whisked me out to the movies when I needed to get away from the work for a few hours! And, as always, Jessica makes me laugh, think, and enjoy life the way only a true sister-friend can. A million thanks to Jessica.

It's no exaggeration to say that this book never would have happened without my mom, Chris Barbone. After high school, when I was supposed to go to college to pursue a degree in teaching, she didn't freak out when I said, "I think I'd rather go do culinary school." While many people thought I'd made a big mistake with this choice, my mom's support never wavered and, to this day, she continues to be my biggest advocate. Thanks, Mom, for being the best mother a woman could ever hope to have.

I'm so incredibly fortunate that my husband, Greg Meuer, is by my side through the unpredictable jumble of heartache and joy that is life. Our relationship is the constant bright spot in my life. There's no one I'd rather spend time with, talk to, and just *be* with. Without his unconditional love, I would have given up on *How to Cook Gluten-Free* before I even started. Thank you, honey, for not letting me do that.

Contents

Introduction

Making dinner. How do those words make you feel? For a while, I felt a little twinge of dread at the thought of putting dinner on the table—but not because I had started eating gluten-free. I mean, I went to cooking school, wasn't I supposed to approach each meal with rapturous wonder? The answer to that: Ha!

Life is the answer to why I started dreading dinner. Life gets busy, doesn't it? I'd work until five-ish, look at the clock, and think, "Hmm . . . what am I making tonight?" This, pardon the pun, is a recipe for dinner disaster—or at least dinner boredom. Over time, I ended up making an increasingly narrow roster of recipes. I got bored and more than a little frustrated with my dinner funk. I needed—no, I *wanted*—to liven things up.

Online, I mentioned my dinner-making problem to my readers. The response was incredible. Many people shared that they too were wrestling with the same problem. They had hungry gluten-free families and needed solutions for getting meals on the table.

I headed into the kitchen, not just for myself but also for my readers who were looking for quick-cook family meals. Although quick recipes have been around forever, many of those recipes rely on convenience products or ingredients that are not gluten-free. My challenge was simple: To create easy recipes for gluten-free eating that I could make on my busiest days.

The recipes in this book are the result of that challenge. Most are quick enough for weeknight meals, a few are perfect for the weekend. And since quick cooking wouldn't be complete without sandwiches, burgers, and pizza, you'll find recipes for those—and breads, buns, and pizza crusts—in the book, too!

All of the recipes reflect my practical cooking style. Even though I'm a graduate of The Culinary Institute of America, I'm not a foodie or whatever it is they are calling folks who cook with rare ingredients these days. All of the ingredients in this book can be found at your local grocery store.

In addition to using easy to-find ingredients, I also use easy cooking techniques throughout the book. If you're new to cooking, look through the book for basic "how-to" lessons. From making bread crumbs to cooking gluten-free pasta, I'll teach you how easy gluten-free cooking can be!

The recipes in this book got me out of my cooking funk. Now when I think about making dinner, I no longer dread it. And that makes my life much tastier! I hope you enjoy making these meals for your family.

Why I Went Gluten-Free

You know that old expression about truth being stranger than fiction? When it comes to my journey to gluten-free living, I feel like I've lived it.

For a long time I was known as the gluten-free baker who didn't need to eat gluten-free. I loved the challenge of baking gluten-free and the joy of serving the gluten-free community. I even wrote a book on gluten-free baking. Having been born with multiple food allergies, I understood firsthand the challenges of living on a medically restricted diet.

Fast forward to 2008. After being diagnosed with thyroid issues and severe anemia, I knew I needed to be tested for celiac disease. It almost seemed silly—I'd spent so long with gluten-free folks and now, here I was, having to be tested.

There was a little hiccup during my testing. I've always had a borderline allergy to wheat. If I ate too much of it I'd get terrible hives, and working with raw wheat flour would make my hands break out. So even before I went gluten-free, my diet didn't include a lot of wheat or gluten. After testing, my blood work came back with elevated numbers, but not clear celiac disease.

My doctor and I talked about how to proceed. There was a good chance that my numbers weren't high because I ate very, very little gluten prior to the test. Together we decided that I should go gluten-free and retest my blood later to see what would happen. The result? My numbers dropped to almost zero. Taking this and everything else into account—my history, my symptoms, the fact that I felt better gluten-free—eating gluten-free was clearly the way to go. Did I have an endoscopy? No, I didn't. Does that bother me? Not really. My follow-up blood work has always been zero since going gluten-free, and on the accidental occasion I get exposed to gluten, I feel terrible. My path to eating gluten-free was a bit unusual. However, working with my doctor I found what was best for me. Since that first blood test, I've been proudly 100 percent gluten-free.

Essential How-to Lessons

Throughout the book, you will find kitchen lessons, referred to as "how-to's," that make cooking a little easier. Below are the lessons I find essential. These techniques are used in various recipes throughout the book. Others lessons, like how to purée soup or make pizza crust, are in the chapters where you'll need them most.

Plan an Easy Meal

You know why I think Thanksgiving is so stressful? If you shouted "The relatives!"—trust me, I understand. But that's not the answer I am looking for—this time. I think Thanksgiving is stressful because of the lack of oven space. You need to roast the turkey, cook the green bean casserole, the dressing, the sweet potatoes. *And* bake pies. Well, you get the point. There is a lot of stuff and only so much space in the oven.

While Thanksgiving is an extreme example, we often plan meals that push our kitchens—and our sanity—to the breaking point. When I think about planning a meal, I think about what equipment I am going to use. And that includes the oven *and* the stove.

Take a look at this meal:

Pan-fried chicken cutlets
Zucchini latkes
Sautéed garlic spinach

Sounds good, right? It does—but I wouldn't want to make it. Let's look at it again:

Pan-fried chicken cutlets (stovetop)
Zucchini latkes (stovetop)
Sautéed garlic spinach (stovetop)

If I had to make this meal, I'd have to cook the chicken while standing at the stove. It requires constant attention. The same goes for the latkes and the spinach. Both require me to stand over the pan. If I want to get all the food on the table at the same time, this meal will be stressful. Instead of making three dishes that require my attention at the stove, I'd tweak the meal to look like this:

Oven-roasted chicken with garlic
Zucchini latkes
Spinach salad

The flavors of the meal are the same, but the preparation is not. While the chicken roasts in the oven, I can put together my spinach salad. (As long as I don't dress the salad, it can hang out in the refrigerator until I am ready to serve it.) After I've made the salad, I can focus on making the zucchini latkes. Once the chicken comes out of the oven and begins its rest, I start frying up my latkes. When the latkes are done, the chicken will be ready to serve. All I need to do is pull the salad out of the refrigerator, toss it with the dressing, and my meal is ready!

Thinking about what each part of the meal requires from you and your kitchen equipment is a key to easy menu planning. In addition to not selecting recipes that all require constant attention, I also stay away from pairing recipes that require the oven to be at different temperatures. It's annoying to have something cooking in the oven only to realize that your side dish needs to be cooked 50 degrees higher than your main course.

Read and Prepare a Recipe

Have you ever been halfway through a recipe only to discover you were out of an essential ingredient? While at The Culinary Institute of America, I learned how to avoid this. It's a technique called "mise en place," which means "everything in its place." When applied to a recipe, it means that you first look over the recipe, set out all the ingredients, prepare any ingredients that call for it (like dicing onions, mincing garlic, and so on), and gather up the required equipment. While it sounds like it might be time consuming, it is actually time saving! If you read and prepare your recipe, you'll never be in the middle of preparing dinner only to discover you are out of an essential ingredient. Mise en place makes cooking easier!

Mise en Place

1. Read the whole recipe—the ingredients list, the instructions, and any notes—to familiarize yourself with the process. Take note of cooking times and make sure they fit into the time you've allotted to the recipe.

2. Gather all the ingredients together. This means *everything*. From the most essential to the smallest amount of spice. Get it all out on your counter. Don't have room on your countertop? Put a rimmed baking sheet or two on the kitchen table and fill them with the ingredients you need.

3. Gather together all the necessary equipment. If you are going to be chopping vegetables, get out the cutting board and knife. Making pasta? Get out your pot and set a colander in the sink. By having all your tools out, you won't need to rummage through your cabinets while your hands are dirty or while something overcooks on the stove because you are hunting for a lid.

4. Adjust the oven racks and preheat the oven when the recipe says to. Making a recipe that calls for the grill to be preheated? This is the time to do it.

5. Prepare all the ingredients. Some recipes call for ingredients like this:

    1 medium onion, finely diced
    8 ounces cheddar cheese, grated
    (2 cups)

    Any instruction that follows an ingredient is your prep work. For these examples, you want to peel and chop the onion and grate the cheese—and you should end up with 2 cups of grated cheese.

    Sometimes you're told to do your prep work *before* you measure the ingredient. In cases like these:

    2 tablespoons diced green bell pepper
    6 cups shredded zucchini

    it means you have to dice part of a green pepper and measure out 2 tablespoons (put the rest away for another use) and shred as many zucchini of whatever size you have on hand to make it to 6 cups.

6. Begin the recipe. And have fun!

Stock Your Kitchen: Cookware

Like everything else, there are a lot of options in cookware. A good rule that holds true from brand to brand is that the heavier the piece of cookware, the better it will perform. If your cookware is really thin, it can overheat easily and cause your food to burn. (The exception to this rule? Woks! They tend to be thin and work beautifully.)

Since it can be expensive to buy new cookware, I like to buy one piece at a time. It is a great way to build a collection. I can see what I like, or don't like, about a piece and let that guide my next purchase.

In this book, you will see me calling for a "small pot," "medium skillet," and so on. The following is a rough guide to finding the best cookware.

Pots

My favorite are heavy-bottomed, thick-walled pots with tight-fitting lids. This ensures that foods heat evenly and will keep food from scorching. What to avoid: thin cookware.

Essentials

- Small pot: 2 quarts
- Medium pot: 4 quarts
- Large pot: $5^1/2$ quarts or more (used mainly to make soup and boil pasta)

Nice to Have

Dutch oven: Only a few recipes in this book call for a Dutch oven. If you need other "essential" cookware, stock your kitchen with those pieces first. A Dutch oven, with its heavy bottom and walls, can go from stovetop to oven. Most are made of cast iron and that is what you want to look for. You'll find both uncoated (black) cast-iron and enameled cast-iron Dutch ovens in stores. While both are great, I tend to prefer the enameled Dutch ovens. If you have a traditional uncoated Dutch oven, be sure to season it well, following the manufacturer's directions, before using. (Bit of cookware trivia: some enameled Dutch ovens are called "French ovens.")

Frying Pans

Skillet versus frying pan versus sauté pan. This can be confusing! Here's the lowdown: Skillets and frying pans are the same. They both have flared sides and flat bottoms. Sauté pans have straight sides and flat bottoms. In this book, I use nonstick frying pans and cast-iron or ovenproof skillets.

I like nonstick frying pans. Most nights I pull one out to cook dinner. I like that I can use less oil when preparing food and, as the name says, nothing sticks to them. My favorite is a heavy-bottomed nonstick frying pan. This helps to ensure even cooking. If you don't use nonstick pans, you might need to increase the amount of oil called for in some of the recipes.

What to avoid: Scratched nonstick pans. If you notice the coating of your nonstick pan is heavily scratched, pitted, or in any way coming off, it's time to replace the pan.

Essentials

- Small frying pan: 8 inches
- Medium frying pan: 10 inches
- Large frying pan: 12 inches
- Cast-iron or enameled ovenproof skillet: 12 inches
- Cast-iron or nonstick grill pan

As much as I love my nonstick pans, they aren't always the best for every recipe—and most can't be used in the oven. For recipes that require a skillet, I like to use either my seasoned cast-iron skillet or my enameled skillet. Both are great for even cooking and go into the oven with no problem. Look for a heavy skillet that states it can be used on both the stovetop and in the oven.

If you don't have an outdoor grill, with a grill pan (it's like a cast-iron skillet with raised ridges instead of a flat bottom) you can grill meats, fish, and vegetables on the stovetop. Living in upstate New York where it gets plenty cold and snowy, I use this a lot! In fact, just about all the grilled recipes here call for using a grill pan.

Cast-iron pots and skillets need to be seasoned with oil for the best results. Follow the instructions from the manufacturer on how to season your pan. I've been using my skillet for many years and now it's dark black and basically nonstick. When well cared for, a seasoned cast-iron pan will serve you a long time.

Nice to Have

Frying pan (11 inches): This is an odd size and can be hard to find. However, sometimes a 10-inch can be too small and a 12-inch a little too large. For times like those, I find myself reaching for my 11-inch pan. Is it necessary? No. But it's a nice addition to the kitchen.

Wok: Only one of the dishes here calls for a wok. If you don't have one, you can use a large frying pan. But if you do, you'll be able to make stir-fry dishes so much more easily.

Baking Pans

I use my rimmed baking sheets (known professionally as "half sheet pans") for everything from pizza to roasting vegetables to making cookies, and other baking pans for many different dishes.

Essentials

- Rimmed baking sheets: 18 by 13 by 1 inch
- Loaf pan: 9 by 5 inches
- Large baking pan: 13 by 9 inches
- Cake pans: 8-inch round and 8-inch square
- Muffin pans: regular (12 cavities) and mini (24 cavities)—for muffins, cupcakes, and individual quiches

My baking sheets aren't nonstick. To make them nonstick, I slip a piece of parchment paper

Cooking Tips for Frying Pans and Skillets

I really like nonstick pans! I use nonstick frying pans for many of the recipes in this cookbook. Here are some tips to heating nonstick pans and skillets safely:

1. No matter what you are cooking, never heat a nonstick pan empty. Always put a little oil, even if it is a tiny amount, into the pan. You don't want to overheat a nonstick pan. Having a little oil in the pan will help you to see how hot your pan is getting.

2. For that matter, unless you are using a cast-iron skillet, never heat *any* frying pan empty. You have no way of knowing if an empty pan has overheated. Having a little oil in the pan will prevent you from overheating your pan.

3. Nonstick pans are best used for cooking that requires low to medium heat. Most nonstick cookware should not be heated over 500°F. (Check with the manufacturer of your cookware for specific guidelines.)

4. A well-seasoned cast-iron pan will have a nice buildup of oil in the pan. (This is what you want!) This means that an empty cast-iron skillet will smoke even if you have not put any additional oil in the pan. That said, I still put a light film of oil in the pan if I don't need to heat it to the smoking point.

into the bottom of the pan when needed. I suggest having two or three (or more!) of these handy pans on hand.

I use my loaf pan for making meatloaf and baking bread. The 13 by 9-inch baking pan has all sorts of uses. Cake pans are for cake (of course!) and also for cornbread and casseroles. And muffin pans aren't just for muffins (and cupcakes!)—they're great for individual quiches, too. If the ones you have aren't nonstick (and for some recipes, even if they are), you can always grease them with gluten-free nonstick cooking spray.

Nice to Have

Roasting pan (15 by 11 inches): Great for baking nachos or roasting a chicken—but so is the large baking pan, so don't worry if you don't have one.

Casserole dish ($1^1/2$ to 2 quarts): A pretty one is nice for bringing your baked casserole to the table; an 8-inch square baking pan will hold about the same amount, though.

Ovenproof dessert cups (6 ounces): Also called custard cups or ramekins, you'll need six of these to make the Cheesecake Cups on page 265—and you should make them!

Pie pans (9 inches): Even if you never bake pie, these are handy for when you're breading foods to fry or bake.

How to:
Stock Your Kitchen: Small Equipment

The smallest tools in your kitchen make the biggest difference when cooking. While there are all sorts of gadgets and gizmos available for the kitchen, I stick to the basics. Here's what I love and use all the time.

Cutting

Knives, in my opinion, are the most personal piece of equipment you will use in the kitchen. What feels great in your hand might not feel right to me. A word of warning: some knives can break the bank. Part of selecting a great knife is to find a workable balance between what you love and what you can afford. What to avoid: knives with thin, flimsy blades.

Essentials

Chef's knife: This is the knife I use most often. My favorite is an 8-inch chef's knife with a straight, not serrated, blade. A chef's knife is used for everything from chopping onions to cutting up meat, and most everything in between. For a chef's knife, I recommend heading to a cookware shop. Ask them to show you some knives. Hold them in your hand and find what works best for you.

Serrated knife: This is *the* knife for slicing bread without squishing it.

Vegetable peeler: I really like "Y" peelers (named because the blade is perpendicular to a handle that looks like the letter Y) because they feel good in my hand. But any peeler that does the job is great.

Cutting board: It's a good idea to have two cutting boards in the kitchen. This way, when you prepare meat, you will have another board ready for vegetables or other foods. Using two boards prevents cross-contamination (the transfer of harmful bacteria to one food from another) and, in addition, makes kitchen prep easier. If you don't have two cutting boards in the kitchen, wash your cutting board after each step of food preparation in a bleach solution of 1 tablespoon chlorine bleach to 1 gallon water.

Nice to Have

Paring knife: I don't use my paring knife often but when I have a small job to do, such as hulling strawberries, the small size is nice to have.

Keys to Working with Cutting Boards

1. Designate one board just for meat. Set it on the counter away from where you will be preparing salads, vegetables, and any other uncooked foods.
2. Wash the cutting board you've used for meat (including chicken and fish) as soon as you are done using it.
3. As soon as your cutting board becomes pitted or develops deep grooves, it is time to replace it.

Decorative cutting board for the table:
Sometimes it's nice to put a loaf of bread or some cheese on the table. I keep a small cutting board in the kitchen for times like this. Mine is a pretty wooden board. When selecting a board for the table, pick one you love to look at.

Measuring

Essentials

Nested measuring cups: In this book, I use volume measurements for dry ingredients such as flour. To measure accurately, you'll want a set of nested measuring cups. Your set should include $1/4$-, $1/3$-, $1/2$- and 1-cup measures. I prefer metal to plastic.

Spouted clear (heatproof glass) measuring cups: For liquids, I use clear measuring cups in 1-cup and 2-cup ($1/2$ quart) sizes, with pouring spouts and markings on the side for fractions. They're also great for measuring larger amounts of things like cubed bread or chopped vegetables. The sturdiest cups are made of heatproof glass—so you can use them in the microwave, too!

Nested measuring spoons: Like nested measuring cups, measuring spoons help to ensure accurate measuring. When a recipe calls for 1 teaspoon salt, for example, you'll want to reach for your measuring spoons. Look for a set that includes $1/8$-, $1/4$-, $1/2$-, and 1-teaspoon and 1-tablespoon measures. Unless otherwise called for, all measurements should be level, not heaping. Run a flat edge across the top of your measuring spoon to level off the ingredient.

Measuring Dry and Wet Ingredients

For dry measuring cups and spoons:
Scoop the dry ingredients into the measuring cup or spoon and level the ingredients with a straight-edge tool. Take care not to pack down the ingredients when measuring.

For liquid measuring cups:
Place the liquid measuring cup on a level surface, like your kitchen counter, and crouch down to check the desired measurement at eye level. Some brands—like the Oxo brand—can be read from a standing or sitting position. These, too, should be placed on a level surface before reading.

Mixing

Essentials

Mixing bowls: A good set of mixing bowls is invaluable in the kitchen. I love my nested set. It includes $1^1/2$-, 2-, and 3-quart bowls and is easy to store.

Wooden spoons: Ah, what would I do without my wooden spoons? Notice I said *spoons*, not spoon, because having a few wooden spoons on hand is a good idea. When making a meal, you might need two. And it's easier to grab another wooden spoon than it is to have to stop and wash your spoon several times while making a recipe. Since wooden spoons can hold on to gluten, any spoons used in your pre-gluten-free days should be tossed or passed along to a non-gluten-free friend.

Whisks: Nothing can do the job of a whisk but a whisk. With all the different styles of whisks available, you could start a whisk collection in your kitchen! But for this book, you really only need one—although a second smaller whisk is nice to have. The essential one is an 8-inch balloon whisk. It is great for whisking together dry ingredients or stirring a sauce while it cooks. Look for the wires to be of different lengths and closely spaced together.

Nice to Have

Small whisk: There are some whisking jobs, such as whisking together one cup of milk and an egg, where an 8-inch balloon whisk is too big. For these jobs, you could use a fork, but I like to use a small whisk. I think it does a better job and makes quicker work of whisking.

Pastry cutter: Use this when you're making a pie crust or biscuits. Or use your fingers.

Prepping, Cooking, and Serving

Essentials

Box grater: If you don't have a food processor, you'll need a grater to grate cheese and shred vegetables.

Instant-read thermometer: Chicken, ground meats, bread, and some other foods have to be cooked to a minimum temperature to be safe or considered done. How do you know when they've reached the right temperature? Use a thermometer! Take the chicken's temperature by inserting the thermometer into the thickest part (don't let it touch bone, if there are any); follow the same procedure for other solid pieces of meat, meatloafs, and loaves of bread. Within a few seconds, it will show you the internal temperature and you'll know for sure that the food is done.

Kitchen string: For trussing chickens.

Kitchen tongs: For turning meats or grabbing foods while they're cooking, a pair of kitchen tongs is your friend. Look for a pair with a scalloped head that will grab food but not crush or pierce it. I find smooth (non-scalloped) kitchen tongs particularly useless. Food seems to slip right out of their grip. Avoid these.

Ladles: I have a large ladle (4 ounces) for serving soup and a small ladle (2 ounces) for making pancakes.

Large colander: I use my colander for draining pasta and washing fruits and vegetables. Look for one with handles. This allows you to give freshly washed or drained foods a good shake.

Parchment paper: For lining pans and rolling doughs, among other tasks.

Pastry brushes: Lightly coating food with oil is easy with a pastry brush. I use one all the time when I make pizza. My current favorite is made of silicone. They are really easy to clean and I don't worry about them holding onto bacteria if washed correctly.

Slotted spoons: I like to use a plastic slotted spoon because then I don't have to worry about using it with my nonstick cookware. Slotted spoons are handy for scooping delicate food out of a pot.

Spatulas: There seems to be endless varieties of spatulas, from rubber spatulas to pancake flippers.

They all share the same name but do different things. If you're using nonstick pans, it's a good idea to buy plastic spatulas. These are the spatulas I can't live without:

Heatproof rubber: Use this for scraping down the sides of bowls or mixing ingredients. I like to have a selection of rubber spatulas—from small to large—at my disposal in the kitchen.

Pancake flipper: This is used for—of course—pancakes! But I also reach for this spatula when I need to flip something and I want the spatula to flex a little.

Stainless-steel: This is great for flipping hamburgers! It doesn't give or bend, allowing it to totally support whatever you need to flip.

Icing spatula: This is made for icing cakes but I use it for much more than that! The small size makes it ideal to use for spreading things like peanut butter or mayonnaise on sandwiches or spreading batter in a pan.

Wire cooling racks: I use my wire racks all the time for cooling baked goods (this prevents them from getting soggy) and for setting down a hot pan fresh from the stovetop or oven. Look for a rack with a tight grid pattern and small legs to allow for air flow.

Nice to Have

Deep-frying thermometer: If you do a lot of frying, the best way to know if your oil is hot enough is to take its temperature.

Kitchen timer: If you are like me and forget about things, you need a timer. If there's no timer built into your microwave, get either a twisty kind or an electronic one.

Microwave bacon cooker: Cooking bacon in the microwave is quick and easy. I can cook just a slice or two whenever I want some for a sandwich. Plus, I don't have to clean a greasy pan! While there are many types of bacon cookers available, my favorite is the flat tray style with a raised cooking area so the bacon can drain.

Rolling pin. Really handy when you need to roll out a pizza crust or cookie dough evenly.

Salad bowl: Just as it's nice to have a pretty cutting board to bring to the table, a salad in a decorative salad bowl (and served with salad tongs) seems to taste better!

Small colander: When rinsing a can of beans or washing a cluster of grapes, I reach for my small colander.

Appliances

You can cook without these, but believe me, they'll make your life much easier. And you'll have more fun cooking, then!

Blender: I don't use my blender all the time, but when I want to make a puréed soup, nothing else can do quite the same job.

Bread machine: While I don't think a bread machine is a requirement for gluten-free baking, one can be nice to have. Look for a machine with a horizontal bread pan and two mixing paddles. I prefer machines that allow for a custom setting rather than machines that have preset gluten-free settings.

Electric mixer (stand or handheld): If you plan on making your own gluten-free bread (not to mention cookies, cakes, crackers!), you'll probably want to use a mixer. It's also great for mashed potatoes.

Food processor: A food processor is one of those tools that isn't really replicated or duplicated by any other tool in the kitchen. It makes great homemade bread crumbs, pesto, and pie crusts and it chops vegetables quickly and effortlessly. In fact, if you don't like chopping vegetables with a knife, you can use a food processor with great results. Since I make bread crumbs a lot, I like the 14-cup size.

Panini grill: If you like panini as much as I do, this will get a workout!

How to:
Stock Your Kitchen: Food

I always have these foods and spices on hand.

A note about ingredients: All ingredients listed in this book are available gluten-free, of course. But ingredients in prepared foods can change frequently. Always read ingredient labels each time you buy a food, even if it's something you've bought before. If you have any questions, check with the manufacturer to ensure a product's gluten-free status. (You can always call the 1-800 number listed on the product right from the store if you carry a cell phone with you.)

PANTRY

Dried Bread Crumbs

Baking Ingredients
   Baking powder
   Baking soda
   Flours
      – Brown rice flour (available at health food stores and some grocery stores)
      – Cornstarch
      – Gluten-free cornmeal
      – Gluten-free oats
      – Sweet rice flour (sometimes called "glutinous rice flour," available at Asian food markets and online)
      – White rice flour (available at Asian food markets and grocery stores)

Xanthan gum (available at health food stores and some grocery stores)

Sugars
Granulated (white)

Dark brown

Powdered

Fats and Oils
Canola oil

Gluten-free nonstick cooking spray

Olive oil

Vegetable oil

Vegetable shortening

Vinegars
Apple cider

Balsamic

Red wine

White wine

Spices and Flavorings
Kosher salt

Table salt

Black peppercorns

Chili powder

Dried basil

Dried dill

Dried oregano

Dried thyme

Granulated garlic

Granulated onion

Ground cinnamon and/or cinnamon sticks

Ground cumin

Ground nutmeg

Paprika (smoked and traditional)

Pure vanilla extract

Red pepper flakes

Condiments
Hot pepper sauce (I like Tabasco)

Ketchup

Maple syrup

Prepared mustard

Gluten-free soy sauce

Dried Fruits
Cherries

Raisins

Gluten-Free Pasta
Elbow macaroni

Fettuccini

Penne

Small shells

Spaghetti

Rice
Brown rice

Long-grain white (basmati, jasmine, Carolina Gold)

Short-grain white (sushi, Arborio)

Canned Goods
Petite diced tomatoes (14.5-ounce cans)

Diced tomatoes (14.5- and 28-ounce cans)

Whole tomatoes (28-ounce cans)

Tomato paste (6-ounce cans)

Tomato sauce (8-, 14.5-, and 28-ounce cans)*

Beans (14- to 15-ounce cans)

Mushrooms (if not using fresh)

Olives

*Don't confuse tomato sauce with spaghetti sauce. Tomato sauce is sold in cans and spaghetti sauce, which is thicker and more heavily flavored, is usually sold in glass jars or is clearly labeled "spaghetti sauce."

Anchovies
Clams (chopped and/or whole baby)
Salmon (pouches are great!)
Tuna

Fresh Vegetables**
Onions
Garlic
Russet potatoes
Red or white potatoes
Sweet potatoes

**Yes, these vegetables are best kept in the pantry! Just don't buy and store so much that they start to sprout and go bad. If you live someplace really hot, it's okay to store them in the refrigerator. But again, use them up soon—especially potatoes, which don't really like the fridge.

REFRIGERATOR
Dairy
Unsalted butter
Milk
Eggs
Cheddar cheese
Feta cheese
Mozzarella cheese (I prefer fresh)
Parmesan cheese (a hunk to grate)
Provolone cheese

Flaxseed meal (ground flaxseed)

Fresh Fruits
Apples (I love Granny Smiths!)
Blueberries (in season)
Lemons (always!)
Peaches (in season)

Fresh Vegetables
Asparagus (in season)
Bell peppers (red and/or green)
Broccoli
Cucumbers
Fresh herbs
Grape tomatoes
Green beans
Lettuce/greens
Mushrooms
Scallions (also called green onions)
Spinach
Zucchini and/or yellow squash

Meats
Sausage (chouriço or chorizo, pepperoni, bratwursts, kielbasa, etc.)
Smoked ham

FREEZER
Baked Goods
Sliced bread
Corn tortillas

Chicken Stock (homemade)

Tomato Sauce (homemade)

Vegetables
Chopped broccoli
Chopped spinach
Corn kernels
Peas and/or peas and carrots

Replace Wheat Flour and Similar Common Ingredients in Cooking

Use this guide to easily replace small amounts of wheat flour or other ingredients in cooking recipes. Replacing wheat flour for baking is different. For baking, only use the gluten-free flour replacements listed in the individual recipes.

If your recipe calls for . . .

- **food to be lightly dusted with flour**:

  - Use white rice flour. White rice flour doesn't impart any flavor to take away from your meal. Look for a finely ground flour for the best texture. The white rice flour found at Asian markets has a wonderful silky texture.

  - Use brown rice flour. Brown rice flour can leave a bit of a coarse texture and a bit of nutty flavor.

  - Use corn flour (very finely ground cornmeal). Just know that corn flour adds a mild corn flavor to a dish.

- **dried bread crumbs for breading or binding foods**: Use gluten-free dried bread crumbs. See page 32 for a how-to.

  - Don't have gluten-free bread crumbs on hand for breading? Use finely crushed nuts, such as almonds. To prepare nuts for breading, pulse whole nuts in a food processor until they are finely ground. (Be sure your guests don't have a nut allergy

when serving something that has been breaded with nuts.) Crushed nuts make a wonderful breading. They can be a little heavy when used as a binder.

  - Don't have gluten-free bread crumbs for binding? Use crushed gluten-free corn or rice cereal.

- **fresh bread crumbs**: Use fresh gluten-free bread. See page 32 for a how-to.

- **canned condensed soup**: Use homemade condensed soup. See page 131 for how to make several varieties.

- **soy sauce**: Use gluten-free soy sauce or gluten-free tamari in equal amounts.

- **white sauce**. Use sweet rice flour to replace the wheat flour in an equal amount when making a white sauce, following the recipe as written. See page 46 for a how-to.

- **gravy thickened with wheat flour**: Use sweet rice flour in an equal amount or half the amount of cornstarch. (If a recipe calls for 2 tablespoons wheat flour, use 2 tablespoons sweet rice flour or 1 tablespoon cornstarch.) A gravy made with cornstarch should not be frozen because it will become watery when thawed. For a how-to on gluten-free gravy and a recipe, see page 47.

How to:
Make Substitutions for Special Diets

In addition to all being gluten-free, some recipes in this book are soy-free and/or nut-free. Unless your diet dictates it, use the ingredients called for in each recipe for the very best results. But if you need to exclude more than gluten, soy, and nuts, use this handy substitution guide.

A quick note about making substitutions: When you replace ingredients, changes to the final dish will occur. I wish this weren't true, but it is. In this substitution guide, I've noted what the original ingredient adds to a dish and what changes to expect when making a replacement. The most dramatic changes occur when eggs are replaced in baked goods. Making several changes at once (both egg- and corn-free modifications, for example) will result in more dramatic changes than replacing just one ingredient.

Milk

Whether powdered or liquid, milk contributes greatly to dishes. Milk:

- Moistens dry ingredients
- Binds ingredients together
- Provides fat, when 1%, 2%, or whole is used
- Contributes to the shelf life
- Adds flavor
- Helps food brown
- Provides structure and texture to baked goods

When milk is replaced, the following effects can occur:

- The item will not brown as much.
- The item might be less creamy.
- The item might be sweeter, depending on which milk substitute is used.
- The item might not rise as well.

Replacing milk in a recipe is easier than you might guess. Find a milk substitute you like the flavor of and use it measure for measure. To substitute for milk in a recipe, try the following:

- Equal amounts of gluten-free rice milk or soy milk. Since rice milk and soy milk are sweeter than cow's milk, you might want to reduce the sweetener in the recipe. Try removing 1 tablespoon of the sugar and adjust the recipe based on your personal taste.
- Equal amounts of Vance's DariFree milk substitute, reconstituted according to the package instructions.

Butter

Butter in Cooking

For cooking, it's pretty straightforward: Replace butter with equal amounts of olive oil or any liquid vegetable oil.

Butter in Baking

Butter in baking works differently than butter in cooking. When butter is present in a baked good, it:

- Tenderizes
- Adds moisture and flavor
- Increases shelf life
- Carries flavor
- Contributes to flakiness
- Provides color

- Adds volume to baked goods when creamed

Recipes made without butter will look more anemic than their butter-filled counterparts. They will also lack some flavor, and they might rise differently. How do you cope with this? You can:

- Replace the butter with another solid fat (shortening or lard).

- If possible, brush the baked good with a beaten egg prior to baking.

- Add an artificial butter flavor. LorAnn Oils makes an imitation butter flavor that is gluten-free and dairy-free

- Add a pinch of salt. You don't want anything you bake to be salty, of course, but salt has the ability to bring out the flavor in baked

---

Solid for Solid: Why NOT To Replace Butter with a Liquid Fat

When you see butter in a baking recipe, you'll want to replace it with another solid fat for the best results. Why? When butter is creamed together with sugar in a baking recipe, the creaming method captures air bubbles and acts as a leavener. If you replace butter with a liquid fat, you lose out on this important benefit. So liquid fats, such as olive oil, can lead to a heavy finished baked good, or one that might spread greatly when baked instead of rising.

Vegetable shortening, palm oil, or lard work well as solid fats in baking, depending on your overall diet.

---

goods. Use this to your advantage.

- Add more flavoring. If you are making muffins, add a splash more vanilla extract, or orange oil, or lemon zest. You get the point.

Here are my favorite butter replacements when baking:

To replace butter with lard: Replace butter equally with lard. If the recipe calls for $1/2$ cup (8 tablespoons) butter, use $1/2$ cup lard. Lard is my favorite butter replacement—it produces the best results. Be sure to use fresh lard. It shouldn't have an off-putting aroma.

To replace butter with vegetable shortening:

$1/4$ cup butter	= $1/4$ cup shortening
	+ $1^1/2$ teaspoons water
$1/3$ cup butter	= $1/3$ cup shortening
	+ 2 teaspoons water
$1/2$ cup butter	= $1/2$ cup shortening
	+ 3 teaspoons water
$2/3$ cup butter	= $2/3$ cup shortening
	+ 4 teaspoons water
$3/4$ cup butter	= $3/4$ cup shortening
	+ 1 tablespoon water
	+ $1^1/2$ teaspoons water
1 cup butter	= 1 cup shortening
	+ 2 tablespoons water

I like Crisco's vegetable shortening. Try Spectrum if you need soy-free.

To replace butter with margarine: Most margarine is not dairy-free. If you find a dairy-free margarine, read the package to make sure it is intended for baking. Margarine contains water and this will cause baked goods to spread. I like Earth Balance's margarine, but I think solid vegetable shortening is a better choice than margarine.

Eggs

Cooking without eggs can be tough. Different rules for replacing eggs in cooking and baking apply.

Eggs in Cooking

For breading (when the recipe calls for meat to be dipped in an egg mixture): Replace each egg with 1 tablespoon ground flaxseed and 3 tablespoons hot water. Whisk the mixture together and allow to stand for 5 minutes before using.

For sauces, custards, puddings, and dishes like penne alla carbonara (where the egg is really important for flavor or body): I don't think egg replacements work well in these recipes. And goodness knows I've tried! There are lots of wonderful recipes in this book that don't use egg-based sauces.

Eggs in Baking

Eggs are a vital element in baked goods. Understanding the many roles they play helps determine the best replacement for eggs in your baked good. Eggs:

- Aid in the leavening process
- Provide critical structure
- Add fat, thereby adding smoothness and flavor
- Add and retain moisture
- Add color and "gloss" when applied as an egg wash
- Impart a delicate flavor

Baking without eggs might produce the following results:

- Items don't rise as well.
- Baked goods don't brown as well.
- The texture might be drier.
- The flavor might be altered.

Depending on your diet, select one of the following egg substitutes for your egg-free baking. All replacements here are for 1 large egg. Therefore, if a recipe calls for 2 large eggs, double the replacement. As mentioned above, egg replacements do not work in custards or puddings.

Flaxseed meal: I think ground flaxseed makes the best egg substitution. For 1 large egg, use 1 tablespoon ground flaxmeal plus 2 tablespoons of hot water. Allow mixture to stand for 8 to 10 minutes.

Ener-G Egg Replacer: To replace 1 large egg, use 1 tablespoon oil, 1 tablespoon Ener-G Egg Replacer, and 2 tablespoons water. (The oil is needed to replicate the yolk.) Whisk all the ingredients together in a small bowl before adding to your recipe.

Flax- and potato-free egg replacer: For those who need to avoid both flaxseed and potato starch (found in Ener-G Egg Replacer), to replace 1 large egg use 1 tablespoon oil, 2 tablespoons water, 2 teaspoons baking powder, and 1 teaspoon cornstarch. Whisk all the ingredients together before adding to your recipe.

Corn

If you are corn allergic, it's probably easier to just leave corn kernels out of your cooking (you can replace them with lots of other vegetables), but cornstarch might show up in recipes you want to cook.

Cornstarch

Replace the cornstarch called for in a recipe with 3 parts potato starch and 1 part tapioca starch.

Powdered Sugar

Cornstarch is added to powdered sugar to prevent it from clumping. To make your own powdered sugar, grind 3 cups granulated sugar in a food processor until fine and powdery. Once you have processed the sugar, stir in 2 tablespoons potato starch. Be sure to whisk to combine thoroughly. Store in an airtight container. If your food processor does not have at least a 3-cup capacity, cut the recipe in half.

Potato Starch

To replace potato starch in a recipe, substitute an equal amount of cornstarch.

Corn-Free and Potato-Free?

Use half arrowroot and half tapioca starch. Therefore, if a recipe calls for $1/4$ cup cornstarch, you would use 2 tablespoons arrowroot and 2 tablespoons tapioca starch.

Cheese

Several of the recipes in this book call for cheese. Often it's fine to omit the cheese from the recipe, as in the recipe for Chicken Tenders, without affecting the recipe. However, if cheese is one of the key ingredients, as in Creamy Macaroni and Cheese, you'll either need to choose a different recipe or use a dairy-free cheese. Some folks don't like the taste and texture of dairy-free cheese and many brands don't melt well. (I've found that Daiya cheese does work well for melting.) If you do enjoy dairy-free cheese, use it. It's best to follow the manufacturer's instructions for the cheese as use varies from brand to brand.

Make Fresh Bread Crumbs

Use fresh bread crumbs the day you make them or discard. They can get moldy very quickly.

For every cup of fresh crumbs you need to make, use 4 to 5 slices of bread ($^1/_4$-inch thick).

▲ 1. Slice bread about $^1/_4$-inch thick and cut slices in half.

▲ 2. Place the slices in a food processor.

◀ 3. Process until the crumbs are as fine as you want them.

Make Dried Bread Crumbs

Making homemade dried bread crumbs is easy! When making bread, I bake an extra loaf of bread for making crumbs. I don't season my crumbs. I prefer to keep them plain until I need them.

1 loaf gluten-free bread (white sandwich bread works best)

◀ 1. Cut the bread into $^1/_2$-inch slices.

◀ 2. Cut each slice into quarters. Don't worry about being perfect. You are making bread crumbs. Perfect slices are not important.

◀ 3. Lay the bread out on one or two rimmed baking sheets in a single layer and bake in a 350ºF oven for about 30 minutes.

▲ 4. Remove the baking sheet(s) from the oven and turn over the pieces of bread. Return the baking sheet(s) to the oven and continue to bake until the bread is golden brown, about 20 minutes more. The pieces should be very dry. (Moisture is the enemy of bread crumbs. If your bread slices are moist, your bread crumbs will get moldy when you store them.)

▲ 5. Transfer the bread pieces to wire racks to cool to room temperature. Put one-third of the pieces in a food processor. If your food processor is small, put in as many as it can hold.

▲ 6. Grind until you have fine crumbs. After I grind continuously for a few seconds, I usually switch to pulsing the crumbs. It helps to break down the few large pieces that remain.

▶ 7. Repeat until you've ground all the bread. If your food processor doesn't grind your bread crumbs until they are all as fine as you want, simply sift them through a sieve and regrind the too-big pieces. Store in an airtight container in the pantry for up to 1 month.

Heat Oil

You'll follow the instructions in each recipe for what level of heat to use. But how do you tell if the oil in your pan is hot enough? Good question! This will vary depending on how much oil you are working with and how you're cooking.

For pan-frying (in a frying pan or skillet, with between $1/2$ and 1 inch oil): Hot oil will begin to shimmer a little. It will look like there are little waves moving across the surface of the oil. You don't want your oil for pan-frying to start to smoke. That's too hot! To test oil for pan-frying, I sprinkle a dusting of white rice flour over the surface of the pan. If the flour sizzles, the oil is hot enough.

For sautéing (in a frying pan, with just a little oil—no more than 3 tablespoons): There are three oil stages for sautéing.

1. *Shimmering*: You'll notice that the oil will move around the pan easily when you carefully rotate the pan and that the oil will shimmer a little. The oil should not be smoking.

2. *Lightly smoking*: The oil will begin to smoke. For this stage, you really want to look at the pan. Can you see smoke rising from it? It's ready!

3. *Heavily smoking*: I only use this for stir-fries. You want the oil in the pan to be clearly smoking.

How to:
Pan-Fry

Pan-frying is a quick way to cook food. When done correctly, food leaves the pan light and crispy.

▶ *1. Add about ¹/₂ inch oil to a frying pan. Heat the oil over medium-high heat until it shimmers.*

▲ *2. Place the food into the hot oil. It should sizzle when it hits the oil. Don't crowd your pan; it is better to only cook a few pieces at a time. This will ensure that the oil stays hot. If cooking oil gets too cold, your food can become greasy. Don't move the food right away. Allow it to brown.*

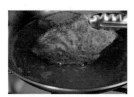

◀ *3. Flip the food (turn it over), using a pair of tongs. Again, allow it to brown.*

◀ *4. Remove the food from the pan and place on a paper towel to drain.*

▶ *5. Check your oil. Has the level in the pan gone down? If it has, add more oil and bring it back up to the right temperature.*

How to:
Bread Foods for Frying or Baking

Breading foods is a simple step that makes a big difference. Often called the "standard breading procedure," this technique is most often used for meat and poultry. In this book, it's also used for mozzarella sticks. No matter what you bread, you want the results to be crispy.

It's fine to bread all the food for a recipe and then fry. You just don't want breaded food to sit around too long, or the breading will get soggy. Have everything else ready to go before you begin breading.

Three large dinner plates or pie pans

White rice flour (seasoned as directed in the recipe)

Egg and maybe milk (amounts as directed in the recipe)

Bread crumbs (seasoned as directed in the recipe)

Rimmed baking sheet

▲ 1. Set up three large dinner plates or pie pans in a line. Fill the first plate with the flour mixture, the next with the egg mixture (you can whisk the egg and other ingredients together right in the plate), and the last plate with the bread crumb mixture. Next to the last plate, place the baking sheet, to hold whatever you are breading.

▲ 2. Dip the item (called "dredging") first in the flour. Be sure to coat the item thoroughly. This helps seal it. Take a look at what you are dredging. If you see bare spots, dredge it again to thoroughly coat. Shake the item lightly to get rid of any excess flour.

▲ 3. Now move on to the egg. Thoroughly coat the item in egg. Again, take a look at what you are breading. Be sure it is thoroughly coated in egg mixture.

▲ 4. Dip the item in the bread crumbs. Pat the food down to ensure the crumbs stick evenly to it.

▲ 5. Set the breaded item on the rimmed baking sheet.

▶ 6. Be sure to throw away the leftover flour, egg, and bread crumb mixtures. They have been contaminated by raw meat and raw eggs and need to be tossed!

NOTE

A few recipes will have you "double dip." This means you will coat the item in flour, then in egg. Then the item goes back into the flour mixture and again into the egg. Then, finally, it's coated with crumbs or gets a third dip in flour. This helps build up a thicker coating of breading. It's important for items such as mozzarella sticks that could otherwise ooze out of the breading. If the recipe calls for a double dip, be sure to do it or your frying results will suffer.

How to:
Peel and Mince Garlic

I love garlic. To prepare it, you can either put it through a garlic press or mince it by hand. Here's how to do the latter:

▲ *1. Remove the garlic skin: Place the garlic clove under a chef's knife blade, a mallet, or a small frying pan. Whichever you use, press down with enough force to crack the garlic clove. Pull away the garlic skin.*

▲ *2. Trim off the end of the clove.*

▲ *3. Slice the garlic as thinly as you can.*

▲ *4. Chop the garlic slices as finely as you like. (I like to chop garlic finely for most recipes.)*

How to:
Select an Onion Size

While measuring is great, sometimes using visual clues works just as well. Take the onion. I rarely measure a diced onion. Instead, I grab a small, medium, or large onion and trust that it is the right amount for my recipe. Here's what I mean by those sizes:

A small onion is about 2 inches across when cut, weighs about 3 ounces before peeling, and yields between $1/4$ and $1/3$ cup diced onion.

A medium onion is about $3 1/2$ inches across when cut, weighs 5 to 6 ounces before peeling, and yields between $1/2$ and $3/4$ cup diced onion.

A large onion is about 4 inches across, weighs about 8 ounces before peeling, and yields between $1 1/4$ and $1 1/2$ cups diced onion.

An extra large onion is about 5 inches across, weighs about 1 pound before peeling, and yields about 2 cups diced onion.

How to:
Dice an Onion

▲ 1. Cut the ends off the onion.

▲ 2. Place the onion cut side down on the cutting board, and cut the onion in half from root to tip.

▲ 3. Peel off the papery skin.

▲ 4. Place the onion halves cut sides down on the cutting board. Hold one onion half steady and slice horizontally until you almost reach the root end. Depending on the size of the onion and how finely you want it diced, you may need to make several horizontal cuts.

▲ 5. Slice the onion vertically, inserting the knife almost to the root. I find it easy to follow the little lines on the onion as a guide.

▲ 6. Slice the onion crosswise, holding on to the root end as you do this.

▶ 7. Repeat with the other half, if necessary.

How to:
Make Caramelized Onions

I really could eat caramelized onions with a spoon. But I have restraint! Instead, I pile them on pizzas, burgers, and sandwiches. I suggest you do the same—in the name of restraint and all, you see.

This may seem like a lot of onion at the start, but they lose a great deal of their volume by the time they're done. You might even decide to make a double or triple batch in a large heavy pot or Dutch oven, to keep in the refrigerator so you'll have them whenever you want them.

---

3 medium yellow onions

2 tablespoons unsalted butter

2 to 3 tablespoons olive oil

1. Cutting onions for caramelized onions is an important part of the process. If they are cut too thin, they won't caramelize nicely. Cut the ends off the onion.

2. Cut the onion in half and remove the papery skin.

3. Cut the onion halves into thick strips, about 1/2 inch at the widest part.

4. In a medium cast-iron skillet, heat the butter and olive oil (or just oil, if you're dairy-free) over medium heat until butter melts. When it stops bubbling, swirl the pan to coat the bottom with the hot butter and oil.

5. Add the onions. Cook, stirring with a wooden spoon, about 5 to 8 minutes. The onions should be translucent and soft. You'll notice them starting to lightly brown. If at any time they start to brown quickly, lower the heat to medium-low.

6. Lower the heat to low and cook, stirring occasionally, until the onions are very, very soft and dark brown. This will take about 45 minutes. The onions will be soft and caramelized, and delicious.

7. Transfer the onions to a container with a tight-fitting lid. Allow to cool to room temperature, then cover and refrigerate for up to 1 week if not using right away.

Makes 3/4 cup caramelized onions

Pit and Peel an Avocado

Avocados can seem tricky to cut thanks to their large pits. You don't want to cut through a pit with your knife; you need to work around it. Many people "whack" the pit with a chef's knife and lift the pit out with the knife. This takes a bit of practice and, as with anything you are whacking at with a knife, can lead to a cut. I prefer to cut my avocado in half and then run a small spoon around the pit. It simply lifts out once loosened.

1. Place the avocado on a cutting board. Hold it in place with the palm of you hand; take care to keep your fingers out of the way of the blade. Insert a chef's knife into the avocado lengthwise until you gently hit the pit.

2. Using your hand, slowly rotate the avocado around the knife; again, be sure to keep your fingers away from the knife blade. Once you've gone all the way around the pit, slide the knife out of the avocado.

3. Gently twist the avocado and pull the two halves apart. The pit will usually remain in one side of the fruit. Sometimes it will pop out on its own. If that happens, think of it as your lucky day and do a little happy dance in the kitchen. If the pit doesn't pop out, don't despair! Grab a spoon.

4. Slide the spoon into the flesh of the avocado as close to the pit as you can get. Move the spoon around the pit until you can lift it out. If any avocado flesh clings to the pit when you've removed it, simply scrape it off with the spoon. Don't let it go to waste!

5. Slide a spoon between the avocado skin and flesh. Gently scoop out the flesh and use as directed.

NOTE

Choose a ripe avocado, one that's soft to the touch but not too mushy. It will be easy to pit and tastes great.

Dice a Potato

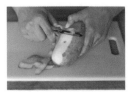 

▲ *1. Peel the potato, if the recipes says to.*   ▲ *2. Cut off a little of one side of the potato to create a flat surface.*

▲ *3. Lay potato on the cut side. Hold and cut in half.*   ▲ *4. Cut each half lengthwise into strips.*

▲ *5. Cut the strips crosswise. The closer the cuts, the smaller the pieces.*

Dice a Bell Pepper

You don't want to bruise the pepper. Be gentle.

▲ *1. Hold the pepper and cut off one side.*   ▲ *2. Place the pepper cut side up on the cutting board. Cut off each side, exposing the core. (Pepper skin can be tough and cause the knife to slip. When you slice through the cut side, the knife won't slip.)*

▲ *3. Discard the core and any seeds that cling to the pepper pieces.*   ▲ *4. Place the quarters flesh side up on the cutting board and flatten the quarters slightly. Cut into strips.*

◀ *5. Cut the strips crosswise into small pieces.*

How to:
Hard-Cook an Egg

I first called this how-to "How To Hard-Boil an Egg." But the best way to cook an egg is to *not* boil it. Cook it this way and you won't get that nasty gray or green around the yolk.

▲ 1. Place the eggs in a pot. Cover with water by about 1 inch.

▲ 2. Bring the water to a boil.

▲ 3. As soon as the water reaches a boil, turn off the heat and cover the pot. Allow the eggs to sit for 10 minutes. (If you are like me and forget about things, use a timer.)

▲ 4. Fill a bowl with cold water and ice. Remove the eggs from the hot water using a slotted spoon and transfer to the cold water.

▶ 5. Peel and enjoy!

How to:
Peel a Hard-Cooked Egg

This is the easiest method I've found.

▲ 1. Tap the cold egg, large end down, on the counter to shatter the bottom of the shell.

▲ 2. Remove a little of the broken shell. Run your thumb over the thin membrane between the shell and the egg to rupture it.

▲ 3. Peel away the membrane, and the shell will come with it!

▲ 4. Slice the egg and enjoy!

How to:
Cook Brown Rice

Did you know that you can cook rice like pasta? I learned this at cooking school and I think it is the best way to do it. When cooked this way, brown rice is fluffy and not mushy.

▶ 1. Fill a large pot three-quarters full with water. Cover and bring to a boil over high heat. Set a colander in the sink for draining the rice later.

▲ 2. When the water reaches a boil, add the rice.

▲ 3. Stir for a few seconds, then boil, uncovered, for about 30 minutes, or until tender. Turn off the heat.

▲ 4. Drain the rice in the colander but don't shake it too vigorously. (You want a little of the water to cling to it so it will steam in the next step.)

▲ 5. Return the rice to the pot and cover it. Allow the rice to stand for 10 minutes.

▲ 6. Fluff with a fork, season with salt, and serve.

NOTE

White rice can be cooked the same way, but boil it for only 10 to 15 minutes and let it stand about 5 minutes before you fluff it. I find that white rice isn't as susceptible to getting mushy as brown rice.

How to:
Cook Bacon

Bacon is delicious no matter how you cook it! There are three ways I like to cook bacon.

In the microwave: If I only have a few pieces to cook, I prefer using the microwave.

▲ *1. Place the bacon on the tray of a microwave bacon cooker, cover with a paper towel, and microwave on HIGH for 2 minutes.*

▲ *2. Check the bacon for crispness and increase cooking time as needed.*

In a frying pan: The classic way to cook bacon.

▲ *1. Heat a little oil in a frying pan. When the oil is shimmering, add the bacon.*

▲ *2. Cook until crisp, turn the slices over with tongs, and cook the second side until crisp.*

◀ *3. Transfer the cooked bacon to a paper towel-lined plate. If you need to cook more bacon, drain almost all the fat from the pan and repeat as needed.*

In the oven: The way to cook bacon for a crowd! The only time I turn on my oven to cook bacon is when I need to make a large batch. This frees me to stand at the stove and flip pancakes.

▲ *1. Adjust oven rack to the middle position and preheat the oven to 400°F. Place the bacon on a rimmed baking sheet.*

▲ *2. Bake for 20 minutes, or until bacon is crisp. Carefully remove the pan from the oven and transfer the bacon to a paper towel-lined plate. Let the fat cool a little before you pour it into the trash (never down the drain!) or into a jar to store in the refrigerator if you want to use it for cooking.*

ESSENTIAL HOW-TO LESSONS   *43*

How to:
Cook Ground Meat

Some of the recipes in this book call for cooked ground turkey or beef. While each one gives you specific instructions, here's the general method to use.

Oil

Ground meat (lean turkey or beef, or extra-lean beef)

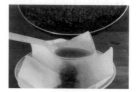

▲ *3. If there is excess fat, place a paper towel-lined bowl next to your stove. Carefully tip the pan and spoon off the excess fat into the bowl. Discard the fat and the towel in the trash. (This shouldn't be a problem with lean ground turkey or extra-lean ground beef. But even some "lean" ground meat may have more fat than you want in the finished dish.)*

▶ *4. Use the cooked meat as needed.*

▲ *1. Heat a little oil in a nonstick frying pan over medium-high to high heat. Add the ground meat and cook, breaking up the clumps with a wooden spoon or heatproof spatula.*

▲ *2. Cook the ground meat until thoroughly browned.*

Cook Chicken Breasts

I love having cooked chicken breasts on hand to add to salads or pasta dishes. If you don't have any chicken breast leftovers, it is easy to quickly cook one for whatever you'd like to use it for.

Boneless, skinless chicken breasts

Olive oil

Salt and freshly ground black or white pepper

To roast in the oven:

1. Adjust oven rack to the middle position and preheat the oven to 375°F. Place the chicken on a rimmed baking sheet and brush lightly with olive oil. Season with salt and pepper.

2. Bake until the internal temperature reaches 165°F.

3. Remove from the pan, let cool, and use as needed.

To pan-fry on the stovetop:

1. Brush the chicken breasts lightly with olive oil. Season with salt and pepper.

2. Heat olive oil in a medium nonstick frying pan over medium heat.

3. When the oil is hot and shimmering but not smoking, place the chicken in the pan. Cook for 5 minutes without moving or turning the chicken.

4. Turn the chicken over and continue to cook until internal temperature reaches 165°F and no pink remains, usually another 5 to 10 minutes depending on the thickness of the chicken.

5. Remove from the pan, let cool, and use as needed.

How to:
Make a White Sauce

Making a white sauce (also called "béchamel") isn't something you are going to do every day. The technique for making a white sauce is used a few times in this book, like in the recipes for Croque Monsieur (page 195), Creamy Macaroni and Cheese (page 140), and, although modified, Chicken-Fried Steak (page 166). It is easy as long as you follow a few steps.

I've found sweet rice flour to be an ideal replacement for wheat flour in a white sauce. If you have any old recipes that use a white sauce or a roux (the combination of cooked butter and flour), simply replace the wheat flour with sweet rice flour.

Warming the milk first makes it easier to whisk in. You can warm it in the microwave just enough to take the chill off.

Butter

Sweet rice flour

Milk, warmed

 1. Place a small, heavy-bottomed pot over medium heat and melt the butter.

2. As soon as the butter melts, add the flour.

3. A thick paste will immediately form.

4. After a few seconds, the paste will relax and begin to bubble.

▲ 5. Cook, whisking constantly, until the paste turns beige. (This is called a "roux.")

▲ 6. Whisking constantly, add the milk in a slow and steady steam. Allow the paste to absorb milk as you add it. You don't want to whisk too quickly because that can incorporate air and cool the white sauce. Just whisk briskly to keep the sauce moving and prevent scorching on the bottom of the pot. Be sure the wires of your whisk are always in contact with the bottom of the pot.

▲ 7. Let the sauce come to a simmer (look for occasional gentle bubbles) and cook until it thickens, stirring constantly, especially at the edges of the pot, so it doesn't burn. (You might want to switch to a wooden spoon for this.) The sauce is ready when it's thick enough to coat the back of the spoon.

How to:
Make Gravy

Making gravy is pretty much the same as making white sauce, but instead of milk, you'll use the pan juices from cooked meat plus stock or broth. Be sure to skim the fat from your pan juices and strain them, or the gravy will be fatty and lumpy.

Sometimes I have enough pan juices to make gravy, (however, avoid burnt juices), but most of the time I need to add chicken broth, especially when making a big batch.

Gravy

This recipe can be doubled or tripled if you have a large gathering.

2^1/$_2$ tablespoons unsalted butter or olive oil

2^1/$_2$ tablespoons sweet rice flour

1^1/$_2$ cups skimmed, strained pan juices
(plus chicken stock if necessary), warmed

▶ 1. In a small (2-quart) pot, melt the butter over medium-high heat.

▶ 2. Add the flour and whisk until a paste forms. Continue whisking for 3 minutes, or until paste turns beige.

▶ 3. In a slow and steady stream, whisk in the pan juices and stock. Continue to whisk until gravy has thickened and begins to bubble. If the gravy is too thick, add more stock.

Makes about 1 ^{1}/$_2$ cups gravy

How to:
Keep Food Safe—The Basics

It goes without saying that food safety is important. Since information (including cooking temperatures for meat) changes, visit the FDA's website (www.fda.org) for accurate, up-to-date information. Here are some good, basic steps to keeping and serving safe food:

1. Keep produce away from raw meat, both on your counter and when storing produce and meat in the refrigerator.

2. Wash your hands often while preparing a meal, especially after touching raw meat.

3. Be aware. This is the most important step, I think, in food safety. When cooking, be aware of where you are placing raw meat and be sure to clean and sanitize any area or utensil that raw meat touches.

Handy Measurement Chart

3 teaspoons	=	1 tablespoon
4 tablespoons	=	$1/4$ cup
5 tablespoons + 1 teaspoon	=	$1/3$ cup
8 tablespoons	=	$1/2$ cup
12 tablespoons	=	$3/4$ cup
16 tablespoons	=	1 cup
2 cups	=	1 pint
4 cups	=	1 quart

1.
Breakfast

Bacon and Marmalade Sandwich

This sandwich is not my invention. It's my mom's. Every Sunday and Wednesday, she has breakfast at Duncan's Dairy Bar, a small restaurant in town. At some point, she put bacon between two slices of rye toast she'd coated with orange marmalade. Now that she is gluten-free, she brings her own rye bread and does the same thing.

▶ *For a how-to on cooking bacon, see page 43.*

Unsalted butter

Orange marmalade

2 slices Rye-ish Bread (page 209), toasted

3 or 4 slices bacon, cooked until crisp

- Spread butter and marmalade lightly on each slice of bread. You can be a little heavier with the marmalade than the butter. Sandwich the bacon between bread, cut, and enjoy.

Makes 1 sandwich

Quiche "Cupcakes"

These little crustless quiches are cute and so easy to make. Plus, they let you have a "cupcake" for breakfast without feeling guilty about it!

Gluten-free nonstick cooking spray

2 teaspoons olive oil

$1/2$ medium onion, finely diced

2 cloves garlic, minced or put through a garlic press

6 large eggs

1 package (10 ounces) frozen chopped spinach, thawed and drained

6 ounces cheddar cheese, shredded ($3/4$ cup)

$1/2$ cup grape tomatoes, halved

1. Adjust oven rack to the middle position and preheat the oven to 350°F. Lightly grease a 12-cavity muffin pan with nonstick cooking spray.

2. In a small (8-inch) nonstick frying pan, heat the olive oil over medium heat until hot and shimmering but not smoking. Add the onion and garlic and cook, stirring, until soft and tender, about 3 minutes. Remove the pan from the heat and transfer onion and garlic to a small plate to cool a little.

3. In a medium bowl, whisk the eggs with a fork. Add the spinach and stir well with the fork to combine. (Chopped spinach likes to clump. Take care to ensure the spinach is "loose" in the eggs.) Add the cheese, tomatoes, and onion and garlic. Stir to combine.

4. Ladle the mixture evenly into the 12 muffin cavities.

5. Bake for 16 to 18 minutes, until the quiches are set and puffy.

6. Remove the pan from the oven and allow to cool for 5 minutes. Run a knife around the edge of each quiche and then carefully lift out using a knife. Serve warm.

Makes 12 quiches

Bacon and Cheddar Strata

Recipes for traditional (read: gluten-filled) strata, a bready breakfast casserole, often call for the bread to be soaked overnight in an egg-milk mixture. I've found that with gluten-free bread, this makes for a really soggy strata. To solve this problem, I soak the bread for only one hour. The texture is creamy without being unpleasantly soggy.

▶ *For a how-to on toasting bread, see page 90.*

▶ *For a how-to on cooking bacon, see page 43.*

5 cups cubed white bread (with crusts), home-made (page 206) or store-bought, lightly toasted

5 ounces sharp cheddar cheese, grated (1^1/4 cups)

8 large eggs

3 cups whole milk

1 teaspoon salt

^{1}/2 teaspoon freshly ground black pepper

8 slices bacon, cooked until crisp, crumbled

1. Lightly butter the bottom and sides of a 13 by 9-inch baking dish. Place the bread cubes in the dish and top with the cheese.

2. In a medium bowl, whisk the eggs until smooth. Add the milk, salt, and pepper and whisk to combine. Pour over the bread. Cover the baking dish with plastic wrap and chill for 1 hour.

3. Adjust oven rack to the middle position and preheat the oven to 350°F. Remove the plastic wrap and sprinkle with the bacon. Bake the strata for 55 to 60 minutes, until golden brown and puffy. If the top of the strata gets too brown during baking, cover with a piece of foil.

4. Remove the pan from the oven and allow to cool for 5 minutes before serving.

Serves 8

Waffles

I created these waffles one morning when I was out of buttermilk. They are delicious, golden brown, and "waffle-y." Of course, they are great with butter and syrup!

Dry Ingredients

1 cup white rice flour

$1/2$ cup cornstarch

$1/4$ cup sweet rice flour

1 tablespoon baking powder

1 tablespoon granulated sugar

$1/2$ teaspoon salt

$1/2$ teaspoon xanthan gum

Wet Ingredients

2 large eggs

$1^1/4$ cups milk

$1/4$ cup vegetable oil

1 teaspoon pure vanilla extract

Gluten-free nonstick cooking spray

1. In a medium bowl, whisk together the dry ingredients. In a small bowl, whisk together the wet ingredients. Pour the wet ingredients over the dry. Blend with a whisk or handheld mixer until smooth.

2. Heat a waffle iron according to the manufacturer's directions. Spray the waffle iron with nonstick cooking spray.

3. When the indicator light shows that the iron is hot enough, spoon batter onto the iron (the amount of batter will vary depending on your iron), close it, and bake until the waffle is golden brown.

NOTE

Waffles are best served as soon as they are cooked, but if you need to wait until all the waffles are cooked before you serve them, preheat the oven to 180°F. As the waffles are done, transfer them to a rimmed baking sheet and keep warm in the oven. Serve as soon as all the waffles are ready.

Serves 4

Pancakes

Light and fluffy are my requirements for pancakes. These pancakes more than meet those requirements. Of course, maple syrup is perfect with them, but if you have a maple allergy, Lyle's Golden Syrup is a nice replacement.

Dry Ingredients

1 cup white rice flour

$1/2$ cup cornstarch

$1/2$ cup sweet rice flour

$1/4$ cup granulated sugar

1 tablespoon baking powder

$1/2$ teaspoon salt

$1/4$ teaspoon xanthan gum

Wet Ingredients

2 large eggs

1 cup milk

$1/4$ cup vegetable oil

1 teaspoon pure vanilla extract

Gluten-free nonstick cooking spray

1. In a medium bowl, whisk together the dry ingredients. In a small bowl, whisk together the wet ingredients. Pour the wet ingredients over the dry and whisk until smooth.

2. Lightly oil a griddle with nonstick cooking spray and heat the griddle over medium-high heat. Pour about $1/4$ cup of batter for each pancake onto the griddle. The batter should sizzle when it hits the griddle.

3. Cook for about 3 minutes, until bubbles appear all over the surface of the pancake and begin to pop. The pancake should begin to look almost dry. Flip and cook for another 1 to 2 minutes, until golden on the bottom. Repeat with remaining batter, adding more oil if your griddle looks dry.

NOTE

If you need to wait until all the pancakes are cooked before you serve them, preheat the oven to 180°F. As the pancakes are done, transfer them to a rimmed baking sheet and keep warm in the oven. Serve as soon as all the pancakes are ready.

Serves 4

Raisin and Bran Muffins

Three gluten-free flours and flaxseed combine to give these muffins a hearty flavor but light texture. I usually use raisins in the muffins but any dried fruit would work well.

Although buckwheat is naturally gluten-free, be sure the bag of flour you purchase is labeled gluten-free.

Dry Ingredients

1 1/2 cups white rice flour

2/3 cup brown rice flour

2/3 cup gluten-free buckwheat flour

2/3 cup flaxseed meal

3/4 cup granulated sugar

1 tablespoon baking powder

2 teaspoons salt

Wet Ingredients

1 1/4 cups milk

3 large eggs

1/2 cup vegetable oil

1/4 cup molasses

1 cup raisins

1. Adjust oven rack to the middle position and preheat the oven to 350°F. Line 24 muffin cavities (2 muffin pans) with paper liners.

2. In a large bowl, whisk together the dry ingredients. Add the wet ingredients and blend until smooth. This batter comes together easily. You can use either an electric mixer or a whisk.

3. Add the raisins and mix until combined.

4. Fill the muffin cavities about two-thirds full. Bake for 20 to 25 minutes, until the muffins spring back to the touch.

5. Remove the muffins from the oven and transfer to a wire rack to cool. Store in an airtight container for up to 3 days or freeze for up to 1 month.

Makes 24 muffins

"Powdered Sugar Doughnut" Muffins

This recipe is my mom's fault. Okay, maybe not "fault" because who would want to blame someone for inspiring something this good? She was watching *The Best Thing I Ever Ate: Snack Attack* on the Food Network and someone mentioned "doughnut muffins." That's right. Muffins that taste like doughnuts. My mouth was already watering when she said, "You should make a gluten-free version."

Since I try to be a good daughter, I listened to my mom. The gluten-filled doughnut muffins from The Downtown Bakery in Healdsburg, CA, are rolled in melted butter and then in cinnamon sugar. While that sounds divine, I love plain powdered sugar doughnuts and wanted to try making a muffin version. (If you'd like cinnamon-sugar muffins, just add $1/2$ teaspoon ground cinnamon to the powdered sugar.) Taking a cue from Mexican wedding cookies, I rolled the muffins in powdered sugar right after they came out of the oven. It worked! The sugar stuck to the warm muffins.

The muffins have a bit of crust that gives way to a tender interior. The next time I make them, I think I'll fill them with a little jam after baking. Jelly doughnut muffins, anyone?

Gluten-free nonstick cooking spray

Dry Ingredients

$3/4$ cup white rice flour

$1/2$ cup cornstarch

$1/4$ cup sweet rice flour

$3/4$ cup granulated sugar

2 teaspoons baking power

$1/4$ teaspoon salt

$1/4$ teaspoon ground nutmeg

Wet Ingredients

$3/4$ cup milk

$1/4$ cup vegetable oil

1 large egg

1 package (1 pound) powdered sugar

1. Adjust oven rack to the middle position and preheat the oven to 350°F. Lightly grease the cavities of a mini muffin pan with nonstick cooking spray.

2. In a medium bowl, whisk together the dry ingredients. Add the wet ingredients and whisk to combine. The batter will be thin.

3. Fill the muffin cavities about half full. Bake for 20 to 25 minutes, until the muffins are golden brown.

(continued)

4. While the muffins are baking, fill an 8-inch square baking dish with the powdered sugar.

5. Remove the muffins from the oven and working in batches, place them directly into the powdered sugar. Gently roll the muffins in the sugar to cover them. The steam from the hot muffins will make the sugar stick to the muffins. Remove the muffins from the sugar and tap off any excess. Transfer the muffins to a wire rack to cool. Store in an airtight container for up to 3 days or freeze for up to 1 month.

Makes 24 mini muffins

2. Starters and Snacks

Pan-Fried Mozzarella Sticks

Even though I've always enjoyed the occasional mozzarella stick, I avoided making them at home. To be honest, I'd rather go without than have to drag out the deep-fryer for just a few sticks. One day I wondered what would happen if I fried them up in a pan instead of the deep-fryer. Success is what happened! With only a little oil in the pan, these mozzarella sticks take very little time to make. The reward? Gooey, cheesy, crunchy heaven!

Double-coating the mozzarella sticks in white rice flour and egg ensures that the fried mozzarella sticks won't leak while cooking. This is an important step; don't skip it. Low-fat and fat-free string cheese do not work well. Use the real thing.

▶ *For a how-to on breading, see page 34.*

▶ *For a how-to on dried bread crumbs, see page 32.*

1 cup white rice flour

Pinch of granulated garlic

$1/4$ teaspoon salt

1 teaspoon dried basil

Pinch of freshly ground black pepper

1 large egg

1 cup gluten-free dried bread crumbs

12 full-fat mozzarella cheese sticks, cold and unwrapped

Vegetable oil, for frying

1. Line up three plates or pie pans on your counter. On the first plate, whisk together the white rice flour, garlic, salt, basil, and pepper. On the second plate, whisk the egg until smooth. On the third plate, place the bread

crumbs. At the end of the line, place a baking pan or dish large enough to hold all the sticks in a single layer.

2. Roll a cheese stick in the white rice flour, coating it well. Take care to coat the ends of the stick with flour, too. You don't want any bare spots. This will prevent the sticks from leaking during frying.

3. Roll the stick in the egg, coating it thoroughly. Return the stick to the flour and coat it again. Return it again to the egg and coat thoroughly. Finally, roll the coated stick in bread crumbs, also coating it thoroughly. Tap off any excess crumbs. Place the coated stick on the baking pan. Repeat until all the sticks are coated. Chill the sticks for 5 minutes.

4. Line a plate with paper towels. Heat $1/2$ inch oil in a small (8-inch) frying pan until it is hot and shimmering but not smoking. Sprinkle a little white rice flour on the surface of the oil. If the flour sizzles, the oil is ready.

5. Place four cheese sticks in the frying pan. Fry for 30 seconds. Using a heatproof spatula, roll the sticks in the oil to turn. Fry 30 seconds more, or until the sticks are golden brown on all sides. If any cheese begins to leak, remove the stick from the oil and place it on the paper towel to drain.

6. Transfer the fried sticks to the paper towels to drain briefly. Repeat with remaining the cheese sticks.

7. Serve the sticks hot.

Makes 12 sticks

SERVING SUGGESTION

These are just perfect for dipping. I like to use marinara sauce.

Loaded Nachos

To be honest, I couldn't decide what chapter nachos should appear in. While many people enjoy nachos as a snack or while watching a game on TV, I like to make a pan of them for dinner. Served with a large salad, this is an easy weeknight meal.

$^1/_4$ cup gluten-free taco seasoning

6 tablespoons water

2 tablespoons olive oil

1 small onion, finely diced

1 pound ground sirloin (90 to 92% lean) or lean ground turkey

1 bag (13 ounces) tortilla chips

1 can (16 ounces) refried beans

1 cup canned black beans, drained and rinsed

$1^1/_2$ cups salsa, homemade (page 64) or store-bought

1 can (2.25 ounces) sliced black olives, drained

8 ounces cheddar, Monterey Jack, or pepper Jack cheese, grated (2 cups)

1. Adjust oven rack to the middle position and preheat the oven to 425°F. Mix together the taco seasoning and water in a small bowl.

2. In a medium (10-inch) nonstick frying pan, heat the olive oil over high heat. When it is hot and shimmering but not smoking, add the onion and cook until tender, about 3 minutes.

3. Add the ground beef and cook, breaking up the clumps with a wooden spoon or heatproof spatula, until thoroughly cooked and browned. If desired, remove and discard any excess fat. (For a how-to on cooking ground meat, see page 44.) Lower the heat to medium. Stir in the taco seasoning and cook for 5 minutes.

4. Line the bottom of a roasting pan (15 by 11-inches) with one-third of the tortilla chips. Spread the chips with one-third of the refried beans. Spoon one-third of the meat on top. On top of that, sprinkle one-third of the black beans, salsa, olives, and cheese. Repeat twice more, until everything has been used.

5. Bake for 15 to 20 minutes, until the cheese is melted and the nachos are hot. Serve immediately.

Serves 6

NOTE

I like to add the salsa to the nacho layers before baking. While tasty, this does make a few chips a little soggy. If you prefer really crisp nachos, add the salsa to the dish after baking.

Pigs in a Blanket

I created this recipe for my friend Jessica after she told me that pigs in a blanket was her secret guilty pleasure at family gatherings. She's not gluten-free, but this recipe got two thumbs up from her. These wieners freeze beautifully, so Jessica can make a batch, freeze some, and then enjoy them whenever the mood strikes!

$1^{1}/_{4}$ cups white rice flour

$^{3}/_{4}$ cup cornstarch

$^{1}/_{4}$ cup sweet rice flour

2 teaspoons baking powder

1 teaspoon granulated sugar

$^{1}/_{4}$ teaspoon salt

$^{1}/_{4}$ cup (4 tablespoons) unsalted butter, chilled and diced

$^{1}/_{2}$ cup plus 1 to 2 tablespoons milk

2 large eggs

1 package (16 ounces) gluten-free cocktail wieners

1. Adjust oven rack to the middle position and preheat the oven to 400°F. Line a rimmed baking sheet with parchment paper.

2. In a medium bowl, whisk together the white rice flour, cornstarch, sweet rice flour, baking powder, sugar, and salt.

3. Add the butter, and using your fingers or a pastry cutter, work it into the flour mixture until no large pieces remain. The mixture should be coarse, with tiny pebbles of butter distributed evenly throughout.

4. Using a wooden spoon, stir in $^{1}/_{2}$ cup of the milk and 1 egg. Blend until a dough forms. If the dough is dry and won't hold together, add a splash (about 1 tablespoon) more milk.

5. Pinch off little balls of dough, about 1 generous teaspoon each. Press the dough evenly around a cocktail wiener to coat the wiener. Leave the ends of the wiener exposed. Don't worry about the dough jacket being perfect. You just want to encase the sausage in dough. Looks don't matter. Place on the prepared pan. Repeat until all the dough and wieners are used.

6. In a small bowl, whisk together the remaining egg and about 1 tablespoon milk with a fork. Using a pastry brush, brush the egg mixture onto each dough wrap.

7. Bake 15 to 18 minutes, until the dough is light golden brown. Serve warm with cocktail sauce.

Makes about 50 pigs

FREEZE IT!

You can make pigs in a blanket in advance and freeze them. Follow the recipe through step five. Place the wrapped wieners on a rimmed baking sheet and freeze. Once they are frozen, transfer to a large plastic bag. Store for up to two months. When you want to make pigs in a blanket, preheat the oven, brush the egg mixture onto the frozen wieners, and bake as directed. Cooking time might increase by a minute or two.

Quick Salsa

Although it is easy to pick up a jar of salsa at the store, I've really come to prefer the flavor of my homemade salsa. For this recipe, I use both canned and fresh tomatoes. I think this combination yields the best flavor and texture. You can use 3 half-pints fresh tomatoes if you don't want to use canned. If you use fresh, use 1 whole jalapeño and a pinch more salt.

If you like your salsa hotter, leave in the jalapeño seeds.

1 small onion, quartered

1 clove garlic, peeled

$1/2$ jalapeño, seeded and coarsely chopped

$1/2$ cup cilantro leaves (about 1 medium bunch), coarsely chopped

1 can (10 ounces) diced tomatoes with green chiles

$1/2$ pint grape tomatoes

Juice of $1/2$ lime

$1/4$ teaspoon salt

1. Put the onion, garlic, and jalapeño in a food processor. Pulse a few times to chop. Add the cilantro. Pulse until the mixture is coarsely chopped.

2. Add the canned and fresh tomatoes, lime juice, and salt. Pulse until the fresh tomatoes are chunky.

3. Use as desired. You can store leftover salsa in a covered container in the refrigerator for up to 24 hours, but leftover salsa tends to break down and get watery, so it's better to make a batch right before you need it.

Makes about 3 cups salsa

Creamy White Bean Dip

Since I'm allergic to sesame seeds, hummus—a blend of chickpeas and sesame paste—has never been an option for me. But I don't mind, since I can enjoy this white bean dip. It comes together in a food processor in seconds. By using different beans, you can change the flavor. Use whatever you love!

2 large cloves garlic, peeled

1 can (15.5 ounces) cannellini beans, drained and rinsed

Juice of $1/2$ lemon

$1/2$ teaspoon ground cumin

3 tablespoons extra virgin olive oil, plus more for drizzling

Salt and freshly ground black pepper

1. In a food processor, pulse the garlic until finely chopped. Add the beans, lemon juice, cumin, and olive oil. Process until smooth. If the dip is too thick, add an additional tablespoon olive oil.

2. Transfer the dip to a serving dish. Season with salt and pepper and stir to combine. Drizzle a little olive oil over the top. Serve right away or store, covered, in the refrigerator for up to 3 days.

Makes a little more than 1 cup dip

SERVING SUGGESTION

Serve any—or all—of these with the dip:

- Chips
- Raw vegetables
- Toasted gluten-free bread

NOTE

If you have fresh rosemary in the kitchen or out in the garden, chop some up for this dip. A scant teaspoon of minced rosemary adds a nice flavor note to the dip without overwhelming it. Stir the rosemary into the dip before transferring it to the serving bowl.

Guacamole

The avocado, it calls to me. I have to keep myself from nibbling on avocado chunks before I mash them into guacamole. This recipe has a little kick, but not enough to take away from the delicate, buttery flavor of my beloved avocado.

Did you know? Avocados don't ripen until after they are picked from the tree.

▶ *For a how-to on pitting and peeling avocados, see page 39.*

---

1 small onion, finely diced

$^1/_2$ jalapeño, seeded and finely chopped

1 small clove garlic or $^1/_2$ large clove, minced or put through a garlic press

2 ripe Hass avocados, pitted and peeled (see Notes)

Juice of $^1/_2$ lime

$^1/_2$ teaspoon salt

• In a serving bowl, stir together the onion, jalapeño, and garlic. Add the avocados and mash with a fork until smooth but with a few chunks still present. Add the lime juice and salt and stir to combine. Guacamole turns brown when exposed to air, so if you aren't serving right away, press a piece of plastic wrap directly onto the surface of the guacamole. Refrigerate for up to 3 days.

Makes about 2 cups guacamole

SERVING SUGGESTIONS

While I could eat guacamole right from the bowl with a spoon, it is better when served with something. Here are a few suggestions:

• With tortilla chips and salsa
• In tacos or fajitas
• As a sandwich spread in place of mayonnaise. One of my favorites is to spread bread with a little guacamole and then make a sandwich with turkey, lettuce, a slice or two of bacon, and a slice of a ripe tomato. Yum!

NOTES

The success of this recipe depends on your avocados being fully ripe. A ripe avocado should be soft to the touch but not mushy. Since I rarely find ripe avocados at the store, I buy them a few days before I plan on making guacamole. Leave them at room temperature to ripen. Once they've ripened, you can store them, whole, in the refrigerator for up to 1 week.

If you like your guacamole hotter, leave in the jalapeño seeds.

Don't use more garlic than called for; too much garlic can overwhelm the guacamole.

VARIATION

Guacamole with Salsa: Add about $^1/_2$ cup salsa to the guacamole. Stir until just combined.

Tortilla "Bread Sticks"

These little tortilla "bread sticks" are a fun change of pace from bagged tortilla chips. I use a blend of chili powder and cumin on them, but you can use whatever spices you enjoy to liven up store-bought corn tortillas.

2 to 3 tablespoons olive oil

2 teaspoons ground cumin

2 teaspoons chili powder

10 (6-inch) corn tortillas, at room temperature

Kosher salt and freshly ground pepper

1. Adjust oven rack to the middle position and preheat the oven to 425°F.

2. In a small bowl, whisk together the olive oil, cumin, and chili powder. Using a pastry brush, lightly brush each tortilla on both sides with the oil. Using a chef's knife or pizza wheel, cut each tortilla into strips about 1 inch thick.

3. Place the tortilla strips in a single layer on a rimmed baking sheet. Bake for 5 minutes. Remove the pan from the oven. Using a spatula, gently turn over the strips. Return to the oven and bake until crisp, about 5 minutes more.

4. Remove from the oven and sprinkle with salt and pepper to taste. Let cool completely.

5. Store the toasted sticks in a sealed plastic bag for a day or two. Depending on the humidity, the sticks might get soft. If they do, return them to a 425°F oven to crisp back up.

Serves 6

SERVING SUGGESTION

These little sticks are great broken up over a salad. They add a little crunch and you don't need to make a batch of croutons.

Easy Herb Crackers

Making crackers isn't hard but they usually require the dough to be rolled thin. Not these! These use a rustic dough that's sliced into rounds instead of being rolled. To vary the flavor, add different herbs to the dough before baking. Thyme, rosemary, and basil (used individually or a blend of all three) are especially nice. For a more peppery cracker, add up to 1 teaspoon pepper.

Dry Ingredients

$3/4$ cup white rice flour, plus more for the counter

$1/2$ cup sweet rice flour

1 teaspoon chopped fresh herbs or $1/2$ teaspoon dried

$1/2$ to 1 teaspoon freshly ground black pepper

$1/4$ teaspoon salt

$1/4$ teaspoon xanthan gum

Wet Ingredients

$1/2$ cup (8 tablespoons) unsalted butter, at room temperature

1 cup freshly grated Parmesan cheese

1 large egg

1 to 2 tablespoons milk (optional)

1. In a small bowl, whisk together the dry ingredients.

2. Cream the butter and cheese in a medium bowl until a thick paste forms, about 1 minute. If using a stand mixer, fit the mixer with the flat paddle attachment and beat on medium speed. Set a handheld mixer to medium-high. Add the egg and beat until light and fluffy.

3. Turn off the mixer. Add the flour mixture. Turn the mixer back on to medium-low. Blend until the dough comes together. It should be thick but not dry. If the dough is dry, add 1 to 2 teaspoons milk.

4. Generously sprinkle your countertop with white rice flour. Turn out the dough onto the counter and roll into a log about 10 inches long. Wrap the dough tightly with plastic wrap or parchment paper. Chill for 2 hours.

5. Adjust oven rack to the middle position and preheat the oven to 375ºF. Line a rimmed baking sheet with parchment paper.

6. Slice the dough into rounds about $1/4$-inch thick and lay them flat on the prepared baking sheet. If the dough crumbles slightly when you cut it, simply squeeze it back together on the baking sheet. If the crackers won't all fit on the baking sheet at one time, bake them in batches, letting the sheet cool between batches.

7. Bake for 20 to 25 minutes, until the crackers are lightly browned. Allow the crackers to cool on the pan for 3 minutes. Using a spatula, transfer the crackers to a wire rack to cool completely.

8. Store the crackers in an airtight container for up to 1 week.

Makes about 24 crackers

3.
Soups

Chicken Stock

Even though there are good gluten-free canned chicken broths available at the store, I try to make my own whenever I have the time. The flavor of homemade really is better and it's worth it to make a batch from scratch. The good news about this recipe? Once you put everything in the pot, you don't need to do much of anything until it is done. It almost makes itself.

    Thanks to the long simmering time, I make sure to start this recipe when I know I will be home for a bit. Chicken stock is one of those recipes that really can't be rushed.

1 cut-up 4-pound chicken (see Notes)
1 large onion, quartered
2 large carrots, peeled and halved crosswise
2 stalks celery, halved crosswise
4 sprigs parsley, or 2 teaspoons dried
1 sprig thyme, or $1/2$ teaspoon dried
1 teaspoon salt
$1/2$ teaspoon freshly ground black pepper
About 4 quarts (16 cups) cold water

1. Put everything in a large ($5^{1}/2$-quart) pot. Fill the pot with enough water to cover the chicken by 1 inch. Bring to a boil over medium-high heat. Skim the top of the broth and discard the scum. (The scum is the foam that will sit on top of the soup. Sometimes there is a lot of scum,

other times hardly any.) Lower the heat to low. Simmer (look for occasional gentle bubbles), uncovered, for 3 hours, skimming as needed.

2. Set a large colander in a large pot near the stove. Strain the stock through the colander into the clean pot. Discard the chicken and other solids. They have done their job.

3. To cool the stock quickly, plug your sink and fill it halfway with ice and cold water. Place the pot of stock into the cold water. Stir occasionally until cool. Cover the pot and refrigerate it overnight.

4. The next day, pop or scrape the fat off the top of the stock and discard. Divide the stock into individual storage containers. I find that 2-cup containers are most helpful, with a few 1-cup containers for when I need just a little. Label and date your containers.

5. Refrigerate for up to 5 days or freeze for up to 3 months.

Makes about 3 quarts stock

NOTES

If your grocery store doesn't carry cut-up whole chickens, you can either ask your butcher to do it for you or use a 50/50 combination of bone-in breasts and thighs.

If you've roasted a chicken, it's a good time to make stock. Add the chicken carcass to the pot for a really rich, flavorful stock.

Homemade stock is a bit gelatinous (jiggly) when cold. This is normal and nothing to be worried about. It comes from the natural collagen that is present in the chicken bones, and adds good flavor to the stock. As soon as you heat up the cold stock, the collagen will melt and you will have a stock that doesn't jiggle but does taste great!

Cheesy Broccoli Soup

Two years ago, before I went gluten-free, my mom had major back surgery. During her three-month recovery, she was unable to drive. So we spent a lot of time together! Each week, we'd go to Panera Bread for lunch and I'd order a bowl of their cheddar-broccoli soup. Since going gluten-free, I've missed that soup. Here is my version.

You might be surprised to see Velveeta in this recipe. I am, too! I was having a hard time with the cheese "breaking" and becoming stringy when I added it to the soup. Using Velveeta changed that. It doesn't become an oily mess when added to the hot broth. Even if you aren't a big fan of Velveeta, give this soup a try. And use whole or 2% milk; 1% and fat-free don't work well in this recipe.

1/4 cup (4 tablespoons) unsalted butter

1 medium onion, finely diced

1 clove garlic, minced or put through a garlic press

1 teaspoon Dijon mustard

1/4 cup sweet rice flour

4 cups homemade chicken stock (page 69) or store-bought reduced-sodium broth

1 1/2 cups whole or 2% milk

1 package (16 ounces) frozen chopped broccoli

1 large carrot, peeled and grated

1 teaspoon hot pepper sauce

1/2 teaspoon freshly ground black pepper

8 ounces Velveeta, cut into small cubes

Salt

1. In a large (5 1/2-quart) pot, melt the butter over medium-high heat. Add the onion and cook, stirring frequently with a wooden spoon, until translucent and soft, about 2 minutes. Add the garlic and cook for 1 minute. Continue to stir frequently. Add the mustard and stir to combine.

2. Switch to a wire whisk. Stir in the sweet rice flour; a paste will form. Cook, whisking constantly, for 4 minutes. The paste should be beige.

3. Add the chicken stock in a slow and steady steam. By doing this slowly and whisking constantly, you will avoid getting lumps in the soup. Whisk in the milk.

(continued)

4. Lower the heat to low. Add the broccoli, carrot, hot pepper sauce, and black pepper. Simmer (look for occasional gentle bubbles) for 30 minutes.

5. Using a slotted spoon, transfer the broccoli from the soup to a blender or food processor. Add a generous splash of soup, about $^1/_2$ cup. (Don't fill the blender more than halfway. Work in batches if you have a small blender.) Blend until the broccoli is almost smooth but not a paste.

6. Return the broccoli to the soup. Stir to combine. Add the Velveeta. Using a wooden spoon, stir until the Velveeta is melted. Season to taste with salt and simmer for 5 minutes. Serve.

Serves 4 for dinner, 6 for lunch

WHY NOT PURÉE ALL THE SOUP?

You'll notice the slightly odd step of puréeing only the broccoli and not the entire pot of soup. When I was testing the recipe, I noticed that if I puréed all of the soup, it became an unappealing color thanks to the broccoli. If I removed the broccoli and puréed it by itself, it added pleasant flecks of green to the soup while the rest of the soup remained an appetizing creamy yellow.

How to: Purèe Soup

1. Remove the cap from the center of the blender's lid and cover the opening with a clean kitchen towel. Only fill the blender halfway— never more. Thanks to the heat of the soup, pressure can build up in the blender. You never want to fill the blender more than half full or it might explode!

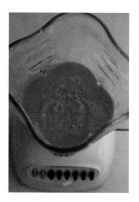

2. Blend until the soup is smooth.

New England Clam Chowder

Somehow I married a man who hates clam chowder. To be more specific, he hates clams. I am still not sure how this happened. Okay, he has other wonderful traits but *he hates clams.* What this means is that I only make this recipe when I have friends over. This creamy clam chowder is so good and so easy to make that I think of lots of excuses to have friends over. And Greg? Well, those nights he usually finds something—anything—that isn't clam chowder in the refrigerator and is happy.

---

4 large russet potatoes, peeled and diced (6 cups)

$1^1/2$ teaspoons salt

$^1/4$ cup (4 tablespoons) unsalted butter

1 medium onion, finely diced

3 stalks celery, thinly sliced

$^1/4$ cup sweet rice flour

4 cups whole milk, warmed

1 bottle (8 ounces) clam juice

2 cans (6.5 ounces each) chopped clams, drained, liquid reserved

$^1/2$ teaspoon freshly ground black pepper

1. Put the potatoes in a medium (4-quart) pot. Add enough cold water to cover the potatoes by 1 inch. Add 1 teaspoon salt. Bring to a boil over high heat, then lower the heat to medium-high. Cook the potatoes until tender but firm, about 10 to 15 minutes. Drain in a colander.

2. Melt the butter in a large ($5^1/2$-quart) pot over medium heat. Add the onion and celery. Cook, stirring frequently with a wooden spoon, until tender, about 5 minutes.

3. Switch to a whisk. Add the sweet rice flour. Whisking constantly, cook for 4 minutes.

4. In a slow and steady stream, whisk in the milk, clam juice, and reserved liquid from the canned clams (not the clams themselves) until the soup is lightly thickened. Stir in the potatoes.

5. Ladle about 3 cups of soup into the blender and purée until smooth. Do not fill the blender more than halfway. Purée the soup in batches and pour the puréed soup into a waiting bowl. (For a how-to on puréeing soup, see page 72.)

6. Return all the puréed soup to the pot. Add the clams, $^1/2$ teaspoon salt, and the pepper. Simmer (look for occasional gentle bubbles) over low heat for 20 minutes. Stir occasionally to prevent the soup from scorching. Serve hot.

Serves 6 to 8

Italian Wedding Soup
(Meatball Soup)

Have you ever eaten Italian Wedding Soup at a wedding? I haven't! And there's a good reason why: the name for this dish most likely comes from a mistranslation of the classic Neapolitan soup *Minestra Maritato*, which translates to "married soup." The soup's name doesn't refer to a marriage between people, but to how well the meat and greens work together in the soup!

▶ *For a how-to on dried bread crumbs, see page 32.*

Gluten-free nonstick cooking spray

Meatballs

1 pound ground sirloin (90 to 93% lean)

$1/4$ cup freshly grated Parmesan cheese

1 large clove garlic, minced or put through a garlic press

2 teaspoons dried parsley

2 teaspoons dried basil

1 teaspoon salt

1 teaspoon freshly ground black pepper

2 tablespoons gluten-free dried bread crumbs

1 large egg

Pasta

2 teaspoons salt

2 cups gluten-free bite-size shells

1 tablespoon olive oil

Soup

1 tablespoon olive oil

2 carrots, peeled and thinly sliced

2 stalks celery, thinly sliced

1 large onion, diced

2 cloves garlic, minced or put through a garlic press

$1/2$ teaspoon salt

8 cups homemade chicken stock (page 69) or store-bought reduced-sodium broth

2 cups water

5 ounces baby spinach

1. Set a rimmed baking sheet on your counter near where you are working. Lightly spray it with nonstick cooking spray.

2. To make the meatballs, in a medium bowl, combine the ground beef, cheese, garlic, parsley, basil, salt, and black pepper. Using your hands or a wooden spoon, mix until all ingredients are evenly distributed. Add the bread crumbs and egg. Mix until combined.

3. For each meatball, pinch off a little less than a tablespoon of the beef mixture and roll it into a ball. Remember, you want these meatballs to be bite-size, so don't pinch off too large a piece. Place the meatballs on the prepared baking sheet. If you aren't going to make the soup right away, wrap the pan of meatballs with plastic wrap and refrigerate.

(continued)

4. To cook the pasta, fill a medium (4-quart) pot three-quarters full with water. Cover and bring to a boil over medium-high heat. Set a colander in the sink for draining the pasta. When the water reaches a boil, add the salt and pasta. Stir with a wooden spoon for about 30 seconds to keep it from sticking, then stir occasionally while the pasta cooks. Set a timer for 6 minutes. (For a how-to on cooking pasta, see page 105.)

5. While the pasta is cooking, begin the soup. Heat 1 tablespoon olive oil in a large (5$\frac{1}{2}$-quart) pot over medium-high heat until hot and shimmering but not smoking. Add the carrots. Cook, stirring occasionally with a wooden spoon, for 3 minutes. Add the celery, onion, garlic, and salt. Cook, stirring occasionally, for 2 minutes more. The vegetables should be soft and aromatic.

6. Add the chicken stock and water and bring to a boil.

7. After about 6 minutes of boiling, check the pasta for doneness. When tender with a little bite (al dente), drain it in the colander. (If it's not ready yet, let it cook a few minutes more and check it again.) Return the pasta to its pot and toss with 1 tablespoon olive oil.

8. Once the soup reaches a boil, add the meatballs, one at a time. After you've added half of them, stir the soup gently with a wooden spoon. Add the remaining meatballs and stir. Allow to boil for 5 minutes.

9. Lower the heat to medium-low and simmer (look for occasional gentle bubbles) for 20 minutes.

10. Add the pasta. Lower the heat to low and simmer the soup, uncovered, for 10 minutes.

11. Stir in the spinach with a wooden spoon. Cook until spinach is wilted and tender, 2 to 4 minutes. Season with salt and pepper to taste and serve.

Serves 6 to 8

MAKE IT EASIER

The meatballs in this soup can be made ahead and frozen. Then, when you are ready to make the soup, simply thaw the meatballs and use as directed.

Cream of Mushroom Soup

It might sound cliché but a bowl of cream of mushroom soup on a cold winter night really is one of my favorite things. I use white mushrooms in this recipe. Feel free to vary the flavor and use whatever mushrooms you love.

6 tablespoons unsalted butter or olive oil

1 small onion, finely diced

8 ounces white mushrooms, thinly sliced

$1/4$ cup sweet rice flour

2 cups gluten-free beef broth

4 cups whole milk

$1/2$ teaspoon dried thyme

Salt and freshly ground black pepper

1. In a large ($5^1/2$-quart) pot, melt the butter over medium heat. Add the onion and cook until soft, stirring occasionally with a wooden spoon. Add the mushrooms and cook until tender, about 7 minutes.

2. Switch to a whisk. Stir in the sweet rice flour; a paste will form. Cook for 3 minutes, whisking constantly. In a slow and steady stream, whisk in the beef broth and milk. Add the thyme. Simmer (look for occasional gentle bubbles) for 20 minutes, letting the soup thicken and the flavors blend.

3. Season with salt and pepper to taste and serve.

Serves 4 to 6

Corn Chowder

You know those foods that you just prefer a certain way? I'm like that with corn chowder. I like the delicate flavor of the corn to be backed up by a little spicy kick. This recipe uses hot pepper sauce to give the soup its kick. If you prefer your corn chowder without the "heat," leave the pepper sauce out.

2 tablespoons unsalted butter

1 small onion, finely diced

2 tablespoons sweet rice flour

3 cups milk, warmed

2 cups homemade chicken stock (page 69) or store-bought reduced-sodium broth

1 bag (12 ounces) frozen corn kernels, thawed

2 medium russet potatoes, peeled and diced (3 cups)

$1/2$ teaspoon dried thyme

Salt and freshly ground black pepper

$1/2$ teaspoon hot pepper sauce

1. Melt the butter in a large ($5^1/2$-quart) pot over medium-high heat. Add the onion and cook, stirring with a wooden spoon, until tender but not brown, about 3 minutes.

2. Switch to a whisk and stir in the sweet rice flour until a paste forms. Whisking constantly, cook for 3 minutes.

3. In a slow and steady steam, add the milk. Allow the paste to absorb the milk as you add it. This will prevent clumping. At first, add the milk slowly; as you add more milk, you can slightly increase the pouring speed until it's all in. Stir in the chicken stock, corn, potatoes, thyme, $1/2$ teaspoon salt, and $1/2$ teaspoon pepper.

4. Bring the soup to a gentle boil. Lower the heat to medium-low and simmer (look for occasional gentle bubbles) for 45 minutes.

5. Ladle 2 cups of the soup into a blender and blend until smooth. The soup shouldn't fill the blender more than halfway. If you have a small blender, do this in batches. (For a how-to on puréeing soup, see page 72.)

6. Return the puréed soup to the pot and stir to combine. Add the hot pepper sauce. Taste and adjust the seasoning with salt and pepper as needed. Simmer over medium heat for 5 minutes or until the soup is hot, and serve.

Serves 4 as a main course

SERVING SUGGESTION

I really like this soup in the summer with a BLT Salad (page 91).

VARIATION

Clam and Corn Chowder: I love corn chowder and I love clam chowder. See where I am going with this? Add a can or two of chopped clams, with their juices, after you've puréed the soup. Simmer the soup for 5 to 10 minutes to warm the clams.

Tomato Soup

Have you ever sat down to a bowl of tomato soup only to discover that it tasted like a tomato *sauce* instead? Unappetizing, right? This soup avoids that pitfall by using dill, not basil or oregano, to flavor the soup. The tomato flavor is vibrant and unlike anything you'd spoon over pasta.

$^1/_4$ cup olive oil

1 medium onion, diced

2 cloves garlic, minced or put through a garlic press

1 teaspoon kosher salt

1 teaspoon dried dill

4 or 5 drops hot pepper sauce

3 cups water

2 cups homemade chicken stock (page 69) or store-bought reduced-sodium broth

2 cans (28 ounces each) diced tomatoes, with juices

1. Heat the oil in a large (5$^1/_2$-quart) pot over medium-high heat until hot and shimmering but not smoking. Add the onion. Cook, stirring frequently with a wooden spoon, until soft and translucent, about 2 minutes. Add the garlic and salt. Cook, stirring, until soft, another 45 seconds.

2. Add the dill, hot pepper sauce, water, stock, and tomatoes and bring to a boil. Lower the heat and simmer (look for occasional gentle bubbles) for 30 minutes.

3. Place a large bowl next to the blender. Purée the soup in batches, never filling the blender more than half full, until all the soup is smooth. Pour each puréed batch into the waiting bowl. (For a how-to on puréeing soup, see page 72.)

4. Pour all the soup back into the pot. Simmer over medium heat for 5 minutes or until the soup is hot, and serve.

Serves 6

Cream of Potato Soup

I always loved the bits of potato in clam chowder but I'd never had cream of potato soup until a friend made it for me. It was filled with tender potato bits. I fell in love immediately. Not only does this soup taste great, but I usually have all the ingredients on hand. Cream of potato soup and a salad is an easy answer to "What's for dinner tonight?"

3 tablespoons unsalted butter

2 medium onions, finely diced

2 scallions (green onions), thinly sliced (white and green parts)

8 medium russet potatoes (3 to 4 pounds), peeled and diced (about 12 cups)

4 cups homemade chicken stock (page 69) or store-bought reduced-sodium broth

2 cups whole milk

Salt and freshly ground black pepper

1. In a large (5^1/2-quart) pot, melt the butter over medium heat. Add the onions and scallions. Cook, stirring occasionally with a wooden spoon, until the vegetables are soft, about 5 minutes.

2. Add the potatoes and chicken stock. Bring to a boil. Lower the heat and simmer (look for occasional gentle bubbles) until the potatoes are soft, about 20 minutes.

3. Add the milk and season with salt and a generous amount of black pepper. Simmer for an additional 5 minutes, until heated through, and serve.

Serves 4 to 6

VARIATION

Cream of Potato Soup with Ham: This soup is great with leftover ham for an even heartier meal. Stir about 2 cups diced ham into the soup along with the milk.

Navy Bean Soup

Every Tuesday when I was a student at The Culinary Institute of America, Senate Bean Soup was served in the dining room. Tuesdays quickly became my favorite day of the week. This is my version of that soup.

1 tablespoon olive oil

1 smoked ham steak (about 12 ounces), diced small

2 large carrots, peeled and thinly sliced

1 medium onion, finely diced

2 cloves garlic, minced or put through a garlic press

8 cups homemade chicken stock (page 69) or store-bought reduced-sodium broth

2 cans (15 ounces each) navy beans, drained and rinsed

1 large russet potato, peeled and diced small

Salt and freshly ground black pepper

1. In a large (5^1/2-quart) pot, heat the olive oil over medium-high until hot and shimmering but not smoking. Add the ham and cook, stirring frequently with a wooden spoon, until the ham is brown on all sides. Add the carrots and cook for 2 minutes, stirring occasionally. Add the onion and garlic and cook, stirring frequently, until the onion is soft and slightly translucent, about 5 minutes.

2. Add the chicken stock, beans, and potato. Simmer for 30 minutes, uncovered, or until the potato pieces are tender.

3. Place a large bowl next to the blender. Purée half of the soup in batches, never filling the blender more than half full, until smooth. Pour each puréed batch into the waiting bowl. (For a how-to on puréeing soup, see page 72.)

4. Return the puréed soup to the pot. Stir to combine. Season with salt and pepper to taste. Simmer over medium heat for 5 minutes or until the soup is hot, and serve.

Serves 8

Sweet Potato Soup

A few years ago, while visiting family in Burlington, Vermont, I stopped at a little restaurant called Smokejacks. I ordered a small bowl of sweet potato soup and after my first spoonful, I wished my bowl were bigger. Sadly, the restaurant has since closed; now I make my sweet potato soup at home and eat as big a bowl as I like!

2 tablespoons unsalted butter

1 medium onion, finely diced

2 stalks celery, thinly sliced

3 cloves garlic, minced or put through a garlic press

2 large sweet potatoes, peeled and diced (about 3 cups)

5 cups homemade chicken stock (page 69) or store-bought reduced-sodium broth

1 cinnamon stick or $^1/_2$ teaspoon ground cinnamon

$^1/_4$ teaspoon ground nutmeg

$^1/_2$ teaspoon salt

$^1/_2$ cup evaporated milk

1. Melt the butter in a large ($5^1/_2$-quart) pot over medium heat. Add the onion, celery, and garlic. Cook, stirring frequently with a wooden spoon, for 8 to 10 minutes, until the vegetables are very soft but not brown. If they begin to brown, lower the heat.

2. Add the sweet potatoes, chicken stock, cinnamon, nutmeg, and salt. Bring the soup to a boil, then lower the heat to medium-low. Simmer (look for occasional gentle bubbles) for 35 minutes, or until the sweet potatoes are very tender. (Test the sweet potatoes with a fork. They should break apart easily when pierced by the tines of a fork.) When the potatoes are tender, remove the cinnamon stick (if using) and turn off the heat.

3. Place a large bowl next to a blender. Purée the soup in batches, never filling the blender more than half full, until the soup is smooth. (For a how-to on puréeing soup, see page 72.) Pour each puréed batch into the waiting bowl. Repeat until all the soup has been puréed.

4. Return the soup to the pot. Add the milk and stir with a wooden spoon. Reheat over medium-low heat but don't bring soup to a boil. Taste and add more salt if you think it needs it.

5. Ladle the soup into individual bowls and serve hot. If desired, garnish as suggested.

Serves 4 to 6

This soup is great on its own, but it's even better with a few easy garnishes. Use as many of these additions as you'd like—they are great alone or combined!

- **Pumpkin seeds**: Sprinkle a few shelled pumpkin seeds on top of each bowl.

- **Sliced scallions** (green onions): Just a few thin slices of scallion can add a different flavor note to the soup. A few slices in the center of each bowl of soup are delightful. Don't add too many or the onion y flavor might overwhelm the soup.

- **Sour cream or crème fraîche**: A dollop of sour cream or crème fraîche transforms this soup into a creamy delight. When using sour cream, I usually make the soup with the chipotle hot sauce variation that follows. This way the creaminess of the sour cream is balanced by the heat of the hot sauce. For a really attractive presentation, put a few drops of chipotle hot sauce on top of the dollop of sour cream.

Chipotle-Spiced Sweet Potato Soup: Chipotle hot sauce adds a smoky heat to the soup but won't overwhelm the delicate sweet potato flavor. For a spicy twist, add 5 or 6 drops of chipotle hot sauce to the soup at the end of cooking when you add the milk.

Hearty Chicken Soup

When I think of homemade soup, chicken noodle is the first soup that springs to mind. Here is the classic, now gluten-free.

At this time, gluten-free egg noodles are not available. I use either shells or elbows.

2 tablespoons plus 2 teaspoons olive oil

2 large carrots, peeled and thinly sliced

1 large onion, finely diced

3 stalks celery, thinly sliced

2 cloves garlic, minced or put through a garlic press

$1^1/2$ teaspoons dried thyme

Salt

$^1/2$ teaspoon freshly ground black pepper

3 pounds split bone-in chicken breasts, skin removed

6 cups cold water

4 cups homemade chicken stock (page 69) or reduced-sodium store-bought broth

8 ounces gluten-free pasta (shells or elbows)

1. In a large ($5^1/2$-quart) pot, heat 2 tablespoons olive oil over medium-high heat. When the oil is hot and shimmering but not smoking, add the carrots. Cook for 2 minutes, stirring frequently with a wooden spoon. Add the onion and celery. Cook for 2 minutes, stirring frequently. Add garlic, thyme, 1 teaspoon salt, and the pepper. Cook until vegetables are soft but not brown, about 5 minutes. Stir occasionally.

2. Add the chicken breasts, water, and chicken stock. Bring to a boil. Once it reaches a boil, skim the top of the soup and discard the scum. (The scum is the foam that will sit on top of the soup. Sometimes there is a lot of scum, other times hardly any.) Lower the heat to low and simmer (look for occasional gentle bubbles) for $1^1/2$ hours. Skim the soup as needed. As the soup cooks, if you notice it is reducing too much (the liquid is evaporating and the chicken is exposed), add an additional cup of water or chicken stock.

3. Once the soup has been cooking about an hour, bring a medium (4-quart) pot of water to a boil and set a colander in the sink. Add 2 teaspoons salt and the pasta to the boiling water. Stir with a wooden spoon for about 30 seconds to prevent the pasta from sticking, then stir occasionally while the pasta cooks. Cook until tender, following the timing on the package. (For a how-to on boiling pasta, see page 105.) Drain the pasta in the colander. Toss the pasta

with 2 teaspoons olive oil to keep the pasta from sticking.

4. Remove the chicken from the soup with a slotted spoon and place on a clean cutting board. Using your hands or a couple of forks, remove the meat from the bones. (Be careful—it is very hot!) It will pull off the bones easily. Discard the bones. Look at the meat. If there is any fat or small bones clinging to it, remove and discard. Using a chef's knife, cut the chicken into small pieces. (Since this is soup, be sure to cut the chicken pieces small. You want the chicken pieces to fit easily on a soup spoon.) Return the chicken to the soup. Stir to combine.

5. Add the pasta to the soup and stir. Taste and adjust the seasoning with salt and pepper as needed. Serve hot.

Serves 6 to 8

How to:
Store and Reheat Soup

▶ *1. Place cooled, leftover soup in a container with a lid and refrigerate. Leftover soup can be refrigerated for up to three days.*

▶ *2. Reheat the soup in the microwave or on the stovetop. If reheating in the microwave, place the soup in a microwave-safe container and heat on HIGH for about one minute; stir. Return the soup to the microwave and continue heating until warm. Do not overheat. On the stovetop, heat the soup in a medium pot over medium-low, stirring occasionally, until warm.*

4.
Salads

How to:
Make a Vinaigrette

The recipe for Basic Vinaigrette (page 88) will give you all sorts of ideas for combinations of oils, vinegars, and seasonings to use. This gives you the basic way to make it.

Vinegar

Mustard

Oil

Seasonings (salt, pepper, herbs, spices)

▲ 1. In a bowl, combine the mustard and vinegar.

▲ 2. Whisk until the mustard and vinegar are smooth.

▲ 3. Whisk in the oil in a slow and steady stream.

▲ 4. Season as directed.

Basic Vinaigrette

Many bottled salad dressings are now gluten-free. Even so, I still like to make vinaigrettes from scratch. The ingredients in the recipes are merely suggestions. Adapt them to fit your tastes and your individual salad.

Measure the oil in a cup with a spout, it's easier to pour. And don't leave out the sugar—it really makes a difference!

1/4 cup vinegar (see Variations for suggestions)
1 tablespoon Dijon mustard
3/4 cup extra virgin olive oil
Kosher salt and freshly ground black pepper
Pinch of granulated sugar

- In a small bowl, whisk together the vinegar and mustard. While whisking vigorously, add oil in a slow and steady steam. Season with salt and pepper to taste. Whisk in the sugar. Store the vinaigrette in an airtight container in the refrigerator for up to 2 weeks.

Makes about 1 cup vinaigrette

VARIATIONS

Using a different vinegar will give you a different vinaigrette:

- Balsamic; Red wine; White wine; Apple cider

Remember that malt vinegar is not gluten-free.

Even the simplest ingredient can change the taste of your vinaigrettes. Using apple cider vinegar and a drizzle of maple syrup instead of the pinch of sugar gives you a maple vinaigrette. Here are some ingredients to have fun playing with.

SWEETENERS, IN PLACE OF THE SUGAR:

- Honey

- Maple syrup (Use pure maple syrup for the best flavor. Imitation maple syrup isn't great in a vinaigrette.)

- Lyle's Golden Syrup (This is a cane syrup with a nice caramel flavor.)

- Molasses

FLAVOR ADDITIONS:

- Minced garlic. In the summer look for garlic scapes, a stalk that grows out of the garlic bulb, at your local farmers' market. Garlic scapes aren't as pungent as regular garlic. A few slivers in a vinaigrette add a fresh garlic flavor.

- Minced red onion, scallion (green onion), yellow onion, or sweet onion like Vidalia

- Grated lemon, orange, or grapefruit zest

- Minced fresh or dried herbs are great in vinaigrettes. I especially like:

    Dill; Chives; Thyme; Basil, any variety; Chervil; Rosemary (Use a little and taste the vinaigrette. A little rosemary is great. Too much can be overwhelming.)

Citrus Vinaigrette

While this vinaigrette can be made all year, I find myself making it more in the summer than any other time. I like the fresh citrus flavor with summer fruits and vegetables.

Any prepared mustard will work, but the bright yellow kind can give your vinaigrette an unattractive hue.

1 lemon

2 teaspoons prepared mustard

6 tablespoons extra virgin olive oil

1 clove garlic, minced or put through a garlic press

Pinch of granulated sugar

Pinch of salt

• Grate the zest (just the yellow outside) from the lemon and set it aside. Cut the lemon in half and squeeze out 2 tablespoons of juice. Whisk together the lemon juice and mustard. Add the oil in a slow and steady stream, whisking constantly. When all the oil is added, whisk in the garlic, sugar, salt, and lemon zest. Use immediately.

Makes about $1/2$ cup vinaigrette

Maple Vinaigrette

This sweet-tart vinaigrette is fantastic on fall salads. Try adding it to a salad with sliced pears, dried cranberries, and toasted almonds.

2 tablespoons maple syrup

2 teaspoons Dijon mustard

2 tablespoons apple cider vinegar

$1/4$ cup extra virgin olive oil

$1/2$ teaspoon kosher salt

$1/4$ teaspoon freshly ground black pepper

• Whisk together the maple syrup, mustard, and vinegar. Add the oil in a slow and steady stream, whisking constantly. When all the oil is added, whisk in the salt and pepper. Use immediately.

Makes about $1/2$ cup vinaigrette

How to: Make Croutons

Croutons are easy to make! I like to use my White Sandwich Bread (page 206) for croutons but any gluten-free bread will work. I use herbs such as parsley, basil, or oregano, but feel free to use any combination of herbs and spices you prefer.

2 cups cubed white sandwich bread

About 3 tablespoons unsalted butter, melted, or olive oil

Minced fresh herbs

Kosher salt

$^1/_8$ teaspoon garlic powder

▶ *1. Adjust oven rack to the middle position and preheat the oven to 325°F.*

▲ *2. In a large bowl, toss together the bread and melted butter. All the bread cubes should be lightly coated. Add more melted butter, if needed.*

▲ *3. Sprinkle the herbs onto the bread and toss until all the cubes have a light dusting of herbs. I start with about 1$^1/_2$ teaspoons and add more if needed.*

▶ *4. Add a couple of pinches of salt and the garlic powder and toss again.*

▲ *5. Transfer the cubes to a rimmed baking sheet and spread them in one layer.*

▲ *6. Bake for 15 minutes. Remove the pan from the oven. Toss the cubes and return to the oven. Bake until the croutons are crisp and golden brown, about 15 minutes more.*

Makes 2 cups croutons

BLT Salad

This salad is a playful take on the classic BLT sandwich. The ingredients are simple, requiring the tomatoes to be at the peak of freshness. This means I only make it in the summer, with tomatoes from the garden or farmers' market.

▶ *For a how-to on cooking bacon, see page 43.*

---

12 to 16 ounces romaine or iceberg lettuce, torn into bite-size pieces (about 8 cups)

Ranch dressing

1 pint cherry tomatoes, halved, or 2 or 3 large tomatoes, sliced

Croutons

8 to 10 slices bacon, cooked crisp, drained, and crumbled

---

1. Place the lettuce in a large bowl. Pour about $^1/_4$ cup dressing over the leaves. You want enough dressing to coat the leaves but not so much that the salad is swimming. It's better to add a little at the beginning and then add more, than to add too much at first. Toss with salad tongs to combine.

2. Add the tomatoes, croutons, and bacon. Toss lightly with the tongs to distribute everything evenly throughout the salad. Divide among plates and serve immediately, with extra dressing on the side.

Serves 4

VARIATIONS

BLTT Salad: Add about 1 cup diced or 4 ounces sliced turkey, either leftover roast turkey or gluten-free deli meat.

BLTC Salad: Add about 1 cup diced or 4 ounces sliced cooked chicken.

Taco Salad

Remember those fried taco bowls that were popular in restaurants? A big, fried, gluten-filled tortilla filled with lots of ground meat, cheese, sour cream and guacamole—and they called this diet-buster a salad! My version uses a few bagged tortilla chips in place of the fried tortilla bowl and ground turkey instead of beef. It celebrates the old taco salad without being too heavy.

2 teaspoons olive oil

1 clove garlic, minced or put through a garlic press

8 ounces lean ground turkey or ground sirloin (90 to 92% lean)

2 teaspoons chili powder

$1/2$ cup salsa, homemade (page 64) or store-bought

1 head romaine or iceberg lettuce, torn into bite-size pieces (about 8 cups)

Ranch dressing, as needed

1 can (15 ounces) black beans, drained and rinsed

$1/2$ green, red, or yellow bell pepper, cored and cut into bite-size pieces

1 pint grape tomatoes, or 2 large tomatoes, sliced

2 scallions (green onions), chopped (white and green parts)

2 ounces cheddar cheese, grated ($1/2$ cup)

1 ripe Hass avocado, pitted, peeled, and sliced

Tortilla chips

1. In a medium (10-inch) nonstick frying pan, heat the olive oil over medium-high heat. Add the garlic and cook until aromatic. Add the ground turkey and cook, breaking up the clumps with a wooden spoon or heatproof spatula, until thoroughly cooked and browned. If desired, remove and discard any excess fat. (For a how-to on cooking ground meat, see page 44.)

2. Add the chili powder and salsa. Remove the pan from the heat to prevent overcooking and let the turkey cool.

3. Put the lettuce in a large salad bowl. Pour about $1/4$ cup dressing over the leaves. (You want enough dressing to coat the leaves but not so much that the salad is swimming. It's better to add a little at the beginning and then add more, than to add too much at first.) Toss with salad tongs to combine.

4. Add the black beans, bell pepper, tomatoes, and scallions. Gently toss to distribute everything evenly throughout the salad.

5. Divide the salad evenly among four plates. Top with the turkey mixture, cheese, and avocado. Crumble a few tortilla chips over the top of the salad and serve with additional chips, if desired.

Serves 4

Fall Chicken, Cherry, Apple, and Almond Salad

When tomatoes and basil go away for the winter, I am usually a bit sad. Then I take one bite of this salad that celebrates fall and suddenly I know I'll be okay!

Don't feel like chopping almonds? Use sliced almonds. Don't have any leftover chicken? For a how-to on cooking chicken, see page 45. And to prevent the apples from turning brown, core and slice them right before you add them to the salad.

3 romaine hearts, chopped or torn into bite-size pieces

2 large cooked chicken breasts, cut into bite-size pieces

$^1/_4$ cup dried cherries

$^1/_2$ cup whole almonds, chopped

Maple Vinaigrette (page 89)

2 large Granny Smith or other tart apples, cored and sliced

• Place the lettuce on a large platter. Top with the chicken, cherries, and almonds. Drizzle the vinaigrette over the salad. Arrange the apples on top and serve immediately.

Serves 4

NOTE

You can also use a rotisserie chicken for this recipe, just make sure it's gluten-free.

Bacon, Sweet Potato, and Onion Spinach Salad

Baked sweet potatoes cubes take the place of croutons in this winter salad. The combination of the sweet potatoes and the saltiness of the bacon is a gentle contrast. If you can find hickory-smoked or cob-smoked bacon, use it in this salad. The smoky flavor it adds is lovely.

I like to add one egg per person. If you like fewer, make two eggs for this salad

▶ *For how-to's on cooking and peeling eggs, see page 41.*

▶ *For a how-to on cooking bacon, see page 43.*

8 ounces baby spinach (8 cups)

Maple Vinaigrette (page 89)

$1/2$ large red onion, cut into thin slivers

1 large sweet potato, roasted (page 251)

8 to 10 slices bacon, cooked crisp, drained, and crumbled

2 to 4 hard-cooked eggs, peeled and sliced

1. Put the spinach in a large salad bowl. Drizzle with vinaigrette and toss with salad tongs. (Start with a light drizzle and add more as needed. You want the dressing to lightly coat the leaves.) Add the onion, sweet potato cubes, and bacon. Toss gently to evenly distribute all the ingredients throughout the salad.

2. Divide the salad evenly among four plates. Place sliced egg on each plate. Drizzle with a little more dressing and serve immediately.

Serves 4

Classic Chicken Caesar

Traditional Caesar dressing uses a raw egg. I've avoided this by replacing the raw egg and oil with mayonnaise. But don't worry—the dressing isn't too heavy or mayo-y. (Use regular or reduced fat mayo. Fat-free doesn't work well in this dressing.) I did leave in the anchovies that are part of a classic Caesar dressing. If you don't like them, leave them out. It's your salad, make it the way you like it! A few capers in their place provide a nice salty-briny flavor in place of the missing anchovies.

If you have them, grilled chicken breasts are really delicious here. If not, just use whatever cooked chicken you have. (For directions on grilling chicken, see Penne with Tomato Cream Sauce and Grilled Chicken on page 119.)

▶ *For a how-to on other ways to cook chicken, see page 45.*

▶ *For a how-to on making croutons, see page 90.*

Dressing

4 anchovy fillets

$1/4$ cup freshly squeezed lemon juice

$1/3$ cup mayonnaise

$1/3$ cup freshly grated Parmesan cheese, plus more for garnish (optional)

1 tablespoon Dijon mustard

1 clove garlic, minced or put through a garlic press

Salt and freshly ground black pepper

Salad

8 ounces romaine hearts, chopped or torn into bite-size pieces (about 8 cups)

2 large cooked chicken breasts, cut into strips

Croutons, as needed

1. Prepare the dressing: On a cutting board, using a chef's knife, mince the anchovy fillets until they are almost a paste. In a small bowl, using a small whisk or fork, whisk together the lemon juice and mayonnaise until smooth. Add the cheese, mustard, and garlic and whisk until smooth. Add the anchovies and stir to just combine. Taste and adjust the seasoning with salt and pepper as needed.

2. In a large salad bowl, toss together the lettuce and dressing with salad tongs. Divide the salad among plates. Top with chicken and croutons. If you feel like it, add a sprinkle more cheese. (I always do!) Serve immediately.

Serves 4

Melon and Prosciutto Salad

My dad loved prosciutto. Since we had a lean food budget, he wasn't able to buy it often but when he did, I remember he'd sometimes wrap paper-thin slices around pieces of very ripe cantaloupe. I thought this was his special thing; I only later learned that melon and prosciutto is a classic pairing. This salad celebrates it.

The success of this recipe really depends on the ripeness of your cantaloupe and the flavor of your balsamic vinegar. Be sure to use a very ripe, very sweet melon and a balsamic vinegar that isn't too tart. Put a little on your pinky finger and taste it. The flavor should be mild and not too acidic, with a gentle sweetness. Using fresh mozzarella really makes a difference, too. You could buy bocconcini (small balls of fresh mozzarella) instead of dicing a ball of cheese.

1 ripe cantaloupe or musk melon, seeded, peeled, and cut into bite-size cubes

8 ounces fresh mozzarella, cut into bite size-pieces

1 tablespoon balsamic vinegar

4 slices prosciutto, cut into thin strips

4 or 5 fresh basil leaves

• In a medium serving bowl, gently stir together the melon and cheese. Sprinkle with the balsamic vinegar and stir to combine. Divide among plates and drape with the prosciutto. Tear the basil into small pieces and sprinkle over the salads. Serve immediately.

Serves 4 to 6

Make-Your-Own Dinner Salad

Dinner really doesn't get any easier than this "make your own" salad. Simply arrange cold cuts on one platter and salad ingredients on another and let everyone have fun creating the salad they want. All the ingredients are mere suggestions; replace them with whatever your family enjoys!

6 ounces baby greens (about 6 cups)

8 ounces sliced gluten-free deli turkey breast, cut into strips

4 ounces sliced gluten-free hard salami, cut into strips

5 ounces sliced provolone cheese, cut into strips

4 ounces fresh mozzarella, cut into bite-size pieces

1 can (14 ounces) artichoke hearts, drained and quartered

$1/2$ pint grape tomatoes, sliced

1 large Granny Smith apple, cored and cubed

A few handfuls of pitted kalamata olives

1 can (14.5 ounces) sliced beets, drained

Basic Vinaigrette (page 88) made with balsamic vinegar, or whatever dressings you like

• Put the greens in a salad bowl with tongs. Place the meats and cheeses on one platter. On another, place the artichoke hearts, tomatoes, apple, and olives. Put the beets in a small bowl (so they don't turn everything else Pepto-Bismol pink!). Let everyone make their own salad and dress it as desired.

Serves 4

Fresh Tomato, Mozzarella, and Basil Salad

This recipe is really a guide for enjoying the summer delights of fresh tomatoes and basil. Be sure to use absolutely the ripest summer tomatoes or this salad will be blah instead of brilliant! Instead of cutting up a ball of mozzarella, you can buy bocconcini, which are small balls of fresh mozzarella.

2 pounds ripe tomatoes (preferably heirloom), sliced

8 ounces fresh mozzarella, cut into bite-size pieces

Basic Vinaigrette (page 88), made with balsamic vinegar

6 to 8 fresh basil leaves

Kosher salt and freshly ground black pepper

• Arrange the tomatoes on a large platter. Scatter the cheese on top. Drizzle with vinaigrette. Tear the basil into small pieces and sprinkle over the top. Season with kosher salt and freshly ground black pepper. Serve immediately.

Serves 4

Winter Storm Salad

Living in upstate New York means that at least once per winter, you will get caught off guard by a snowstorm. During one unexpected storm, I threw this salad together because I was hungry and wanted a quick lunch. Funny thing happened—I really liked the salad and found myself making it on non-snow days. It's a great winter salad for one. The crisp Granny Smith apple brings a nice sweet-tart balance to the saltiness of the olives and pickle. (A pickle on a salad? Yes!) Even if you aren't snowed in, this salad is worth a try.

Handful of lettuce (whatever is in the house) torn into bite-size pieces

$1/2$ Granny Smith apple, chopped into bite-size pieces but not peeled

A few green olives, chopped

1 small pickle, chopped

Handful of cheddar cheese cubes

Dried fruit (optional; I like dried cranberries or dried cherries)

Dressing, whatever you are in the mood for that day (I usually use a vinaigrette)

• Place the lettuce on a plate. Top with remaining ingredients and dress to taste.

Serves 1

Greek Salad

Some days if I am really busy, I forget to eat lunch. Then I get really, *really* hungry and run into the kitchen with the goal of "find food!" As luck would have it, those are often the days when leftovers are scarce. So on those days I make a "sort of" Greek salad. I usually have lettuce, feta, olives, and a cucumber in the refrigerator. I omit the onions but because I don't love raw onions on my salad. If you do, add some to this simple salad.

You can use whatever lettuce you have in the house, but romaine is especially nice.

Handful of bite-size pieces lettuce
Chunk of feta cheese, cubed
Handful of pitted kalamata olives, chopped (I usually eat one or two while making the salad)
A few slivers of red onion
$1/2$ small cucumber, peeled and diced
Vinaigrette (whatever is in the refrigerator)

• Place the lettuce on a plate. Top with the feta, olives, cucumber, and onion. Dress to taste.

Serves 1

Grapefruit and Avocado Salad

I had this salad for the first time when I was a student at the CIA. I've loved it ever since. For the dressing, use grapefruit juice in the Citrus Vinaigrette (page 89).

▶ *For a how-to on pitting and peeling avocados, see page 39.*

5 ounces baby spinach (about 5 cups)
Citrus Vinaigrette (page 89)
2 large Hass avocados, pitted, peeled, and sliced
1 large red grapefruit, peeled and sectioned

1. Put the spinach in a large bowl. Drizzle a little of the vinaigrette over the top and toss with salad tongs to combine. Add more vinaigrette as needed. You want the vinaigrette to lightly coat the leaves. Reserve a little of the vinaigrette for drizzling over the top of the salad.

2. Arrange the spinach on a platter or individual plates. Top with the avocado slices and grapefruit sections. Drizzle with the remaining vinaigrette.

Serves 4

Feta and Watermelon Salad

Sweet watermelon pairs really well with salty feta and kalamata olives. It is a slightly unusual combination but one of my favorite refreshing meals during the summer. For the best salad, be sure to use a sweet, juicy watermelon. The better the melon, the better the salad.

6 ounces arugula (about 6 cups), torn into bite-size pieces

Basic Vinaigrette (page 88), made with white wine vinegar or lemon

4 ounces feta cheese, cut into bite-size cubes

Handful of pitted kalamata olives (optional)

3 cups peeled, seeded, cubed watermelon

• In a salad bowl, toss together the arugula and vinaigrette using salad tongs. Start with a light drizzle of vinaigrette and add more as needed. You want the dressing to lightly coat the leaves, not soak them. Add the feta and the olives, if using. Toss again to combine. Divide the salad among plates. Scatter the watermelon over the top and serve immediately.

Serves 4

5.
Pastas

Pasta Essentials

Gluten-free pasta cooks differently than wheat pasta. Here are some things you should know.

Use a large pot. You'll want to use a pot that is $5^1/2$ quarts or larger; an 8-quart pot is big enough for 1 pound of pasta.

Why a large pot? A large pot with lots of water gives the pasta enough room to boil and not stick together as gluten-free pasta has a tendency to do.

Cover the pot to keep in the heat so it comes to a boil faster.

Use lots of salt. There is an old Italian cooking adage about how pasta water should be as salty as the sea. Isn't that lovely? Adding salt to the cooking liquid helps to boost the flavor of the pasta. On its own, gluten-free pasta is pretty boring. You'll want to use 1 to $1^1/2$ tablespoons salt per pound of pasta. I bring my water to a boil, add the salt, and then finally the pasta. This brings me to . . .

Cook your pasta in vigorously boiling water. I know, I know. On some bags of gluten-free pasta it states that you can "cook" your pasta in a covered pot of hot water. I've found this makes for sticky pasta. If you want silky pasta, cook it in boiling water. Be sure your water is at a boil when you add the pasta and returns to a bubbling boil while the pasta cooks.

Don't add oil to the cooking water. There is this cooking myth that adding oil will prevent your pasta from sticking together. Not true! Oil in pasta water floats to the top of the pot. When you drain the pasta, it will coat your cooked noodles. And you know what this means? It means the sauce won't stick to them! You'll end up with noodles that can't hold sauce and, when chilled, will take on a weird crunchy texture. Ew! So no oil in the cooking water, thank you!

Stir. Gluten-free pasta sticks to itself if you don't prevent it. How to prevent this from happening? Stir it! As soon as you drop the pasta into the boiling water, begin to stir. Keep doing this for about 30 seconds. Then stir occasionally while the pasta cooks. The first 3 to 5 minutes are the most important for stirring. This is when your pasta releases the most starch and is the stickiest.

Taste. The cooking time printed on the back of the bag or box never, ever seems to be right. After about 10 minutes, check your pasta. If you are doing other things while the pasta cooks, set a timer. For gluten-free pasta, you want it to be cooked thoroughly—al dente doesn't really work well. Rice, which is what makes up most gluten-free pasta, isn't soft. When you bite into the pasta, look at it. If there is a dark spot in the center, it is not done. The texture and color should be the same all the way through.

Check it. When overcooked, gluten-free pasta becomes mushy. After the initial tasting, check it every 2 minutes. This will ensure that you don't overcook it.

Reserve. Reserve some cooking water for the sauce. Right before you drain the pasta, ladle out about 1 cup. Gluten-free pasta really soaks up sauce.

Drain and return to the pot. Once most of the hot water has drained, return the pasta to the cooking pot.

Sauce and enjoy! To loosen your sauce, add a bit of the reserved cooking liquid to your pasta when you add the sauce. In fact, you want enough sauce so that it looks like too much. This prevents your pasta from becoming dry.

Cook Gluten-Free Pasta

▷ *1. Bring a large, covered pot of water to a boil.*

◁ *2. Uncover and add a generous amount of salt and the pasta.*

◁ *3. Stir the pasta for 30 seconds, then stir occasionally while the pasta cooks.*

△ *4. After the pasta has been cooking for about 10 minutes, check your pasta for doneness. If it's done, reserve some of the cooking water.*

△ *5. Drain the pasta in a colander and return it to the cooking pot.*

◁ *6. Add your sauce and some of the cooking liquid if the pasta seems dry.*

Reheat Pasta

Gluten-free pasta often gets hard when chilled. Upon reheating, its soft texture returns.

Reheating Pasta Dishes

▷ *Spoon the desired amount of pasta onto a microwave-safe plate. Cover with plastic wrap and heat on HIGH for 1 minute. Remove the pasta and stir. Recover the pasta and continue heating until the pasta is warm. Microwave times will vary.*

Reheating Baked Pasta Dishes

Use this technique when reheating baked dishes such as baked ziti and macaroni and cheese.

▷ *For individual portions: It's easiest to reheat in the microwave. Cut a portion of pasta and place it on a microwave-safe dish. Cover with plastic wrap and heat on HIGH for 1 minute. Gently stir the pasta then recover and continue heating until the pasta is warm. Microwave times will vary.*

▷ *For multiple portions: Adjust oven rack to the middle position and preheat the oven to 325ºF. Reheat pasta for about 20 minutes; time will vary depending on how much you are reheating.*

Baked Gluten-Free Meatballs for Pasta

Poor meatballs! They have such a bad reputation for being hard to make. As this recipe proves, they aren't hard to make at all. All you need to do is squish together some ingredients, roll into balls, and bake. To make life even easier, meatballs can be frozen either raw or baked. Place raw or cooked meatballs on a pan in a single layer. Freeze for a few hours until firm and then transfer them to a freezer bag. Frozen, the meatballs will keep for up to three months. If you freeze them raw, simply bake from frozen, as directed in the recipe; they will take a little longer. If you freeze them baked, allow them to thaw and then heat in a 350°F oven.

Meatloaf mix is usually one-third each ground beef, pork, and veal. Be sure your store doesn't add bread to theirs.

▶ *For a how-to on making dried bread crumbs, see page 32.*

Gluten-free nonstick cooking spray

1^1/$_2$ pounds meatloaf mix or ground round (85 to 90% lean)

2 large eggs

^{1}/$_4$ cup milk

1 cup gluten-free dried bread crumbs

^{1}/$_2$ medium onion, finely diced

Generous 1 teaspoon dried basil

^{1}/$_2$ teaspoon dried oregano

Pinch of garlic powder

Pinch of salt

Pinch of freshly ground black pepper

1. Adjust oven rack to the middle position and preheat the oven to 400°F. Spray a rimmed baking sheet lightly with cooking spray or brush lightly with olive oil.

2. In a large bowl, combine all the ingredients. Stir with a wooden spoon or use your hands.

3. Roll the mixture into balls, about 2 tablespoons each. (I use a cookie scoop.) Place the meatballs on the prepared baking sheet.

4. Bake for 20 to 25 minutes, until the meatballs are firm and no longer pink. The internal temperature should read 165°F on an instant-read thermometer.

Makes enough meatballs for 1 pound of pasta (about 4 servings)

Pasta and Meatballs

You can't go wrong with a big bowl of pasta and meatballs; it's comfort food, plain and simple.

Gluten-free meatballs (page 106)

Basic tomato sauce (page 126)

1 tablespoon salt

1 pound gluten-free pasta, such as penne

1. Bake or reheat the meatballs according to the recipe. While the meatballs are heating, warm the sauce.

2. Fill a large ($5^1/2$-quart) pot three-quarters full with water. Cover and bring to a boil over high heat. Set a colander in the sink for draining the pasta.

3. When the water reaches a boil, add the salt and pasta. (Set a timer for 10 minutes.) Stir with a wooden spoon for about 30 seconds, then stir occasionally while the pasta cooks. After about 10 minutes, check the pasta for doneness. Cook the pasta until tender. (For a how-to on cooking pasta, see page 105.)

4. When the pasta is tender, ladle out about 1 cup of the pasta cooking water into a small heatproof bowl and set aside. Drain the pasta in the colander and return it to its pot over very low heat.

5. Add half of the sauce to the pasta. Stir to combine. If the pasta seems dry, stir in about $1/4$ cup of the cooking water.

6. Pour the pasta into a large serving bowl. Top with the meatballs and the remaining sauce. (Of course, you could place the pasta on individual plates and top with a few meatballs and sauce instead.) Serve immediately.

Serves 4

Pasta with Summer Vegetables

It seems to happen every summer: vegetables start calling to me, whether from my own garden or from the abundant stands at the local farmers' market. This pasta is a great way to answer their call.

Fresh onions from a farmers' market have a milder flavor than the onions found at the grocery store, so you'll need twice as many.

Salt
1 pound gluten-free pasta
$1/3$ cup olive oil
2 large fresh onions or 1 large yellow onion, thinly sliced
1 clove garlic, minced or put through a garlic press
$1/4$ teaspoon red pepper flakes (or more or less)
2 small zucchini, halved lengthwise and sliced $1/2$-inch thick (about 1 cup)
2 small yellow summer squash, halved lengthwise and sliced $1/2$-inch thick (about 1 cup)
2 cups grape tomatoes, halved
$1/2$ cup chopped fresh basil
Kosher salt and freshly ground black pepper
Freshly grated Parmesan cheese, for garnish

1. Fill a large (5$1/2$-quart) pot three-quarters full with water. Cover and bring to a boil over high heat. Set a colander in the sink for draining the pasta.

2. When the water reaches a boil, add 1 tablespoon salt and the pasta. (Set a timer for 10 minutes.) Stir with a wooden spoon for about 30 seconds, then stir occasionally while the pasta cooks. (For a how-to on cooking pasta, see page 105.)

3. While the pasta is cooking, make the sauce. In a large (12-inch) nonstick frying pan, heat the olive oil over medium-high heat until hot and shimmering but not smoking. Add the onions and cook, stirring frequently with a wooden spoon, until the onions are soft and translucent, about 3 minutes. Add the garlic, pepper flakes, and $1/2$ teaspoon salt. Cook until garlic is soft, stirring occasionally, about 45 seconds.

4. Add the zucchini and summer squash. Cook, stirring occasionally, until tender but not mushy, about 5 minutes. Lower the heat to low to keep warm.

5. After about 10 minutes of boiling, check the pasta for doneness. When the pasta is tender, ladle out about 1 cup of the pasta cooking water into a small heatproof bowl and set aside. Drain the pasta in the colander and return it to its pot over very low heat.

6. Add the squash mixture to the pasta and toss. Add the tomatoes and basil and toss well to

combine. If the sauce seems too thick, loosen it with a little of the pasta cooking water; stir in $^1/4$ cup to start, adding more if needed.

7. Season to taste with kosher salt, black pepper, and more pepper flakes, if you like. Pour pasta into a large serving bowl or spoon onto individual plates. Top with cheese. Serve and enjoy!

Serves 4

Chouriço and Spinach-Garlic Pasta

In my house, this pasta has become the answer to "I don't know what to make for dinner." I always keep the ingredients on hand. Since the pasta and sauce can be made in about 20 minutes, it's great for those nights when I'm hungry and want to eat *now*. The fact that this dish is also incredibly delicious doesn't hurt either!

Chouriço is a Portuguese sausage similar to Spanish chorizo, but not as spicy. If you can't find either one, use your favorite fully-cooked sausage.

$^1/3$ cup olive oil

7 ounces baby spinach (about 7 cups)

Salt

1 pound gluten-free penne pasta

1 pound gluten-free chouriço sausage, halved lengthwise and cut into bite-size pieces

4 cloves garlic, minced or put through a garlic press

$^1/4$ teaspoon red pepper flakes (optional)

8 ounces mozzarella, grated (2 cups)

$^1/4$ cup freshly grated Parmesan cheese

1 pint grape tomatoes, sliced

1 can (15.5 ounces) great Northern or cannellini beans, drained and rinsed

About 1 tablespoon chopped fresh basil or 1 teaspoon dried, or to taste

Kosher salt and freshly ground black pepper

1. Fill a large (5^1/$_2$-quart) pot three-quarters full with water. Cover and bring to a boil over high heat. Set a colander in the sink for draining the pasta.

2. While you wait for the water to come to boil, cook the spinach. Heat 1 teaspoon of the olive oil in another large (5^1/$_2$-quart) pot over high heat. When the oil is hot and shimmering but not smoking, add the spinach. Cook, tossing with tongs, until wilted and tender. The spinach will lose most of its volume during cooking. Remove from the heat and set aside. (Don't have another large pot? Cook the spinach in batches in a smaller pot or in a large frying pan. Transfer each batch to a heatproof bowl as it finishes cooking.)

3. When the water reaches a boil, add 1 tablespoon salt and the pasta. (Set a timer for 10 minutes.) Stir with a wooden spoon for about 30 seconds, then stir occasionally while the pasta cooks. (For a how-to on cooking pasta, see page 105.)

4. While the pasta is cooking, heat 1 tablespoon of the oil in a large (12-inch) nonstick frying pan over medium-high heat. When the oil is hot and shimmering but not smoking, add the chouriço and cook until golden brown, stirring occasionally with a wooden spoon.

5. Using a slotted spoon, remove the cooked sausage from the pan and place it in a bowl or on a plate. Wipe out the frying pan with a paper towel and return it to the stovetop.

6. Heat the remaining olive oil (about 4 tablespoons) over medium heat in the frying pan until hot and shimmering but not smoking. Add the garlic and pepper flakes, if using. Cook until the garlic is light golden brown. Once it reaches the desired color, lower the heat to low.

7. After about 10 minutes of boiling, check the pasta for doneness. When the pasta is tender, ladle out about 1 cup of the pasta cooking water into a small heatproof bowl and set aside. Drain the pasta in the colander and return it to its pot over very low heat.

8. Pour the olive oil and garlic over the pasta. Toss with a wooden spoon to coat. Stir in the mozzarella and Parmesan. When the mozzarella is melted, stir in the spinach, chouriço, tomatoes, beans, and basil.

9. Season with salt and pepper to taste. If the sauce seems too thick, loosen it with a little of the pasta cooking water; stir in ^{1}/$_4$ cup to start, adding more if needed. Serve immediately.

Serves 4

Penne alla Carbonara

I think spaghetti alla carbonara is not only one of the easiest pasta dishes to make, but also one of the tastiest. There are countless excellent carbonara variations.

You'll notice my recipe uses penne and not spaghetti. Why? I found that the carbonara got a bit clumpy with gluten-free spaghetti but penne produced a silky sauce. The next time you want a rich pasta dish that is easy to make, give this recipe a try.

Kosher salt

1 pound gluten-free penne pasta

4 large eggs

$^1/_4$ cup milk

$^1/_2$ cup freshly grated Parmesan cheese

1 teaspoon olive oil, plus more if needed

7 or 8 slices bacon

2 cloves garlic, minced or put through a garlic press

Freshly ground black pepper

1. Fill a large (5$^1/_2$-quart) pot three-quarters full with water. Cover and bring the water to a boil over high heat. Set a colander in the sink for draining the pasta. Line a plate with paper towels to drain the bacon, and line a bowl with paper towels for disposing of excess bacon fat.

2. When the water reaches a boil, add 1 tablespoon salt and the pasta. (Set a timer for 10 minutes.) Stir with a wooden spoon for about 30 seconds, then stir occasionally while the pasta cooks. (For a how-to on cooking pasta, see page 105.)

3. In a small bowl, whisk together the eggs, milk, and cheese.

4. Heat the oil in a medium (10-inch) nonstick frying pan over medium-high heat until hot and shimmering but not smoking. Add the bacon and cook, turning with tongs when the first side is golden. Remove the bacon from the pan when it's crisp and place it on the paper towel–lined plate to drain. Pour out all but 2 to 3 teaspoons of bacon fat from the frying pan into the bowl to discard when it's cool. (If you don't want to cook the garlic in bacon fat, discard all the bacon fat and heat 2 to 3 teaspoons of olive oil in the frying pan.)

4. Return the frying pan to the stovetop. Heat the fat over medium-high heat until hot but not smoking. Add the garlic and cook until golden brown and aromatic, about 45 seconds. Remove from the heat.

5. After about 10 minutes of boiling, check the pasta for doneness. When the pasta is tender, ladle out about 1 cup of the pasta cooking water into a small heatproof bowl and set aside. Drain the pasta in the colander and return it to its pot over very low heat.

6. Add the garlic and fat to the pasta. Toss with a wooden spoon to combine. Pour the egg mixture over the pasta. Working quickly, stir the pasta to evenly coat it. The heat from the pasta will cook the eggs.

7. Using your hands, crumble the bacon over the pasta. Stir to combine. If the sauce seems too thick, loosen it with a little of the pasta cooking water; stir in $1/4$ cup to start, adding more until the sauce is creamy.

8. Season with salt and pepper to taste. (Carbonara usually has a generous helping of freshly ground black pepper.) Serve immediately.

Serves 4

VARIATIONS

Penne alla Carbonara with Onions: I love adding onions to carbonara. They add a sweet flavor that goes really well with the salty bits of bacon. Cook the onions before you start cooking the pasta.

1 tablespoon unsalted butter

1 tablespoon olive oil

1 large onion or 2 medium onions, halved and sliced about $1/8$-inch thick

Pinch of salt

Tiny pinch of granulated sugar

• In a large (12-inch) nonstick frying pan, heat the butter and olive oil over medium heat until the butter is melted and the oil is hot. You don't want the butter to begin to brown. Add the onion, salt, and sugar. Stir to combine. Cook for 5 minutes. Lower the heat to low. Cook, stirring occasionally, until the onions are soft and brown, about 10 to 15 minutes. Keep the onions warm over very low heat while you prepare the

Penne alla Carbonara. Add the onions to the pasta after you've added the eggs and bacon.

Penne alla Carbonara with Bratwurst: Since bratwurst reminds me a little of breakfast sausage, I thought it would go well with eggy carbonara sauce. One day I had a few cooked brats in the refrigerator and decided to test my theory. It worked! You can either use leftover bratwursts or you can cook some up while you bring the water for the pasta to a boil. I'll leave it up to you if you want to include both bacon and bratwurst in this dish or omit the bacon and use only the bratwurst (If you do, cook the garlic in olive oil.)

2 tablespoons olive oil

4 bratwurst sausages

1. In a large (12-inch) nonstick frying pan, heat the olive oil over medium-high heat until hot and shimmering but not smoking. Add the bratwursts. Cook, turning occasionally with tongs, until cooked through, about 10 minutes.

2. Remove the bratwursts from the pan and place on a cutting board. Using a sharp knife, cut each bratwurst into $1/4$-inch slices. If your pasta isn't ready, return the sausage to the pan and keep warm over low heat. Once you've added the eggs to the pasta and tossed them, add the sausage. Toss to combine, season to taste, and serve.

Penne alla Carbonara with Bratwurst and Onions: Combine both variations for a great pasta dish!

Baked Ziti

Baked ziti is similar to lasagna (they both contain a ricotta filling) but ziti is a little easier to make. This recipe makes a pan of what I think of as the ultimate comfort food.

Gluten-free nonstick cooking spray

Filling

16 ounces ricotta cheese

1 cup freshly grated Parmesan and/or Romano cheese

2 large eggs

2 teaspoons dried basil

Sauce

$1/4$ cup olive oil

$1^1/2$ pounds ground sirloin (90 to 92% lean)

1 medium onion, finely diced

$1/2$ green bell pepper, seeded and finely diced

3 cloves garlic, minced or put through a garlic press

1 can (14.5 ounces) petite diced tomatoes

1 can (29 ounces) tomato sauce

1 can (6 ounces) tomato paste

$3/4$ cup water

1 tablespoon dried basil

Salt and freshly ground black pepper

Pasta

Salt

1 pound gluten-free ziti or penne pasta

Topping

8 ounces mozzarella cheese, shredded (2 cups)

$1/4$ cup grated Parmesan and/or Romano cheese

1. Adjust oven rack to the middle position and preheat the oven to 400°F. Lightly spray a 13 by 9-inch baking dish with nonstick cooking spray.

2. In a medium bowl, combine the ricotta, Parmesan, eggs, and basil for the filling. The mixture will be thick.

3. Fill a large ($5^1/2$-quart) pot three-quarters full with water. Cover and bring to a boil over high heat. Set a colander in the sink for draining the pasta.

4. While you wait for the pasta water to come to a boil, begin the sauce. In a medium (4-quart) pot, heat the olive oil over high heat until hot and shimmering but not smoking. Add the ground beef and cook, breaking up the clumps with a wooden spoon or heatproof spatula, until thoroughly cooked and browned. If desired, remove and discard any excess fat. (For a how-to on cooking ground meat, see page 44.)

5. Add the onion, bell pepper, and garlic. Stirring constantly, cook until the vegetables are soft, about 3 to 4 minutes.

6. Lower the heat to medium. Stir in the diced tomatoes, tomato sauce, tomato paste, and water until thoroughly combined. Stir in the basil. Raise the heat slightly and bring the sauce to a boil. Once it reaches a boil, lower the heat to medium-low. Allow the sauce to simmer while you cook the pasta.

7. When the pasta water reaches a boil, add 1 tablespoon salt and the pasta. (Set a timer for 10 minutes.) Stir with a wooden spoon for about 30 seconds, then stir occasionally while the pasta cooks. After about 10 minutes of boiling, check the pasta for doneness. When the pasta is tender, ladle out about 1 cup of the pasta cooking water into a small heatproof bowl and set aside. Drain the pasta in the colander and return it to its pot over very low heat. (For a how-to on cooking pasta, see page 105.)

8. Add three-quarters of the sauce to the pasta. Stir to combine with a wooden spoon.

9. Pour half of the pasta in the baking dish. Using a large spoon or ladle, spoon the cheese filling over pasta. Smooth the filling with the back of the spoon, or a spatula if it is easier. Evenly spoon remaining pasta into the baking dish.

10. Cover the pasta with the remaining sauce. Sprinkle the mozzarella and Parmesan evenly over the top of the pasta.

11. Bake, uncovered, until the cheese is golden brown and the sauce is bubbling, about 1 hour. Remove from oven and allow to stand for 5 minutes before serving.

Serves 8

Penne with Roasted Garlic Cream Sauce

I love culinary magic tricks. Roasted garlic is one of them. Sharp, pungent raw garlic is transformed into something totally different. It becomes silky, almost sweet. If you've never roasted garlic, you are in for a treat! This sauce is wonderful for the winter. There are no sharp edges to it. Cream and roasted garlic combine to create a sauce that even a vampire would love.

2 heads garlic (the entire head, not the individual cloves)

Olive oil

Salt

1 pound gluten-free penne pasta

1 1/2 cups half-and-half

3 tablespoons butter

1/4 teaspoon freshly ground black pepper

1/2 cup freshly grated Parmesan cheese

1. Adjust oven rack to the middle position and preheat the oven to 400°F. Cut two large squares of aluminum foil.

2. Place a garlic head on its side on a cutting board. Hold it firmly in place with one hand. Using a chef's knife, cut about one-third off the top of the head to expose the very tips of the garlic cloves. Place the head on a piece of foil, cut side up. Drizzle the top of the garlic head lightly with olive oil. Try to get a little oil on each exposed clove. Gather the foil around the head, bunching and twisting the foil tightly over the top. (It should look like a little handle.) Repeat with the second head. Place the foil packets on a rimmed baking sheet and bake the garlic for 35 minutes, or until the cloves are fork-tender. Remove the garlic from the oven. Open the foil packets to allow the garlic to cool as you begin the pasta. Turn off the oven; you are done with it.

3. Fill a large (5 1/2-quart) pot three-quarters full with water. Cover and bring to a boil over high heat. Set a colander in the sink for draining the pasta.

4. When the water reaches a boil, add 1 tablespoon salt and the pasta. (Set a timer for 10 minutes.) Stir with a wooden spoon for about 30 seconds, then stir occasionally while the pasta cooks. (For a how-to on cooking pasta, see page 105.)

5. While the pasta cooks, prepare the sauce. Separate the roasted garlic heads into individual cloves. Squeeze the garlic out of the papery skins into a small bowl. Mash the cloves with a fork until a thick paste forms. Set aside.

6. Combine the half-and-half, butter, 1/2 teaspoon salt, and the pepper in a small (2 quart) pot over medium heat. Once the butter has melted, whisk in the garlic paste with a small whisk or fork. Whisk vigorously to distribute the garlic paste evenly throughout sauce. The garlic paste should almost disappear into the sauce. You

don't want any large chunks floating around.

7. Add the cheese and whisk to combine. Lower the heat under the sauce to low. This is a good time to check the pasta if you haven't already.

8. After about 10 minutes of boiling, check the pasta for doneness. When the pasta is tender, ladle out about 1 cup of the pasta cooking water into a small heatproof bowl and set aside. Drain the pasta in the colander and return it to its pot over very low heat.

9. Add the sauce and toss with a wooden spoon to combine. If the sauce seems too thick, loosen it with a little of the pasta cooking water; stir in $1/4$ cup to start, adding more if needed, until the sauce is creamy. Serve immediately.

Serves 4

Penne with Roasted Garlic Cream Sauce and Artichoke Hearts: I really love this pasta with artichoke hearts. It might be because it's similar to the first pasta dish my husband ever made for me. Or it could be because I love artichokes. Maybe it's a little of each!

• Drain 1 can (14 ounces) of artichoke hearts (8 to 10 count) and cut the artichokes into quarters. Prepare the sauce as directed above. After adding the cheese and lowering the heat, stir the artichokes into the sauce.

Penne with Roasted Garlic Cream Sauce and Sautéed Spinach: Spinach is a nice addition to this pasta. Cook the spinach while you bring the pasta water to a boil.

• Rinse 8 ounces baby spinach (about 8 cups) but leave a little water still clinging to the leaves when you drain it. Heat 1 teaspoon olive oil in a large ($5^{1}/2$-quart) pot over medium-high heat. When the oil is hot and shimmering but not smoking, add the spinach and cook, tossing with tongs, until the spinach is tender, about 2 minutes. (Cooked fresh spinach really reduces in volume quite dramatically. This is normal.) Turn off the heat and set spinach aside. Stir the spinach into the pasta after you've added the sauce.

Penne with Tomato Cream Sauce

Recipes, like people, are always full of surprises. Take this tomato cream sauce. When you take a bite, you think you understand it. It's creamy and soft. Then it surprises you with a little bit of spice. That little kick keeps me coming back, forkful after forkful. Of course, if you are having a day that requires your pasta sauce to be creamy and not spicy (aka a rough day), you can omit the red pepper flakes. Without them, the sauce has no sharp edges.

Be sure to use cream for this sauce. Don't use milk. It will curdle.

Salt

1 pound gluten-free pasta

2 tablespoons olive oil

4 cloves garlic, minced or put through a garlic press

$1/4$ teaspoon red pepper flakes (optional)

1 large can (28 ounces) petite diced tomatoes or 2 medium cans (14.5 ounces each)

1 teaspoon dried basil

$1/3$ cup heavy cream or half-and-half

$1/2$ cup freshly grated Parmesan cheese

---

1. Fill a large (5$1/2$-quart) pot three-quarters full with water. Cover and bring to a boil over high heat. Set a colander in the sink for draining the pasta.

2. When the water reaches a boil, add 1 tablespoon salt and the pasta. (Set a timer for 10 minutes.) Stir with a wooden spoon for about 30 seconds, then stir occasionally while the pasta cooks. (For a how-to on cooking pasta, see page 105.)

3. While the pasta is cooking, make the sauce. In a large (12-inch) nonstick frying pan, heat the olive oil over medium-high heat until hot and shimmering but not smoking. Add the garlic and pepper flakes. Cook, stirring frequently with a wooden spoon, for 2 minutes, or until garlic is soft and translucent. Keep your eye on the pan. If the garlic begins to brown, lower the heat to medium.

4. Add the tomatoes, basil, and $1/4$ teaspoon salt. Stir with a wooden spoon to combine. Cook for about 5 minutes or until the sauce boils and begins to thicken.

5. Lower the heat to medium-low. Add the cream. Simmer for 3 to 4 minutes, until the sauce thickens. (This is a good time to check the pasta if you haven't already.) Lower the heat to low. Stir in the cheese with a fork.

6. After about 10 minutes of boiling, check the pasta for doneness. When the pasta is tender, ladle out about 1 cup of the pasta cooking

water into a small heatproof bowl and set aside. Drain the pasta in the colander and return it to its pot over very low heat.

7. Add the sauce to the pasta and stir with a wooden spoon to combine. If the sauce seems too thick, loosen it with a little of the pasta cooking water; stir in $1/4$ cup to start, adding more if needed until the sauce is the right consistency. Serve immediately.

Serves 4

VARIATION

Penne with Tomato Cream Sauce and Grilled Chicken: Sometimes I like to serve this dish with grilled chicken breasts. Cook the chicken while you bring the pasta cooking water to a boil.

Olive oil

2 medium boneless, skinless chicken breasts, trimmed of any fat

Kosher salt and freshly ground black pepper

1. Heat a lightly oiled cast-iron grill pan over high heat until hot and just beginning to smoke.

2. While the pan is heating, place the chicken breasts on a cutting board. Cover with a piece of parchment paper. Using a meat mallet, pound out the chicken to $1/2$-inch thickness. (If you don't have a meat mallet, use a heavy skillet to pound the meat.) Remove the parchment paper and brush each chicken breast lightly with olive oil. Season lightly with salt and pepper.

3. Grill the chicken for 6 minutes without moving it. Flip with tongs and cook for an additional 6 minutes or until the internal temperature reaches 165°F and no pink remains. Remove from the pan. Allow chicken breast to rest on a clean cutting board for 5 minutes. (Remember to use a different cutting board from the one you used for pounding out the chicken. If you don't have another board, wash your cutting board thoroughly with a bleach solution before placing the cooked chicken on it.) Cut the chicken into strips with a chef's knife.

4. After you've added the cheese to the sauce, add the chicken strips to the sauce. Follow recipe as directed.

Clam Pasta
with Anchovy Variation

My first memories of this pasta come from Christmas Eve dinners. My grandmother always made the anchovy variation and even when I was little, I loved it! I realize that anchovies are not everyone's favorite, so I replaced them with canned clams. Heck, I love anchovies but sometimes I make the clam version of this dish because it's so good. There's no better reason, right?

Salt

1 pound gluten-free pasta

$1/2$ cup olive oil

4 cloves garlic, minced or put through a garlic press

1 small onion, finely diced

1 teaspoon dried parsley

1 teaspoon dried oregano

2 cans (6.25 ounces each) chopped clams, or 1 can (10 ounces) whole baby clams

1. Fill a large (5$1/2$-quart) pot three-quarters full with water. Cover and bring to a boil over high heat. Set a colander in the sink for draining the pasta.

2. When the water reaches a boil, add 1 tablespoon salt and the pasta. (Set a timer for 10 minutes.) Stir with a wooden spoon for about 30 seconds, then stir occasionally while the pasta cooks. (For a how-to on cooking pasta, see page 105.)

3. While the pasta is cooking, begin the sauce.

In a small (2 quart) pot, combine the oil and garlic. Turn on the heat to medium-low. (Yes, start the garlic in cold oil. You want to cook it very gently.) When the garlic begins to sizzle, add the onion, parsley, and oregano. Cook, stirring occasionally with a wooden spoon, until the onions are translucent. Lower the heat to low. (This is a good time to check the pasta if you haven't already.)

4. Add the clams and their juices to the oil mixture and heat through. Don't let the sauce boil, or the clams will get tough.

5. After about 10 minutes of boiling, check the pasta for doneness. When the pasta is tender, ladle out about 1 cup of the pasta cooking water into a small heatproof bowl and set aside. Drain the pasta in the colander and return it to its pot over very low heat.

6. Add the clam sauce to the pasta and toss with a wooden spoon. If the pasta seems dry, add a little of the pasta cooking water; stir in $1/4$ cup to start, adding more if needed. Serve immediately.

Serves 4

VARIATION

Anchovy Pasta: Replace the clams with 2 jars (2.8 ounces each) anchovy fillets with oil. Mince them before adding to the oil mixture, and let the sauce cook until the anchovies "melt." If you like, add the oil from the anchovy jars and a pinch of red pepper flakes, too. Not for the faint of heart, but oh so good!

Upstate "Goulash"

Traditional Hungarian goulash is made with meat, vegetables, and a generous helping of paprika. But that isn't what I think of when someone says goulash. The first thing I think of is a pasta dish made with tomato sauce, ground beef, and cheddar cheese. In upstate New York, this casserole was always called "goulash." No matter what you want to call it, it's a recipe for easy comfort food.

Gluten-free nonstick cooking spray

Salt

1 pound gluten-free elbow macaroni

2 tablespoons olive oil

1 medium onion, finely diced

1 clove garlic, minced or put through a garlic press

1 pound ground sirloin (90 to 92% lean)

1 can (28 ounces) tomato sauce

6 ounces cheddar cheese, grated (about 1^1/$_2$ cups)

1. Adjust oven rack to the middle position and preheat the oven to 375°F. Lightly spray a 13 by 9-inch baking dish with nonstick cooking spray.

2. Fill a large (5^1/$_2$-quart) pot three-quarters full with water. Cover and bring to a boil over high heat. Set a colander in the sink for draining the pasta. When the water reaches a boil, add 1 tablespoon salt and the pasta. (Set a timer for 10 minutes.) Stir with a wooden spoon for about 30 seconds, then stir occasionally while the pasta cooks. (For a how-to on cooking pasta, see page 105.)

3. In a large (12-inch) nonstick frying pan, heat the oil over high heat until hot and shimmering but not smoking. Add the onion. Cook, stirring frequently with a wooden spoon, until the onion is soft, about 3 minutes. Add the garlic and ^{1}/$_2$ teaspoon salt. Cook, stirring frequently, until soft and aromatic, about 45 seconds.

4. Add the ground beef and cook, breaking up the clumps with a wooden spoon or heatproof spatula, until thoroughly cooked and browned, about 4 to 5 minutes. If desired, remove and discard any excess fat. (For a how-to on cooking ground meat, see page 44.)

5. Stir three-quarters of the tomato sauce into the beef. Lower the heat to low.

6. After about 10 minutes of boiling, check the pasta for doneness. Drain the pasta in the colander and return it to its pot over very low heat.

7. Add the meat sauce to the pasta and stir with a wooden spoon to combine. Pour into the prepared baking dish. Top with the remaining tomato sauce and sprinkle evenly with the cheese.

8. Bake, uncovered, until the cheese is golden brown and the sauce is bubbling, about 25 minutes.

Serves 4

Smoked Mozzarella and Roasted Vegetable Pasta

I hesitate to call a dish perfect, but to be honest, this one comes pretty close! The ingredients are simple: pasta, smoked mozzarella, and roasted vegetables. Since the vegetables roast while you are heating the pasta water, this dish comes together quickly. The smoky flavor of the cheese highlights the slightly smoky, slightly sweet flavor of the vegetables. If you can't find smoked mozzarella, replace it with fresh mozzarella. Your pasta will still be wonderful, I promise!

---

6 tablespoons olive oil

1 pound asparagus, tough bottoms trimmed off, remaining spears cut into thirds

1 pint grape tomatoes, sliced

1 large sweet onion, halved and sliced $1/4$-inch thick

1 teaspoon dried basil

1 teaspoon dried oregano

Kosher salt

$1/2$ teaspoon freshly ground black pepper

1 pound gluten-free penne pasta

8 ounces smoked mozzarella, shredded (about 2 cups)

4 to 6 fresh basil leaves

---

1. Adjust oven rack to the middle position and preheat the oven to 450°F. Lightly brush a rimmed baking sheet with oil.

2. In a large bowl, combine the asparagus, tomatoes, onion, dried basil, oregano, 1 teaspoon salt, and pepper. Add 2 teaspoons of the olive oil. Using a wooden spoon, stir to combine. Spread vegetables on the baking sheet in a single layer. Bake for 25 to 30 minutes, stirring and flipping the vegetables with a spatula about halfway through, until the vegetables are tender and soft. Some black spots will appear on the roasted vegetables. (This is a good thing!)

3. While the vegetables are roasting, fill a large ($5^1/2$-quart) pot three-quarters full with water. Cover and bring to a boil over high heat. Set a colander in the sink for draining the pasta. When the water reaches a boil, add 1 tablespoon salt and the pasta. (Set a timer for 10 minutes.) Stir with a wooden spoon for about 30 seconds, then stir occasionally while the pasta cooks. Cook the pasta until tender. (For a how-to on cooking pasta, see page 105.)

4. As the pasta cooks, remember to check the roasting vegetables. If they are done, remove the pan from the oven and set it on a wire rack. Turn off the oven; you are done with it.

5. After about 10 minutes of boiling, check the pasta for doneness. When the pasta is tender, ladle out about 1 cup of the pasta cooking water into a small heatproof bowl and set aside. Drain the pasta in the colander and return it to its pot over very low heat.

6. Add the remaining oil (about 4 tablespoons), vegetables, and cheese to the pasta. Stir with a wooden spoon to combine. If the sauce seems too thick, loosen it with a little of the pasta cooking water; stir in $^1/_4$ cup to start, adding more if needed. You can also add a splash more olive oil if you like.

7. Transfer the pasta to a serving dish. Chop the basil leaves and sprinkle over the top. Serve immediately.

Serves 4

Penne with Ham and Spinach

Whenever macaroni and cheese get together, you know the dish is going to be good. This version of mac and cheese uses fontina and Parmesan cheeses and pairs them with ham and spinach. The combination is a decidedly grown-up version of the classic comfort food.

Be sure to use whole or 2% milk; 1% and fat-free don't work well in this recipe.

▶ *For a how-to on making fresh bread crumbs, see page 32.*

Gluten-free nonstick cooking spray

3 teaspoons olive oil

1 bag (10 ounces) spinach

1$^1/_2$ cups cubed ham

1 tablespoon salt

1 pound gluten-free penne pasta

3 tablespoons unsalted butter

2 cloves garlic, minced or put through a garlic press

3 tablespoons sweet rice flour

3 cups whole or 2% milk, warmed

8 ounces fontina cheese, grated (2 cups)

$^1/_3$ cup plus 1 tablespoon freshly grated Parmesan cheese

$^1/_2$ teaspoon freshly ground black pepper

$^3/_4$ cup gluten-free fresh bread crumbs

1 tablespoon unsalted butter, melted

1. Adjust oven rack to the middle position and preheat the oven to 350°F. Lightly spray a 13 by 9-inch baking dish with nonstick cooking spray.

(continued)

2. Fill a large (5$\frac{1}{2}$-quart) pot three-quarters full with water. Cover and bring to a boil over high heat. Set a colander in the sink for draining the pasta.

3. In another large (5$\frac{1}{2}$-quart) pot over high heat, heat 2 teaspoons of the olive oil until hot and shimmering but not smoking. Add the spinach and cook, tossing constantly with kitchen tongs, until the spinach is soft and tender, 2 to 3 minutes. The spinach will lose most of its volume during cooking. Remove the pot from the heat. (Don't have another large pot? Cook the spinach in batches in a smaller pot or in a large frying pan. Transfer each batch to a heatproof bowl as it finishes cooking.)

4. Heat the remaining 1 teaspoon of olive oil in a medium (10-inch) nonstick frying pan until hot and shimmering but not smoking. Add the ham and cook, stirring occasionally, until cubes are browned on all sides. Remove the pan from the heat.

5. When the water reaches a boil, add the salt and pasta. (Set a timer for 10 minutes.) Stir with a wooden spoon for about 30 seconds, then stir occasionally while the pasta cooks. (For a how-to on cooking pasta, see page 105.)

6. While the pasta cooks, start the sauce. In a small (2-quart) pot, melt the 3 tablespoons butter over medium heat. Add the garlic and cook, stirring occasionally, until garlic is soft and aromatic, about 2 minutes. Whisk in the sweet rice flour. Cook, whisking constantly, for 3 minutes. The flour should become a beige paste. Add the milk in a slow and steady steam, whisking briskly but not too fast. Cook until the sauce is thickened and begins to bubble, 3 to 4 minutes. Once it bubbles, remove from the heat. (For a how-to on making white sauce, see page 46.)

7. After about 10 minutes of boiling, check the pasta for doneness. When the pasta is tender, drain it in the colander and return it to its pot. Add the sauce, ham, spinach, fontina, 1/3 cup of the Parmesan, and the black pepper. Stir with a wooden spoon to combine. Pour into the prepared baking dish.

8. Toss together the remaining 1 tablespoon Parmesan, the bread crumbs, and melted butter in a small bowl. Sprinkle evenly over the top. Bake, uncovered, for 35 minutes, or until the topping is golden brown and the sauce is bubbling. Let sit for a few minutes, then serve.

Serves 4

Make Your Own Pasta Dish

One of the things I love about pasta is that you can make a great pasta dish without a recipe. Some of the best pasta dishes I've made have come from looking around the refrigerator and seeing what looked good. This chart helps you play with your pasta! Simply select a pasta and a sauce and then have fun adding different meats, cheeses, and vegetables. Whatever you cook up will be delicious!

Start with one pound of pasta to serve four to six. Pick as many vegetables as you like, but when combining several vegetable choices, you might want to reduce the amounts called for so you don't end up with too much "stuff" in your pasta.

Pasta (pick one)	Sauce (pick one)	Cheese (optional)	Meat/Fish (optional)	Vegetables
Penne	Basic Tomato Sauce (page 126)	Feta, 4 ounces, crumbled	Cooked chicken, 1 breast, diced or cut in strips	Spinach, 8–10 ounces, sautéed
Spaghetti	Basic Cream Sauce (page 127)	Fresh mozzarella, 8 ounces, cut into bite-size pieces, or grated traditional mozzarella	Cooked sausage 2 links, crumbled or sliced	Fresh tomatoes, sliced; halved or whole grape tomatoes; or drained canned diced tomatoes, about 1 cup
Shells	Garlic Oil (page 128)	Parmesan, grated, 1/3 cup	Baked Gluten-Free Meatballs (page 106) *meatballs and garlic oil do not go well together	Asparagus, 1 bunch, steamed, boiled, or roasted
Fettuccini	Nut-Free Pesto (page 127)	Ricotta salata, 4 ounces, grated	Bacon, 4 slices, cooked and crumbled (see page 43)	Beans, 1 can (14 to 15 ounces), drained and rinsed
		Asiago, grated, 1/3 cup	Anchovy fillets, 1 can (2 ounces) drained and chopped	Mushrooms, 8 ounces, sliced or quartered and sautéed
		Fontina, grated, 1/3 cup	Chopped clams, 1 can (6.25 ounces)	Artichoke hearts, 1 can (14.5 ounces), drained and sliced
		Gorgonzola, 4 ounces, crumbled	Salmon, 4 to 6 ounces, cooked and flaked	Frozen peas, 1 cup, thawed
				Broccoli florets, 2 to 3 cups, steamed or boiled

Four Essential Pasta Sauces

Basic Tomato Sauce

Everyone needs a basic tomato sauce in their repertoire. This is mine.

2 tablespoons olive oil

1 large onion, finely diced

2 cloves garlic, minced or put through a garlic press

1 teaspoon salt

$1/4$ teaspoon red pepper flakes (optional, for a spicier sauce)

$1/2$ cup red wine

2 cans (28 ounces each) diced tomatoes

$1/2$ teaspoon dried oregano

1 bay leaf

2 teaspoons dried basil

$1/4$ teaspoon freshly ground black pepper

1. In a medium (4-quart) pot, heat the olive oil over medium heat until hot and shimmering but not smoking. Add the onion. Cook, stirring occasionally with a wooden spoon, until the onion is soft, 3 to 5 minutes. Add the garlic, salt, and pepper flakes, if using. Cook, stirring frequently, until the garlic is aromatic, about 1 minute. Add the wine and cook until wine almost, but not fully, evaporates. Add the tomatoes, oregano, bay leaf, basil, and pepper and stir to combine.

2. Bring to a boil, then lower the heat to medium-low and simmer the sauce (look for occasional gentle bubbles) for 30 minutes to $1^1/2$ hours (see Note).

3. Remove the bay leaf. Serve as is for a chunky pasta sauce.

4. If you want a smooth sauce, let the sauce cool to room temperature. Place a large bowl next to the blender or food processor. Working in batches, ladle the sauce into blender and purée until smooth. Take care not to fill the blender more than halfway. Purée until smooth. Pour the puréed sauce into the waiting bowl. Repeat until all the sauce has been puréed. Return the sauce to the pot and simmer to reheat. Use as desired on pasta.

Makes about $3^1/2$ cups sauce, enough for 1 pound of pasta

NOTE

This sauce can either be cooked quickly in about 30 minutes, or slowly. When cooked quickly, the sauce has a fresh taste. A longer cooking time provides a deeper tomato taste. Vary the cooking time and see which you prefer! If cooking the pasta sauce for a long time, stir occasionally. If the sauce is too thick, add a splash of water, about $1/4$ cup.

Nut-Free Pesto

For years I never sampled pesto because of my nut allergy. Then one day I scanned the recipe and decided it would be fine without the addition of pine nuts.

If you have lots of basil around during the summer, this recipe freezes really well. I like to freeze the pesto in individual muffins cups: line the muffin cups with paper liners, fill with pesto, and freeze. Pop the frozen pesto out of the cups and into a freezer bag, and keep frozen for up to 6 months. Then when I need a burst of summer flavor in the winter, I thaw a batch and all is right in my world. If you plan on freezing your pesto, omit the cheese; add when the pesto has defrosted.

2 cloves garlic, peeled
$1^1/2$ cups fresh basil leaves, tightly packed
1 teaspoon salt
$1/2$ cup extra virgin olive oil
$2/3$ cup freshly grated Parmesan cheese

1. Chop the garlic in a food processor until finely minced. A few quick pulses should do the trick.

2. Add the basil and salt. Process until basil is finely chopped. With the food processor running, add the olive oil in a slow and steady steam. (Many food processors have a feed tube that will do this for you. Pour the oil into the feed tube and it will drizzle into the basil mixture while the processor runs.)

3. After all the oil has been added, turn off the processor. Add the cheese and pulse a few times until sauce is smooth.

4. Toss together with hot pasta.

Makes 1 cup pesto, enough for 1 pound of pasta

Basic Cream Sauce

If I could pick one pasta sauce that is my absolute favorite, it would be cream sauce. Of course, cream sauce isn't something that I can eat often; it wouldn't do my waistline any favors. When I splurge and decide to have it, I want it to be excellent. This cream sauce is excellent; no sharp edges, just rich and luxurious.

This sauce doesn't store well, but it's so easy, you can make it fresh whenever you want to.

$1/4$ cup (4 tablespoons) unsalted butter
1 cup heavy cream
$1/4$ teaspoon salt
$1/4$ teaspoon freshly ground black or white pepper
$1/2$ cup freshly grated Parmesan cheese

1. Melt the butter in a small (2 quart) pot over low heat. Add the cream, salt, pepper, and cheese. Stir with a whisk to combine. Bring

to a light simmer (look for occasional gentle bubbles), stirring often.

2. Toss with hot pasta and serve.

Makes about 1¹/2 cups sauce, enough for 1 pound of pasta

Garlic Oil

This sauce is my jumping off point for many great pasta dishes. I'll make garlic oil and add grape tomatoes, fresh mozzarella, and basil one night. Another night, browned chorizo, cooked spinach, white beans, and a sprinkle of Parmesan. No matter what you add to this sauce, you are guaranteed to have a great meal.

---

6 to 7 tablespoons olive oil

4 large cloves garlic, minced or put through a garlic press

$1/8$ teaspoon crushed red pepper flakes

Kosher salt and freshly ground black pepper

Chopped fresh herbs, such as basil or parsley

---

1. In a medium (10-inch) nonstick frying pan, combine the olive oil, garlic, and crushed pepper. Cook over medium-high heat until garlic begins to brown, about 45 seconds. (The oil will be bubbling.) Lower the heat to low and cook for an additional 2 minutes. If your pasta isn't ready at this point, allow sauce to remain in the pan over low heat. Keep your eye on the garlic. If it starts to get too brown, remove the pan from the heat.

2. Toss the sauce together with drained pasta and season with salt and pepper to taste. Add freshly chopped herbs to pasta and stir to combine.

Makes about $1/2$ cup, enough for 1 pound of pasta

6.
Casseroles

Casserole Essentials: Condensed Soup

I'll be honest: even before I went gluten-free, I didn't make recipes that called for condensed soup. It wasn't that I had something against these dishes; it was that these recipes—usually casseroles—simply never made it into my cooking repertoire. So when I started getting emails from readers asking for a gluten-free condensed soup recipe, I was happy to help. It sounds silly but working with condensed soup was new to me. And I love new foods—even classic-American-retro foods such as condensed soup casseroles.

My goal for creating a gluten-free condensed soup was that it had to be almost as easy as opening a can. It turned out to be more challenging than I originally thought it would be. But I reminded myself that if I could conquer gluten-free bread, I could make condensed soup!

I tried many (many, many, many) different recipes until I created one that could be made in two minutes. Two minutes! And while the finished "soup" achieves the same consistency and results as canned condensed soup, the ingredients are much better! My homemade version isn't loaded with sodium or fat. To make it, you simply whisk together milk, cornstarch, and spices in a microwave-safe measuring cup. The mixture gets microwaved for two minutes and, like magic, you have homemade condensed soup. I really don't think it can get any easier than that!

As I worked on the condensed soup conversion, I experimented with different recipes that called for condensed soup. While they were good, I didn't fall in love with most of them. There were two exceptions: Tuna Noodle Casserole and a casserole simply called Meat and Potatoes. These two dishes were good enough to make it into this book, on pages 132 and 133. Creating oodles of new casseroles calling for homemade condensed soup isn't why I created a homemade version; I created it so you can again make a cherished recipe from your pre-gluten-free days that calls for condensed soup. Or if you stumble on a recipe that calls for condensed soup and you want to give it a try, you can. For me, the best kind of eating involves the freedom to eat what you want.

Note that foods thickened with cornstarch should not be frozen. They will become watery. Leftover casseroles made with cornstarch—or my homemade condensed soup—can be stored in the refrigerator for a few days.

Make Condensed Soup

Milk

Cornstarch

Flavorings and seasonings

▲ 1. Measure 1¹/₄ cups milk. I like to use a 2-cup measure because then I don't have to dirty a measuring cup and a bowl. In fact, you can make the entire recipe in the 2-cup measure. Add the cornstarch and whisk. This is important. Be sure to whisk until the cornstarch is fully dissolved. You don't want any lumps. Add the flavorings and seasonings required by the recipe.

▶ 2. Microwave for 2 minutes.

▲ 3. The mixture needs to reach a boil to thicken. When it's done, it will have the consistency of canned condensed soup. See how thick the milk has become? That is what you want. If your soup hasn't thickened, return it to the microwave and cook for another minute, or until it boils and thickens.

Barbone's Condensed Cream-of Soup

Start with the milk and cornstarch, then add the seasonings for one of the variations below.

1¹/₄ cups milk

2 tablespoons cornstarch

Cream of Chicken

1 teaspoon gluten-free chicken bouillon granules (regular, low-sodium, or no-sodium)

¹/₄ teaspoon garlic powder

Cream of Mushroom

¹/₂ teaspoon gluten-free chicken bouillon granules (regular, low-sodium, or no-sodium)

¹/₄ teaspoon salt

¹/₄ teaspoon dried thyme

¹/₈ teaspoon garlic powder

1 can (4 ounces) mushroom stems and pieces, drained and chopped fine

Cream of Celery

¹/₄ teaspoon gluten-free chicken bouillon granules (regular, low-sodium, or no-sodium)

¹/₂ teaspoon celery salt

1. In a 2-cup microwave-safe liquid measuring cup, whisk together the milk and cornstarch until the cornstarch is thoroughly dissolved. Add the bouillon and other ingredients for your choice of flavor. Combine thoroughly.

2. Microwave on HIGH for 2 minutes, or until mixture reaches a boil. After 2 minutes, mixture should be thick. If it isn't, return it to the microwave for an additional minute.

3. Let cool and use as directed.

Makes about 1¹/₄ cups condensed soup, equivalent to 1 can (10.75 ounces)

NOTE

Store-bought condensed soups usually have a lot of salt; you might want to add ¹/₂ teaspoon of salt to your recipe, since you won't have the salt from the condensed soup. I will leave this up to you.

Tuna Noodle Casserole

The American classic, made gluten-free.

At this time, gluten-free egg noodles are not available. I use either shells or fusilli.

▶ *For a how-to on making dried bread crumbs, see page 32.*

Gluten-free nonstick cooking spray

2 teaspoons salt

2 cups gluten-free pasta shapes

2 tablespoons gluten-free dried bread crumbs

2 tablespoons freshly grated Parmesan cheese

Barbone's condensed cream of mushroom or celery soup (page 131)

1 cup milk

1 cup frozen peas, thawed

2 tablespoons chopped pimientos

2 cans (5 to 6 ounces each) tuna in water, drained

1. Adjust oven rack to the middle position and preheat the oven to 400°F. Lightly spray a 1^1/$_2$-quart baking dish with nonstick cooking spray. Fill a medium (4-quart) pot three-quarters full with water. Cover and bring to a boil over high heat. Set a colander in the sink for draining the pasta.

2. When the water reaches a boil, add the salt and pasta. (Set a timer for 10 minutes.) Stir with a wooden spoon for about 30 seconds, then stir occasionally while the pasta cooks. Cook the pasta until tender. (For a how-to on cooking pasta, see page 105.)

3. While the pasta cooks, stir together the bread crumbs and cheese in a small bowl with a fork.

4. After about 10 minutes of boiling, check the pasta for doneness. When the pasta is tender, drain the pasta in the colander and return it to its pot over very low heat. Add the condensed soup and milk. Stir with a wooden spoon until thoroughly combined. Stir in the peas, pimientos, and tuna. Pour into the prepared baking dish. Sprinkle the bread crumb mixture evenly over the top.

5. Bake, uncovered, until the crumb topping is golden brown and the sauce is bubbling, about 25 minutes. Serve hot.

Serves 4

NOTE

This casserole is *not* suitable for freezing.

Meat and Potato Casserole

You know that old saying about people loving meat and potatoes? That's what I thought when I had this casserole for the first time. It's a simple name for a simple but delicious meal.

▶ *For a how-to on making dried bread crumbs, see page 32.*

2 large russet potatoes, peeled and cut into bite-size pieces (about 2 cups)

2 tablespoons plus 2 teaspoons olive oil

$1/4$ teaspoon salt

$1/2$ teaspoon freshly ground black pepper

1 medium onion, finely diced

1 clove garlic, minced or put through a garlic press

1 pound ground sirloin (90 to 92% lean) or lean ground turkey

1 cup milk

1 bag (10 ounces) frozen corn kernels, thawed

3 ounces cheddar cheese, grated ($3/4$ cup)

Barbone's condensed cream of mushroom soup (page 131)

2 tablespoons gluten-free dried bread crumbs

1. Adjust oven rack to the middle position and preheat the oven to 425°F.

2. In a 13 by 9-inch baking dish, toss together the potatoes, 2 tablespoons of the oil, and the salt and pepper. Bake for 35 to 40 minutes, turning the potato cubes over occasionally with a pancake flipper, until the potatoes are golden brown and tender. Remove the baking dish from the oven but leave the oven on.

3. After the potatoes have been cooking for about 25 minutes, cook the ground beef. In a medium (10-inch) nonstick frying pan, heat the remaining 2 teaspoons of oil over medium-high heat until hot and shimmering but not smoking. Add the onion. Cook, stirring frequently with a wooden spoon, until soft and aromatic, about 3 minutes. Add the garlic. Cook, stirring frequently, until garlic is soft, about 45 seconds. Add the ground beef and cook, breaking up the clumps with a wooden spoon or heatproof spatula, until thoroughly cooked and browned, about 4 to 5 minutes. If desired, remove and discard any excess fat. (For a how-to on cooking ground meat, see page 44.) Remove the pan from the heat.

4. In a small bowl, whisk together the milk, corn, cheese, and condensed soup with a fork or small whisk.

5. Top the potatoes with the beef. Pour the milk-soup mixture evenly over the top. Sprinkle the bread crumbs evenly over the casserole.

6. Bake until the crumbs are golden brown and the sauce is bubbling, about 25 minutes. Serve hot.

Serves 4

NOTE
This casserole is *not* suitable for freezing.

Easy
Taco Casserole

This recipe is a fun cross between tacos, enchiladas, and lasagna. The filling and corn tortillas are layered, creating a lasagna of sorts, using all the ingredients you'd usually find in tacos. Like tacos, you can vary the ingredients to suit your taste. Want more heat? Increase the chiles! Love olives? Add more!

Gluten-free nonstick cooking spray

2 teaspoons olive oil

1 medium onion, finely diced

2 cloves garlic, minced or put through a garlic press

$^1/_4$ teaspoon salt

1 pound ground sirloin (90 to 92% lean) or lean ground turkey

12 (6-inch) corn tortillas

1 can (4 to 4.5 ounces) chopped green chiles, drained

$1^1/_2$ cups salsa, homemade (page 64) or store-bought

1 can (2.25 ounces) sliced black olives, drained

6 ounces cheddar cheese, grated (about $1^1/_2$ cups)

1 can (10 ounces) gluten-free enchilada sauce

1. Adjust oven rack to the middle position and preheat the oven to 375°F. Spray the bottom and sides of a 13 by 9-inch baking dish with nonstick cooking spray.

2. In a medium (10-inch) nonstick frying pan, heat the olive oil over medium-high heat until hot and shimmering but not smoking. Add the onion and cook, stirring frequently with a wooden spoon, until soft and aromatic, about 3 minutes. Add the garlic and salt. Cook until the garlic is soft but not brown, stirring occasionally with a wooden spoon, about 45 seconds. Add the ground beef and cook, breaking up the clumps with the wooden spoon, until thoroughly cooked and browned, 4 to 5 minutes. If desired, remove and discard any excess fat. (For a how-to on cooking ground meat, see page 44.) Remove the pan from the heat.

3. Place 4 corn tortillas in the bottom of the prepared baking dish. They will overlap. Spoon one-third each of the beef, chiles, salsa, and olives and one-quarter of the cheese over the tortillas. Add 4 more tortillas to the pan and repeat with fillings. Repeat once more, until you have three layers of everything. Pour on the enchilada sauce and sprinkle the remaining cheese on the top of the casserole.

4. Bake until the cheese is golden brown and the sauce is bubbling, about 20 minutes. Serve hot.

Serves 4

Chicken and Cheesy Biscuit Casserole

Rarely do I get a recipe right the first time around. I always need to tinker with it a little—or a lot—to get it "just right." This recipe is the exception. I was testing it when I got a call from my mom. She needed me to bring her something at work. Since I just pulled the casserole out of the oven, I decided to bring it with me. I went through my whole spiel about how this was the first time I'd tested the recipe and not to expect it to be very good. Then I watched as my mom and her coworkers gobbled (there is no other word for it) down plate after plate of the casserole. I thought they were only being nice! Then I tried it myself. To say I fell a little in love with it would not be an understatement. The chicken filling and cheesy biscuits were just right. I've tested it many times since to ensure that it was "just right" and I've never changed a thing about it. I almost called it "The Perfect Chicken and Cheesy Biscuit Casserole." But I didn't want the casserole to get a big ego!

Gluten-free nonstick cooking spray

Cheesy Biscuits

$1^1/2$ cups white rice flour

$1/2$ cup sweet rice flour

$1/2$ cup tapioca starch

$1/4$ teaspoon xanthan gum

4 teaspoons baking powder

1 teaspoon salt

6 tablespoons unsalted butter, chilled and diced

$3/4$ cup milk

1 large egg

4 ounces cheddar cheese, grated (about 1 cup)

Chicken Filling

4 cups diced cooked chicken or turkey (see Note)

1 package (12 ounces) frozen mixed broccoli, cauliflower, and carrot mix, thawed

1 cup frozen peas, thawed

3 tablespoons unsalted butter

3 tablespoons sweet rice flour

2 cups milk, warmed

1 cup homemade chicken stock (page 69) or store-bought reduced-sodium broth

1 teaspoon salt

Freshly ground black pepper

$1/8$ teaspoon garlic powder

(continued)

1. Adjust oven rack to the middle position and preheat the oven to 400°F. Lightly spray a 13 by 9-inch baking dish with nonstick cooking spray.

2. Prepare the biscuits: In a food processor, pulse together the white rice flour, sweet rice flour, tapioca starch, xanthan gum, baking powder, and salt. (Don't have a food processor? Use a medium bowl and whisk them together.)

3. Pulse the food processor to work the butter into the dry ingredients until no large pieces remain. The mixture should be coarse, with tiny pebbles of butter distributed evenly throughout. (If you are making this without a food processor, use a fork or pastry cutter.)

4. Add the milk, egg, and cheese and pulse just until the dough forms a ball. Don't overmix. (Stir with the fork to combine if doing this by hand.) Set the dough aside while you prepare the sauce and filling.

5. Make the filling: Combine the chicken and vegetables in the prepared baking dish. Stir to combine.

6. In a medium (4-quart) pot, melt the butter over medium-high heat. Add the sweet rice flour. Cook, whisking constantly, for 3 minutes until the paste turns beige. Add the milk in a slow and steady stream, whisking constantly. Whisk in the chicken stock. Reduce the heat to medium and cook, whisking constantly, until mixture thickens and begins to bubble. Lower the heat to low. (For a how-to, see page 46.)

Season with the salt, pepper, and garlic powder. Stir to combine.

7. Pour the sauce evenly over the chicken and vegetables. Using a large spoon, drop the biscuit dough evenly over top of the casserole.

8. Bake until the biscuits are golden brown and the sauce is bubbling, about 35 minutes. Serve hot.

Serves 4, with leftovers

NOTE

I usually make this when I have leftover roast chicken or turkey. If you don't happen to have any in your refrigerator, see page 45 for a how-to on cooking chicken. Or see page 149 for a recipe for roast chicken.

Shepherd's Pie

One of the many things I love about cooking is that there are seemingly endless variations of different dishes—and endless arguments about which dish is "the best." Shepherd's pie is either made with lamb—hence the name—or with ground beef. Since I grew up eating the ground beef version, it is the one I prefer. Usually I make shepherd's pie when I have leftover mashed potatoes. If you don't have leftover mashed potatoes on hand, you can always boil some up before making the pie. It doesn't really take too much longer!

2 tablespoons olive oil

1 medium onion, finely diced

2 small cloves garlic, minced or put through a garlic press

1¼ pounds ground sirloin (90 to 92% lean) or meatloaf mix (see Notes)

1 can (15 ounces) tomato sauce

½ teaspoon salt

¼ teaspoon freshly ground black pepper

1 bag (12 ounces) frozen corn or peas and carrots, thawed

3 cups mashed potatoes, leftover or freshly made (page 237)

¼ cup freshly grated Parmesan cheese

1. Adjust oven rack to the middle position and preheat the oven to 375°F.

2. Heat the oil in a large (12-inch) nonstick frying pan over medium-high heat. Add the onions. Cook, stirring frequently with a wooden spoon, until soft and translucent, about 3 minutes. Add the garlic and cook until soft, about 2 minutes. Add the ground beef and cook, breaking up the clumps with a wooden spoon or heatproof spatula, until thoroughly cooked and browned, about 5 minutes. If desired, remove and discard any excess fat. (For a how-to on cooking ground meat, see page 44.)

3. Add half the tomato sauce and stir to combine. Season with the salt and pepper. Spoon the mixture into an 8-inch square baking pan. Sprinkle the corn evenly over the top.

4. Using a spatula, spread the potatoes over the corn. Take a fork and draw lines in the potatoes, this will help the topping get nice and crispy. Sprinkle the cheese evenly over the top of the potatoes.

5. Bake for 20 minutes, or until the filling is bubbling and the mashed potatoes are golden brown.

6. Warm the remaining tomato sauce and serve with the casserole.

Serves 4

NOTES

Meatloaf mix is usually one-third each ground beef, pork, and veal. Be sure your store doesn't add bread to theirs.

If you have leftover roast from the recipe on page 165, use it in place of the ground beef. Shred the leftover meat with a fork; you'll need about 4 cups. Instead of adding tomato sauce, use the leftover roast cooking liquid to moisten the meat, about 1 cup. Top with vegetables and mashed potatoes and bake as directed.

Creamy Macaroni and Cheese

One day while thumbing through an old issue of *Cooks Illustrated* I noticed a recipe for a mac and cheese that promised to yield a creamy sauce. Intrigued, I set out to make it gluten-free. My first attempt was good but the sauce was a little too runny. After some tweaking, I reduced the amount of milk they used and upped the amount of chicken stock. Along with some other modifications, I created, in my opinion, the most outrageously delicious gluten-free macaroni and cheese ever!

Is this an everyday dish? I don't think so. But it is wonderfully decadent. If you love macaroni and cheese and have been disappointed by other recipes, you must give this recipe a try. And while you are grating the 1¹/₂ pounds of cheese, just close your eyes. Okay, don't close your eyes—you might hurt yourself. But you know what I mean!

▶ *For a how-to on making dried bread crumbs, see page 32.*

Gluten-free nonstick cooking spray

1 tablespoon salt

1 pound gluten-free elbow macaroni

6 tablespoons unsalted butter

1 clove garlic, minced or put through a garlic press

1 teaspoon prepared mustard (any kind will do)

¹/₄ teaspoon ground chipotle chile or cayenne (optional)

6 tablespoons sweet rice flour

2¹/₂ cups homemade chicken stock (page 69) or reduced-sodium store-bought broth, warmed

2 cups whole milk, warmed

1 pound Colby cheese, grated (about 4 cups)

8 ounces extra-sharp cheddar cheese, grated (about 2 cups)

¹/₃ cup gluten-free dried bread crumbs

1. Adjust oven rack to the middle position and preheat the oven to 375°F. Spray a 13 by 9-inch baking pan with nonstick cooking spray. Fill a large (5¹/₂-quart) pot three-quarters full with water. Cover and bring to a boil over high heat. Set a colander in the sink for draining the pasta.

2. When the water reaches a boil, add the salt and macaroni. (Set a timer for 10 minutes.) Stir with a wooden spoon for about 30 seconds, then stir occasionally while the macaroni cooks. (For a how-to on cooking pasta, see page 105.)

(continued)

3. While the macaroni cooks, start the sauce: In a medium (4-quart) pot, melt the butter over medium heat. Add the garlic, mustard, and chipotle, if using. Cook, stirring constantly, until garlic is soft, about 1 minute.

4. Switch to a wire whisk. Add the sweet rice flour. Cook, whisking constantly, until thick and beige, about 3 minutes.

5. In a slow and steady steam, add 1 cup of the chicken stock. Whisk until mixture thickens. Repeat, stopping after each addition of chicken stock, until all of the stock is incorporated. Add the milk, 1 cup at a time, until mixture is thick and bubbling. Turn off the heat. (For a how-to, see page 46.)

6. After about 10 minutes of boiling, check the macaroni for doneness. When the macaroni is almost tender, drain it in the colander and return it to its cooking pot.

7. Return to making the pasta sauce: Add the cheeses, one handful at a time. Stir until the cheese is almost melted and smooth, it will finish melting in the oven.

8. Pour the sauce over pasta. (It will seem like a lot of sauce. Don't worry.) Stir to combine. Pour the mixture into the prepared pan and sprinkle the bread crumbs evenly over the top.

9. Bake until the edges start to turn golden brown and the sauce is bubbling, 25 to 30 minutes.

10. Remove from the oven and allow to cool for 10 minutes. Enjoy.

Serves 6 to 8

Cornbread Chili Bake

I've taken the classic combination of chili and cornbread and turned it into an easy casserole. This recipe uses chili and adds ground beef. If you'd prefer to keep it a meatless dish, double the amount of chili.

Gluten-free nonstick cooking spray

Cornbread Topping

1 cup gluten-free cornmeal

$1/2$ cup white rice flour

$1/2$ cup sweet rice flour

$1/4$ cup granulated sugar

1 tablespoon baking powder

$1/2$ teaspoon salt

$1/4$ teaspoon xanthan gum

2 large eggs

1 cup milk

2 tablespoons olive oil

Chili Filling

2 teaspoons olive oil

1 small onion, finely diced

2 cloves garlic, minced or put through a garlic press

1 pound ground sirloin (90 to 92% lean) or lean ground turkey

3 cups Easy Veggie Chili (page 180)

$1/2$ cup water

4 ounces cheddar cheese, grated (about 1 cup)

1. Adjust oven rack to the middle position and preheat the oven to 425°F. Spray a 13 by 9-inch pan with nonstick cooking spray

2. To make the cornbread topping, in a medium bowl, whisk together the cornmeal, white rice flour, sweet rice flour, sugar, baking powder, salt, and xanthan gum. In a small bowl, whisk together the eggs, milk, and oil. Set aside.

3. To make the filling, in a large (12-inch) nonstick frying pan, heat the oil over medium-high heat until hot and shimmering but not smoking. Add the onion and cook, stirring frequently with a wooden spoon, until the onion is soft and tender, about 3 minutes. Add the garlic and cook, stirring occasionally, until the garlic is soft and aromatic, about 1 minute. Add the ground beef and cook, breaking up the clumps with the wooden spoon, until thoroughly cooked and browned, about 4 to 5 minutes. If desired,

remove and discard any excess fat. (For a how-to on cooking ground meat, see page 44.)

4. Add the chili and water. Stir until combined and cook until it begins to bubble. The mixture should be loose but not watery. Add an additional $1/4$ cup water if it seems dry.

5. Pour the chili filling into the prepared pan. Sprinkle the cheese evenly over the top.

6. Finish the cornbread topping: Pour the egg mixture into the cornmeal mixture. Stir with a fork to combine. Pour the batter evenly over the cheese. Use a spatula or the back of a spoon to spread batter evenly.

7. Bake the casserole for 20 to 25 minutes, until the cornbread topping is light golden brown and no longer jiggles. Serve hot.

Serves 6

7. Main Dishes

Easy Chicken Parmigiana

I love traditional chicken parmigiana, but on weeknights I don't always have the time to make it. This dish celebrates the flavors of chicken parmigiana but is made in one pan. In addition to being easier, it is also a bit lighter. The chicken is sautéed instead of breaded and pan-fried.

You want to use chicken breasts no more than 1-inch thick. If the chicken breasts are thicker than 1 inch, you can either pound them down slightly with a meat mallet or increase the cooking time.

4 boneless, skinless chicken breasts (about $1^{1}/2$ pounds), patted dry

Salt and freshly ground black pepper

1 tablespoon olive oil

$1/2$ cup Basic Tomato Sauce (page 126), or store-bought tomato sauce

2 ounces mozzarella cheese, grated ($1/2$ cup), or 4 thin slices fresh mozzarella

4 fresh basil leaves

1. Season the chicken breasts on both sides with salt and pepper.

2. Heat the oil in a large (12-inch) nonstick frying pan over medium-high heat until the oil is hot and shimmering but not smoking. Add the chicken and cook undisturbed for 6 minutes. Using tongs, flip the chicken and cook for an additional 6 minutes, or until internal

temperature reaches 165°F. (For a how-to on cooking chicken, see page 45).

3. Lower the heat to medium. Spread 2 tablespoons tomato sauce on each chicken breast. Top each breast with 2 tablespoons cheese. (If you are using fresh mozzarella, lay the slice over the sauce-coated breast.) Put 1 basil leaf on the center of each breast.

4. Cover the frying pan and cook for about 4 minutes, or until cheese is melted. Serve immediately.

Serves 4

Classic Chicken Parmigiana

Before I went gluten-free, chicken parmigiana was one of my favorite meals to order at the little Italian family restaurants that can be found all over upstate New York. It was always served with a small bowl of ziti, and my love for it never wavered. This recipe reflects the way chicken parmigiana was prepared in those restaurants. The chicken breast is pounded, breaded, and pan-fried. It's then topped with sauce and cheese and put in the oven to melt the cheese. This dish isn't hard to make but it takes a little bit of time. The results are more than worth it.

▶ *For a how-to on making dried bread crumbs, see page 32.*

4 boneless, skinless chicken breasts (about $1^1/2$ pounds)
$1/3$ cup white rice flour
$1/3$ cup cornstarch
Pinch of salt
Pinch of freshly ground black pepper
2 large eggs
$1/4$ cup milk
Hot pepper sauce
$1^1/2$ cups dried gluten-free bread crumbs
1 teaspoon dried basil, plus additional for sprinkling (optional)
1 teaspoon dried oregano
Olive oil
1 cup Basic Tomato Sauce (page 126), or store-bought tomato sauce
4 ounces mozzarella cheese, grated (1 cup)

Pictured at right with Classic Chicken Parmigiana: Red Potatoes with Olive Oil and Vinegar, recipe on page 231.

1. Adjust oven rack to the middle position and preheat the oven to 425°F.

2. Place the chicken breasts on a cutting board. Cover with parchment paper. Using a meat mallet or the bottom of a clean frying pan, pound the breasts about 1/2-inch thick.

3. Set up three large dinner plates or pie pans in a line on your counter. At the end of the line, place a rimmed baking sheet.

4. Place the white rice flour, cornstarch, and salt and pepper on the first plate. Whisk with a fork to combine. Whisk together the egg, milk, and a dash of hot sauce on the middle plate. On the last plate, whisk together the bread crumbs, basil, and oregano.

5. Coat the chicken one piece at a time in the following order: first in the white rice flour mixture, next in the egg mixture, and finally in the bread crumb mixture. Be sure to coat each chicken piece thoroughly in every coating. (For a how-to on breading food, see page 34.) Place the coated chicken on the baking sheet.

6. Fill a large (12-inch) cast-iron frying pan with 1/4 inch of olive oil. Heat over high heat until the oil is hot and lightly smoking. Cook each chicken piece undisturbed for 5 minutes. (Don't crowd the pan. There should be space between the pieces of chicken. If necessary, cook the chicken in batches.) Using tongs, flip the chicken and cook until internal temperature reaches 165°F and the breading is golden brown, about 4 more minutes.

7. Remove the chicken from the pan and place on a clean baking sheet. Don't use the pan that held the raw chicken.

8. Top each piece of chicken with a light layer of tomato sauce. The amount of sauce will vary depending on the size of the chicken breasts. Sprinkle the cheese on top of the sauce. Bake until the cheese is golden brown and bubbly, about 8 minutes. Serve warm.

Serves 4

SERVING SUGGESTION

For a classic meal, serve chicken parmigiana with gluten-free pasta. For a how-to on cooking pasta, see page 105. Red Potatoes with Olive Oil and Vinegar (page 231) also make a great meal.

Classic
Roast Chicken

What is it about roast chicken? It's easy to make and when it comes out of the oven, I feel as if I've made something special. The best part of a roast chicken, to me, are the leftovers. In fact, sometimes, I will roast a chicken solely to have the meat for other dishes. The wonderful first meal almost seems like a bonus.

2 large carrots, peeled and cut into large chunks

3 stalks celery, peeled and cut into large chunks

1 large onion, cut into wedges

4 cloves garlic, peeled

1 whole 4- to 5-pound chicken, giblets removed, patted dry

Kosher salt and freshly ground black pepper

Dried basil

About 2 tablespoons unsalted butter, melted

1. Adjust oven rack to the middle position and preheat the oven to 425°F.

2. In the bottom of a roasting pan or 13 by 9-inch baking dish, toss together the carrots, celery, onion, and garlic.

3. Sprinkle the inside of the chicken cavity with salt, pepper, and basil. Place the chicken on the vegetables in the pan, breast side up.

4. Using kitchen string, tie the drumsticks (legs) together snugly. Tuck the tips of the wings under the chicken's body. Brush the chicken all over with melted butter. Sprinkle generously with more salt, pepper, and basil.

5. Bake for 1¹/₂ hours, or until an instant-read thermometer inserted into the thigh reads 165°F.

6. Remove from the oven. Place on a cutting board and loosely tent a piece of foil over the chicken. Let rest for 10 minutes.

7. Discard the vegetables, they've done their job. Carve and serve.

Serves 4 to 5

NOTES

If you want, add the chicken carcass to the recipe for chicken stock. It will make for a flavorful addition to the stock.

If the pan juices are not burnt, use them to make gravy: Allow the pan to cool slightly, then pour the juices into a 2-cup measuring cup or a small bowl. With a ladle, skim the fat from the top and discard. Use the remaining liquid in gravy. For a how-to, see page 47.

Mom's Chicken Stir-Fry

This was one of my favorite dinners to eat growing up. My mom made it fairly often. Since the vegetables and chicken require chopping, start the rice before you get out the cutting board. This way, the rice can cook as you chop.

1 cup white or brown rice

1 tablespoon plus 1 teaspoon olive oil

1 1/2 pounds boneless, skinless chicken breasts, cut into bite-size pieces

2 cups fresh broccoli florets

2 tablespoons water

2 cloves garlic, minced or put through a garlic press

2 scallions (green onions), finely chopped (white and green parts)

1 large red bell pepper, cored and thinly sliced

5 teaspoons gluten-free soy sauce

1/2 cup homemade chicken stock (page 69) or reduced-sodium store-bought broth

1. Prepare the rice according to package directions. When the rice is cooked, turn the heat to its lowest setting to keep rice warm while you prepare the chicken. (For a how-to on cooking rice, see page 42.)

2. In a large (12-inch) nonstick frying pan, heat 1 tablespoon of the olive oil over high heat until the oil is hot and shimmering but not smoking. Add half the chicken. Cook, stirring occasionally with a wooden spoon, for 5 minutes, or until the chicken is lightly browned and cooked through with no pink remaining. Remove the cooked chicken from the pan and place on a plate. Repeat with the remaining chicken, adding a little more oil if none remains in the pan. Set the chicken aside with the first batch.

3. Add the broccoli florets to the hot pan. Stir occasionally for 2 minutes. Pour the water over the broccoli and immediately cover the pan. Cook for about 4 minutes, until the broccoli turns bright green and is slightly tender when pierced with a fork. The cooking time will vary depending on the cut of your broccoli florets. Remove the broccoli from the pan and place on the same plate with the chicken.

4. Wipe out the pan with a paper towel. Return the pan to the stovetop and add the remaining 1 teaspoon olive oil. Heat until the oil is hot and shimmering but not smoking. Add the garlic and scallions and cook for 1 minute. Add the bell pepper and cook for 5 minutes, stirring occasionally, until the pepper is tender. Pour the soy sauce and chicken stock over the peppers. Stir. Lower the heat to medium. Return the chicken and broccoli to the pan. Be sure to add any juices that have accumulated on the plate. Cook until all ingredients are warm, about 3 minutes.

5. Serve with the cooked rice.

Serves 4

Chicken with Red Peppers and Onions

This dish was inspired by the classic Italian sausage and peppers. I've replaced the sausage with chicken and the green bell peppers with red. The red pepper lends a nice sweetness to the meal. Green peppers can be successfully substituted for red, however. This meal comes together in about 30 minutes.

1 tablespoon olive oil

4 boneless, skinless chicken breasts (about 1^1/2 pounds)

Salt and freshly ground black pepper

1 large red bell pepper, cored and cut into strips

1 medium onion, halved crosswise and thinly sliced

^{1}/2 cup homemade chicken stock (page 69) or reduced-sodium store-bought broth

4 to 6 fresh basil leaves, chopped

1. In a large (12-inch) nonstick frying pan, heat the olive oil over medium-high heat. Pat the chicken breasts dry and lightly season both sides with salt and pepper.

2. When oil is hot and shimmering but not smoking, place the chicken in the pan in a single layer. Don't move or turn the chicken for 5 minutes.

3. Using tongs, flip the chicken breasts and cook for an additional 5 to 10 minutes, until the internal temperature reaches 165°F. (If your chicken breasts are thin, the cooking time will be a shorter. For a how-to on cooking chicken, see page 45.)

4. Remove the chicken from the pan and place on a clean plate. Cover. (I usually invert a large bowl over the plate. If you don't have a bowl that fits, use a piece of aluminum foil.)

5. With the heat still on medium-high, add the red pepper to the pan. Cook for about 2 minutes, or until the strips are light brown. Add the onion. Cook, stirring occasionally, until the onion and pepper are soft, about 4 minutes.

6. Pour ^{1}/4 cup of the chicken stock into the pan. Cook until it almost fully evaporates and thickens. Add the remaining ^{1}/4 cup stock, lower the heat to medium, and return the chicken to the pan. Sprinkle the basil over the top of each chicken breast. Cover the pan and simmer for 3 minutes. Serve hot.

Serves 4

SERVING SUGGESTION

I really like this dish with brown rice and a salad.

Roasted Vegetable and Chicken Wraps

These chicken wraps had me at the first bite. When I make them, I usually use zucchini, yellow squash, onion, and red pepper. Changing the vegetables, however, changes the flavor of these wraps. Use whatever vegetables you like. Roasted asparagus and tomatoes are also especially good.

---

1 large zucchini, diced (about 2 cups)

1 large yellow squash, diced (about 2 cups)

1 large onion, halved crosswise and thinly sliced

1 large red bell pepper, cored and cut into strips

2 tablespoons olive oil

1 1/2 pounds chicken tenders

Kosher salt and freshly ground black pepper

1/2 cup mayonnaise

1/2 teaspoon ground chipotle chile (more or less depending on how spicy you like it)

8 (6-inch) corn tortillas

8 slices provolone cheese

---

1. Adjust oven rack to the middle position and preheat the oven to 400°F.

2. On a rimmed baking sheet, toss together the zucchini, squash, onion, and red pepper with about 1 tablespoon of the olive oil. You just want the vegetables lightly coated with oil. You don't need much. Roast for 20 to 25 minutes, stirring about halfway through, until the vegetables are golden brown and soft.

3. Heat the remaining 1 tablespoon olive oil in a grill pan or large (12-inch) nonstick frying pan until shimmering. Season the chicken lightly with salt and pepper. Cook undisturbed for 5 to 7 minutes. Using tongs, flip the chicken and cook until brown, 4 to 6 more minutes. (Remember not to crowd your pan. If you need to cook the chicken in two batches, that's fine!) Remove the cooked chicken from the pan and place on a clean plate. (For a how-to on cooking chicken, see page 45.)

4. In a small bowl, stir together the mayonnaise and chipotle with a spoon.

5. Remove the roasted vegetables from the oven. Leave the oven on. Place the tortillas on a clean baking sheet. Warm them in the oven for 3 to 5 minutes, until they are soft and starting to brown.

6. Spread a thin layer of chipotle mayonnaise on each tortilla and top with 1 slice of provolone. Divide the vegetables and chicken among the tortillas, wrap, and serve.

Makes 8 wraps

Chicken with Broccoli

This recipe really makes me happy. With a few select ingredients, including rice vinegar, the flavor of this dish sings. While the recipe might look time consuming, I promise you it isn't. The chicken marinates while you cook the broccoli and then the chicken is quickly cooked in two batches. By cooking the chicken in two batches, you'll have moist, flavorful chicken that isn't rubbery or dry.

Marinated Chicken

$1/4$ cup water

3 tablespoons gluten-free soy sauce

2 tablespoons unseasoned rice vinegar

2 tablespoons cornstarch

2 cloves garlic, minced or put through a garlic press

3 scallions (green onions), thinly sliced (white part only)

$1/4$ to $1/2$ teaspoon crushed red pepper flakes

$1^1/2$ pounds boneless, skinless chicken breasts, cut into 1-inch cubes

Broccoli

1 tablespoon vegetable or olive oil

$1^1/2$ pounds fresh broccoli florets, cut into individual pieces (5 to 6 cups)

$1/2$ cup water

Finishing

2 tablespoons vegetable or olive oil

1 clove garlic, minced or put through a garlic press

1 scallion, thinly sliced (white and green parts)

$1/4$ cup water

1. To marinate the chicken, in a large bowl, whisk together the water, soy sauce, vinegar, cornstarch, garlic, scallions, and crushed pepper (add more if you like it spicier). Add the chicken and stir to coat the chicken evenly. Allow to stand for 15 minutes.

2. While the chicken is marinating, cook the broccoli: In a wok or large (12-inch) nonstick frying pan, heat the oil over high heat until heavily smoking if using a wok, or until hot and shimmering but not smoking if using a nonstick pan. Add the broccoli and cook for 1 minute, stirring constantly with a wooden spoon. Add the water and cover. Cook for 7 minutes, or until broccoli is tender but still bright green. Remove the broccoli from the pan and place on a large dish.

3. Wipe out the wok with a paper towel. Return it to the stovetop.

4. To finish, remove the chicken from the marinade using a slotted spoon. Do not discard the marinade. Heat 1 tablespoon of the oil in the wok over high heat until hot and shimmering but not smoking. Add half the garlic and half the scallion slices and cook, stirring constantly, for 30 seconds or until aromatic but not brown. Add half the chicken and cook, stirring often, until lightly browned with no pink spots remaining, 5 to 6 minutes. (Cooking time will vary depending on the thickness of your chicken.) Place the cooked chicken on the same platter with the broccoli.

5. Repeat with the remaining scallions, garlic, and chicken, using the remaining 1 tablespoon of oil. Set aside with the first batch.

6. Lower the heat to medium-low. Whisk the water into the reserved marinade. Pour into the wok and bring to a boil. Cook, stirring occasionally, until the marinade thickens. Return the chicken and broccoli to the wok. Toss to combine with the sauce and cook for 1 minute to warm. Serve hot.

Serves 4

SERVING SUGGESTION

I always serve this with rice, either white or brown. As soon as I get home, I start cooking the rice. This way, the rice is done when I am ready to serve dinner.

Baked Chicken Tenders

While chicken tenders are a mainstay of children's menus, many adults love them, too. Most of the gluten-y chicken tenders sold in restaurants are fried. I bake my tenders, and before baking I coat them with crushed gluten-free cornflakes or gluten-free Corn Chex. The cereal provides a really crunchy crust. No one ever misses the fried version!

Gluten-free nonstick cooking spray

2$^1/_2$ cups gluten-free corn cereal

$^1/_4$ cup freshly grated Parmesan cheese

About $^1/_8$ teaspoon garlic powder

Pinch of freshly ground black pepper

$^1/_3$ cup milk

5 or 6 dashes hot pepper sauce

1 pound boneless, skinless chicken breasts, cut into strips, or 1 pound chicken tenders

1. Adjust oven rack to the middle position and preheat the oven to 350°F. Lightly spray a rimmed baking sheet with nonstick cooking spray.

2. Crush the cereal to coarse crumbs in a food processor or a large heavy-duty plastic bag. If using a bag, hit the bag with a rolling pin or frying pan a few times to crush the cereal.

3. Add the cheese, garlic powder, and pepper to the crumbs. Pulse to combine or shake the bag a few times.

4. Set up two large dinner plates or pie pans in a line on your counter. At the end of the line, place the prepared baking sheet. In the first plate, combine the milk and enough hot sauce to turn milk a light pink. On the other plate, put the cereal mixture.

5. Dip the chicken into the milk. Roll to coat thoroughly. Lift out and let any excess drip back onto the plate. Place the chicken in the crumb mixture and roll to coat evenly with crumbs.

6. Place the chicken on the prepared baking sheet in a single layer. Lightly spray with nonstick cooking spray.

7. Bake for 15 minutes, or until the strips are crisp and the internal temperature reaches 165°F. Serve hot.

Serves 4

Pictured at left with Baked Chicken Tenders: Corn, Peas, and Bacon, recipe on page 244.

Chicken Piccata

Fresh lemon juice ensures that this chicken dish has a nice, tart flavor. Since the lemon is so important to the dish, you don't want to replace it with bottled lemon juice or the flavor will suffer.

For this recipe you'll butterfly the chicken breasts, which just means cutting them in half horizontally. Take your time, and be careful not to cut yourself!

4 boneless, skinless chicken breasts

Salt and freshly ground black pepper

$^1/_3$ cup white rice flour

$^1/_4$ cup cornstarch

$^1/_4$ cup (4 tablespoons) unsalted butter

$^1/_4$ cup olive oil

$^1/_4$ cup freshly squeezed lemon juice (about 2 lemons)

$^1/_3$ cup dry white wine

3 tablespoons brined capers, drained and rinsed

Chopped fresh parsley, for serving

Thin lemon slices, for serving (optional)

1. Put 1 chicken breast on a cutting board. Place your hand on top of it very lightly, to hold it steady. Holding a chef's knife parallel to the cutting board, starting at the long, thin end, slice the chicken breast in half almost all the way through. Open the chicken like a book, flatten it slightly, and cut the two halves apart. Set aside on a plate. Repeat with the remaining chicken. (Wash your hands thoroughly when you're done!)

2. Season the chicken on both sides with salt and pepper.

3. Combine the white rice flour, cornstarch, $^1/_2$ teaspoon salt, and $^1/_4$ teaspoon pepper on a large dinner plate. Whisk to combine. Set a rimmed baking sheet next to the plate.

4. One piece at a time, drag the chicken through the white rice flour mixture, coating it thoroughly on both sides. Shake off any excess and set the chicken aside in a single layer on the baking sheet.

5. In a large (12-inch) nonstick frying pan over medium-high heat, heat 2 tablespoons butter and 2 tablespoons olive oil until the butter is melted and the oil begins to shimmer.

6. Add 4 pieces of chicken (2 breasts) in a single layer. Cook undisturbed for 4 to 5 minutes, until the bottom is golden. Using tongs, flip the chicken and cook for an additional 4 to 5 minutes, until golden brown. Remove the chicken from the pan and place on a plate.

7. Add the remaining 2 tablespoons butter and 2 tablespoons oil to the pan and cook the remaining chicken the same way. Set the chicken aside with the first batch.

8. Add the lemon juice, wine, and capers to the pan and bring to a boil. Taste and adjust the seasoning with salt and pepper if necessary. Return all the chicken to the pan, along with any juices from the plate. Simmer for 5 minutes, turning the chicken in the sauce to coat all the pieces.

9. Place the chicken on a platter or individual plates and spoon the sauce over it. Sprinkle chopped parsley over the top of the chicken and serve with lemon slices, if desired

Serves 4

Tomato and Chouriço Paella

For a long time I thought that paella meant seafood and rice. But seafood is only one variation of this classic Valencian dish. This recipe, made with chouriço and tomatoes, is hearty and a nice meal for a cold winter night. The saffron is expensive but it does add an indescribably wonderful flavor to paella. If it fits into your budget, add it to this dish. If not, omit it. The dish will still be tasty!

If you don't have smoked paprika, regular paprika works just fine.

2 tablespoons olive oil

1 pound gluten-free chouriço or chorizo sausage, cut into bite-size pieces

1 medium onion, finely diced

2 cloves garlic, minced or put through a garlic press

2 teaspoons smoked paprika

2 cups short-grain rice (I use Arborio)

$1/2$ teaspoon saffron threads (optional)

2 cups water

4 cups homemade chicken stock (page 69) or reduced-sodium store-bought broth

1 can (15 ounces) petite diced tomatoes, with juices

1. Adjust oven rack to the middle position and preheat the oven to 425°F.

2. Heat the olive oil in a large (12-inch) ovenproof skillet over high heat until lightly smoking. Add the sausage. Cook until browned, stirring frequently with a wooden spoon. Using a slotted spoon, remove the sausage from the pan and set aside on a plate. Lower the heat under the skillet to medium and let it cool down for a minute or two.

3. Add the onion and garlic to the fat in the skillet. Cook, stirring frequently, until soft and translucent, about 3 minutes. Add the paprika and cook for 1 minute. Stir in the rice. Cook, stirring constantly, for 2 minutes. The rice will get shiny as it cooks.

4. Stir the saffron into the water. Pour the chicken stock and water over the rice. Stir to combine. Scrape the bottom of the pan with the wooden spoon to dislodge any tasty brown bits. Add the sausage and tomatoes, including the juice.

5. Place the skillet in the oven and cook, uncovered, for 40 minutes, or until all the liquid is absorbed and the rice is fluffy. Serve hot.

Serves 4 to 6

Pork with Apples and Onions

This is sort of an autumnal stir-fry. The pork is cooked in two batches to ensure it gets nicely brown and flavorful. Since the pork is thin, each batch only takes about 3 minutes to cook. Prior to cooking, the pork marinates for 20 minutes. I use that time to make my side dishes. Before I know it, the pork is ready to be cooked.

1^{1}/$_{2}$ pounds thin boneless pork chops (about ^{1}/$_{4}$-inch thick)

2 tablespoons olive oil

2 teaspoons balsamic vinegar

1^{1}/$_{2}$ teaspoons kosher salt

^{1}/$_{4}$ teaspoon freshly ground black pepper

1 large onion, halved and thinly sliced

1 large Granny Smith apple, peeled, cored, and thinly sliced

1 teaspoon dark brown sugar

^{1}/$_{2}$ cup apple juice

1. Trim any fat from the pork. Cut the pork into strips about ^{1}/$_{2}$-inch wide. In a bowl, combine pork, 1 tablespoon of the olive oil, the balsamic vinegar, ^{1}/$_{2}$ teaspoon of the salt, and the pepper. Allow to marinate for 20 minutes.

2. Drain the pork and discard any remaining marinade. Put a clean plate near the stove. Heat 1 teaspoon of the remaining olive oil in a large (12-inch) nonstick frying pan over high heat until the oil is hot and shimmering but not smoking. Add half the pork. Cook, stirring occasionally with a wooden spoon, for 2 to 3 minutes, until meat is brown. (Cooking time will vary depending on the thickness of the pork pieces.) Place the cooked pork on the waiting plate. Repeat with remaining pork and set aside with the first batch.

3. Add the remaining 2 teaspoons olive oil to the pan. Add the onion and apple. Sprinkle the sugar and the remaining 1 teaspoon salt evenly over the mixture. Stir. Lower the heat to medium-low and cook for 10 minutes, stirring occasionally, until the onion and apples are soft and fragrant. Add the apple juice and cook until the liquid is reduced by half, about 4 minutes.

4. Return the cooked pork to the pan. Stir together with the apples and onions. Lower the heat to low. Cover the pan and cook for 1 to 2 minutes, until warm. Serve.

Serves 4

SERVING SUGGESTION

I like this dish with either brown rice or Roasted Sweet Potatoes (page 251).

Kielbasa with Sauerkraut and Onions

I've always loved kielbasa and sauerkraut. Don't worry about the sauerkraut being too aggressive in this dish. When cooked with the onions, it gets really mellow and loses the bite usually associated with it.

If you're using wine, Riesling or Gewürztraminer work best.

---

2 tablespoons olive oil

---

1 pound kielbasa (beef or pork), halved lengthwise and cut into 2-inch-long pieces

---

1 large onion, halved and thinly sliced

---

2 cups sauerkraut, drained

$1/2$ cup white wine, gluten-free beer, or water

---

1. In a large (12-inch) nonstick frying pan, heat the oil over medium-high heat until hot and shimmering but not smoking. Place half of the kielbasa, cut side down, into the frying pan. Cook for 3 minutes. Turn and cook for an additional 2 minutes. Remove the kielbasa from the pan and set aside on a plate. Repeat with the remaining kielbasa. Cover the plate of cooked kielbasa with a piece of aluminum foil.

2. Add the onion to the hot pan. Lower the heat to medium-low. Cook, stirring occasionally with a wooden spoon, until the onions are soft and brown, 15 to 20 minutes.

3. Add the sauerkraut. Stir to combine. Increase the heat to high. Once the pan is hot, add the wine. Cook until wine is almost fully evaporated and looks thick, 2 to 3 minutes.

4. Lower the heat to medium. Return the kielbasa to the pan. Cook for 5 minutes, until the kielbasa is heated through. Serve immediately.

Serves 4

SERVING SUGGESTION

This dish is great served with mustard, roasted potatoes, and a green salad.

Saltimbocca

Have you ever noticed that some dishes seem like one amazing taste layered on top of another? For me, saltimbocca is one of those dishes. Veal topped with prosciutto and sage in a white wine sauce—how can you go wrong with that? Some saltimbocca recipes call for breading the veal and sautéing it. I've taken out the breading for a quicker and lighter saltimbocca.

If veal doesn't fit into your food budget, you can make this with chicken. I love both versions.

1^{1}/$_{2}$ pounds veal scaloppini or cutlets, about ^{1}/$_{2}$-inch thick, patted dry

Kosher salt and freshly ground black pepper

2 tablespoons unsalted butter

^{1}/$_{3}$ cup dry white wine

4 thin slices prosciutto

4 fresh sage leaves

1. Season the veal with salt and pepper on both sides.

2. Melt the butter in a large (12-inch) nonstick frying pan over medium-high heat. When the butter begins to brown, add the veal in a single layer. Cook for 4 minutes. Using tongs, flip the veal and cook for an additional 4 minutes, or until it reaches 150°F.

3. Pour the wine into the pan and cook for 1 minute.

4. Place 1 piece prosciutto and 1 sage leaf on each piece of veal. Lower the heat to low, cover the pan, and cook for 3 minutes. Serve immediately.

Serves 4

VARIATION

Chicken Saltimbocca: Veal can be expensive! This dish is delicious made with chicken breasts. Use boneless, skinless chicken breasts, pounded ^{1}/$_{2}$-inch thick. Cook until the chicken breasts are golden brown and cooked through with no pink spots remaining.

Veal with White Wine Sauce

This is a quick-cook meal that doesn't taste "quick-cooked" at all! After cooking the veal, you make a simple pan gravy, which transforms this easy meal into pure comfort food. The gravy is phenomenal with the veal but always seems to be extra special when spooned over mashed potatoes.

1 pound veal scaloppini or cutlets, cut into 1-inch-wide strips

2 tablespoons plus 1 teaspoon olive oil

Salt and freshly ground black pepper

$1/4$ cup (4 tablespoons) unsalted butter

2 tablespoons sweet rice flour

$3/4$ cup white wine, homemade chicken stock (page 69), or store-bought reduced-sodium broth

$1/2$ cup water, plus more as needed

Garlic powder

$1/4$ cup chopped flat-leaf parsley

1. In a medium bowl, stir together the veal with 2 tablespoons of the olive oil. Lightly season with salt and pepper. Stir to combine.

2. Place a large bowl near the stove. Heat the remaining 1 teaspoon olive oil in a large (12-inch) nonstick frying pan over high heat until the oil is hot and shimmering but not smoking. Cook the veal in batches, about 3 minutes, stirring frequently, until brown. The veal will cook quickly. Transfer the cooked veal to the waiting bowl. Repeat with remaining veal until all of it is cooked, and set aside.

3. Add the butter to the pan and allow to melt. Add the sweet rice flour. Lower the heat to medium. Cook, stirring constantly with a whisk, for 3 minutes, until the paste is beige. Combine the wine and water and whisk into the paste in a slow and steady stream. Cook for 1 to 2 minutes, until smooth and thick. (For a how-to, see page 46.)

4. Tilt the bowl with the veal and spoon the juices into the pan. Whisk into the sauce. Adjust the thickness of the sauce. If it seems too thick, add more water as needed. The sauce should have a nice body but not be gluey. Season the sauce to taste with salt, pepper, and garlic powder. Lower the heat to low, add the veal, and simmer for 2 to 4 minutes, until warm.

5. Place on a serving platter and sprinkle with the parsley.

Serves 4

Easy Beef Roast

There are two types of "quick cooking." One is quick in the pan; the other takes a long time to cook but is quick to prepare. This roast is the latter. It only takes about 15 minutes to prepare, then you leave it alone for 3 to 4 hours. The reward for this type of "fast slow cooking?" Absolutely flavorful, tender meat that can't be rushed. Often people stop cooking a roast too soon and then it's tough. Braising, which is how this roast is cooked, allows tough pieces of meat to become tender during long, slow cooking. So test the roast. If the meat is tough, pop it back into the oven.

If you don't have a Dutch oven, brown the meat in a skillet. Then transfer it to a casserole, add the vegetables, cover, and finish in the oven.

Kosher salt and freshly ground black pepper

2 tablespoons olive oil

1 boneless chuck roast (3 to 4 pounds), patted dry

4 carrots, peeled and cut into large chunks

2 medium onions, quartered

6 cloves garlic, peeled

1 can (28 ounces) diced tomatoes, with juices

---

1. Adjust oven rack to the middle position and preheat the oven to 325°F. Season the roast all over with salt and pepper.

2. Heat the oil in a large (8-quart) Dutch oven over high heat until it begins to smoke. Brown the roast, undisturbed, for 7 minutes. Turn over with tongs and brown the other side for an additional 7 minutes. Turn off the heat.

3. Add the carrots, onions, garlic, and tomatoes. Cover and place in the oven. Cook for 3 to 4 hours. The finished roast should be very tender. Test it with a fork. If the meat is tender and pulls apart easily, it is ready. If the meat seems tough when you test it, cook the roast longer.

4. Remove the roast from the Dutch oven and place on a cutting board. Reserve the cooking liquid and skim off any excess fat, if you want to. Allow the roast to stand for at least 5 to 10 minutes before slicing. (Slices might fall apart as you cut them. This is a good thing—it means the roast is very tender.)

5. Place the sliced meat and the vegetables on a serving platter and spoon a little of the cooking liquid over the top. Serve with the cooking liquid alongside.

Serves 6, with leftovers

SERVING SUGGESTION

With a roast, I like to serve mashed potatoes with a ladle of the roast's cooking liquid spooned over the top. I'll start the mashed potatoes (page 237) as soon as I take the roast out of the oven. If the slices of meat have cooled off too much by the time the potatoes are ready, I return the meat to the warm cooking liquid to reheat.

Chicken-Fried Steak

Chicken-fried steak. The name alone lets you know this is a rich recipe. And it doesn't stop with frying a piece of cube steak. Nope—a rich pan gravy goes on top of the fried steak. This isn't light eating but, oh my, it is delicious! Since this recipe requires several steps, I usually make it on the weekend when I don't have to rush.

My grocery store sells two kinds of cube steak. One is marked for "braising," and the other states "pan-frying." Be sure to get the one for pan-frying. If you aren't sure, ask the butcher.

Steak

1 cup white rice flour

$^3/_4$ cup tapioca starch

$^3/_4$ cup sweet rice flour

$^1/_2$ teaspoon dried parsley

$^1/_4$ teaspoon garlic powder

$^1/_4$ teaspoon cayenne or ground chipotle chile

$^1/_4$ teaspoon smoked or regular paprika

$^1/_4$ teaspoon xanthan gum

2 large eggs

$1^1/_2$ cups 2% or whole milk

$^1/_2$ cup vegetable oil, for frying

$1^1/_2$ pounds cube steak for pan-frying, cut into 8 pieces

Gravy

$^1/_4$ cup reserved cooking oil

$^1/_4$ cup sweet rice flour

2 cups milk, warmed

Freshly ground black pepper

1. Line a rimmed baking sheet with several layers of paper towels and place it near the stove. Adjust oven rack to the middle position and preheat the oven to 180°F.

2. Set two large dinner plates or pie pans in a line on your counter. Place a small bowl in between the two plates. At the end of the line, place a rimmed baking sheet. In a medium bowl, whisk together the white rice flour, tapioca starch, sweet rice flour, parsley, garlic powder, cayenne, paprika, and xanthan gum. Divide the mixture between the two dinner plates at the ends. In the small bowl, whisk together the eggs and milk.

3. Heat the oil over medium-high heat in a large (12-inch) cast-iron skillet. Test the oil by sprinkling a tiny bit of flour over it. If the flour sizzles, the oil is hot enough.

4. One piece at a time, drag a steak through the first plate of white rice flour mixture, coating well on both sides. Dip the steak into the egg mixture, coating it well, and then into the second plate of flour. Return the steak to the egg mixture and again coat it thoroughly.

Coat again in the second plate of flour. (You only want the egg-coated meat going into the second flour plate. The first flour plate should remain dry, only dip uncoated meat into it. If you start to run out of flour in the second plate, transfer some from the first plate.)

5. Shake the steak slightly to get rid of excess flour and transfer to the baking sheet at the end of the line (not the baking sheet lined with paper towels). Repeat with 2 more steaks. (If your steaks are large and only 2 will fit in your frying pan at once, prepare 1 more steak.) Place the steaks into the hot oil and fry for 3 to 4 minutes, then flip with a pair of tongs. Cook for an additional 4 to 5 minutes. Depending on the size of the steaks, you can fry 2 or 3 at a time.

6. Using tongs, remove the cooked steaks from the hot oil and place on prepared baking sheet. Put the baking sheet in the oven to keep the steaks warm. Repeat with the remaining steaks.

7. When you've fried all the steaks, turn off the burner. Carefully pour the hot oil into a heatproof bowl. Measure out $1/4$ cup oil. (Let any remaining oil cool completely before you dispose of it in the trash—never down the drain!)

8. To make the gravy, return the $1/4$ cup of oil to the skillet. Turn the heat back on to medium-high. Sprinkle the sweet rice flour over the hot oil. Using a whisk, stir constantly for 1 minute, until a beige paste forms.

9. Whisk in the milk in a slow and steady steam. Be sure to go slowly, whisking the entire time; if you don't the gravy will be lumpy.

10. After the last of the milk has been added, simmer the gravy for an additional minute. If gravy seems too thick, add additional milk to thin. Season with pepper to taste. (For a how-to on making gravy, see page 47.)

12. Place the steaks on individual plates and spoon gravy over each steak. Serve immediately.

Serves 4

NOTE

It's important to keep your baking sheets separate—use one for holding the breaded, raw steak, and the other, lined with paper towels, for the fried steak.

Beef Stew with Peppery Dumplings

Dumplings! They are one of the kings of comfort food. In this recipe they sit atop a really flavorful beef stew. The secret to fluffy dumplings is not peeking at them while they cook. After you've put the dumplings on the top of the stew, set a timer and don't look for 20 minutes.

You can buy the beef cubes precut from your butcher, which is what I do, or you can cut them yourself. If you cut the meat yourself, be sure to remove the thin layer of silverskin, the tough, silvery-white tissue, that coats the meat. To do this, run the blade of a thin knife under the silverskin, cutting away as little of the beef as possible.

Beef Stew

3 tablespoons olive oil

3 pounds boneless beef chuck, cut into 1-inch cubes and patted dry

2 medium onions, finely diced

3 cloves garlic, minced or put through a garlic press

2 tablespoons sweet rice flour

2 cups red wine or water

3 cups low-sodium gluten-free beef broth

4 carrots, peeled and cut into large chunks

Peppery Dumplings

1 cup white rice flour

$1/2$ cup cornstarch

$1/2$ cup sweet rice flour

4 teaspoons baking powder

1 teaspoon salt

1 teaspoon freshly ground black pepper

$1/4$ teaspoon xanthan gum

$3/4$ cup milk

2 large eggs

1. To make the stew, place a medium bowl near the stove. In a large (5^1/$_2$-quart) Dutch oven or heavy pot, heat 1 tablespoon of the olive oil over high heat until it begins to smoke. Cook half of the beef until brown, 1 to 2 minutes. Turn the cubes over with a wooden spoon and cook for an additional 1 minute. Transfer the beef to the bowl. Repeat with another 1 tablespoon oil and the remaining beef. Set aside with the first batch.

2. Add the remaining 1 tablespoon oil to the Dutch oven. Add the onions and garlic and cook for 3 minutes, stirring occasionally with a wooden spoon.

3. Return the beef and any juices from the bowl to the Dutch oven. Add the sweet rice flour. Stir with a wooden spoon to thoroughly coat the pieces of meat. Cook for 3 minutes. Add the wine, beef broth, and carrots. Bring to a boil, then lower the heat to low, cover, and simmer the stew (look for occasional gentle bubbles) until beef is tender, about 2 hours. Stir occasionally so the stew doesn't scorch on the bottom of the pot.

4. When the beef is fork-tender, start the dumplings. In a medium bowl, whisk together the white rice flour, cornstarch, sweet rice flour, baking powder, salt, pepper, and xanthan gum. Add the milk and eggs and stir to combine.

5. Increase the heat to medium. Scoop the dough, about 3 tablespoons at a time, onto the top of the stew. You will get about 12 dumplings.

6. As soon as you've added the last dumpling to the pan, cover the pot. Cook—no peeking!—for 20 to 22 minutes, then check if the dumplings are light and fluffy. A tester inserted into the center of a dumpling should come out clean.

7. Spoon into individual bowls or plates and serve hot.

Serves 6

Classic Meatloaf

Meatloaf seems to inspire strong feelings in people. They either love it or, well, they don't. Personally, I am a big fan. I like mine made with half ground beef and half ground pork. If you can't find ground pork, replace it with all ground beef. The meatloaf will still be delicious.

▶ *For a how-to on making dried bread crumbs, see page 32.*

12 ounces ground sirloin (90 to 92% lean)
12 ounces ground pork
$3/4$ cup gluten-free dried bread crumbs
1 can (15 ounces) tomato sauce
1 large egg
1 medium onion, finely diced
1 clove garlic, minced or put through a garlic press
1 teaspoon salt
$1/2$ teaspoon freshly ground black pepper

1. Adjust oven rack to the middle position and preheat the oven to 350°F.

2. In a large bowl, combine the beef, pork, bread crumbs, half of the tomato sauce, the egg, onion, garlic, salt, and pepper. Blend, using your hands or a wooden spoon, until thoroughly combined. I prefer to use my hands and "squish" the mixture together to blend it.

3. Shape into a loaf and place in a 9 by 5-inch or $8^1/2$ by $4^1/4$-inch loaf pan. Pour the remaining tomato sauce over the top.

4. Bake for 1 hour and 15 minutes, or until internal temperature reaches 165°F. Serve hot.

Serves 4

Pictured at left with Classic Meatloaf: Mashed Potatoes, recipe on page 237, and Tomatoes and Green Beans, recipe on page 247.

Cod Cakes

I dislike cod cakes that are more bread crumbs than fish. This recipe doesn't suffer from that problem. I use just enough crumbs to hold together the flakes of cod, making for really tender and flavorful cod cakes. If you can't find cod, any other mild white fish works well in the recipe.

▶ *For a how-to on making dried bread crumbs, see page 32.*

1 teaspoon salt
2 pounds skinless fresh cod fillets
$1^{1}/4$ to $1^{1}/2$ cups gluten-free dried bread crumbs
$1/3$ cup mayonnaise
$1/4$ cup freshly squeezed lemon juice (about 2 lemons)
1 large egg
2 scallions (green onions), thinly sliced (see Note)
3 tablespoons chopped fresh basil
2 tablespoons chopped fresh parsley
1 teaspoon freshly ground black pepper
Vegetable oil for frying

1. Fill a large (12-inch) frying pan with about 1 inch of water. Add $1/2$ teaspoon salt and bring the water to a simmer (look for occasional gentle bubbles).

2. Place the cod into the simmering water and cover. Cook for 8 to 10 minutes, until the fish is firm, flakes easily with a fork, and is no longer translucent. The cooking time will vary depending on the thickness of the fish. Turn off the heat under the pan.

3. Remove the cod from the pan with a slotted spoon and place it in a large bowl. Set aside the pan to cool. Using a fork, flake the cod into small pieces. Add $1/2$ cup of the bread crumbs, the mayonnaise, lemon juice, egg, scallions, basil, parsley, pepper, and the remaining $1/2$ teaspoon salt. Using a fork, gently stir to combine. The mixture should hold together. If not, add up to $1/4$ cup additional bread crumbs.

6. Set up a line with the bowl of cod mixture, a rimmed baking sheet, a large dinner plate, and another baking sheet. Fill the plate with $3/4$ cup bread crumbs.

7. Using your hands, shape the mixture into 12 cakes (use about $1/3$ cup of the mixture for each cake). Be sure to press the mixture together as you shape the cake. If you don't, you risk it falling apart when you fry it. Set the cakes onto the first baking sheet.

8. Coat the cod cakes on both sides with the bread crumbs. Press to make sure the crumbs stick. Place the coated cakes on the second baking sheet. Set a large paper towel–lined plate next to the stove.

9. Carefully pour the water out of the frying pan. (Down the drain is okay.) Wipe the pan dry with a paper towel. Pour about $1/2$ inch of oil in the frying pan and place over medium-high heat until the oil is hot and shimmering but not smoking. Place half of the cod cakes into the oil. (The cod cakes should sizzle when they hit the oil.) Fry until golden brown on the bottom, about 3 minutes. Flip with a spatula or pancake flipper and cook for an additional 3 minutes.

10. Remove the cod cakes from the pan and drain on the paper towels. Fry remaining cakes. Serve and enjoy!

Serves 6

NOTE

I usually use only the white part of the scallions in these cakes, but you can include the green tops as well for more flavor (and color).

Salmon Cakes

I never knew canned salmon could be really tasty until I had these salmon cakes. To make this recipe even easier, buy boneless, skinless canned salmon. This way you can open the can and use the salmon with no cleanup to deal with.

▶ *For a how-to on making dried bread crumbs, see page 32.*

$3/4$ cup plus 2 tablespoons gluten-free dried bread crumbs

2 cans or pouches (5 ounces each) boneless, skinless salmon, drained and flaked

1 large egg

2 tablespoons finely diced green bell pepper

$1/4$ small onion, finely diced

2 tablespoons finely chopped dill pickle

2 tablespoons finely chopped green olives

2 tablespoons mayonnaise

2 tablespoons freshly grated Parmesan cheese

1 teaspoon freshly ground black pepper

1 tablespoon olive oil

1. Place $3/4$ cup bread crumbs on a plate. Place a rimmed baking sheet lined with parchment paper next to the plate.

2. In a medium bowl, combine the remaining crumbs, the salmon, egg, green pepper, onion, pickle, olives, mayonnaise, cheese, and pepper. Stir well with a fork to combine.

3. Scoop out about $1/3$ cup at a time and shape into cakes using your hands. (When I form the cake, I squeeze it with my hands to get rid of extra liquid and help the cake hold together.) You should get 5 cakes.

4. Coat the salmon cakes on both sides with the bread crumbs. Place the cakes on the prepared baking sheet.

5. Heat the olive oil in a large (12-inch) nonstick frying pan over medium-high heat until the oil is hot and shimmering but not smoking. Fry the cakes until golden brown on the bottom, 3 to 4 minutes. Flip with a spatula or pancake flipper and cook for an additional 3 minutes. Serve hot.

Serves 2 hungry adults

SERVING SUGGESTION

I like to pile some baby greens on a plate and nestle 2 salmon cakes on top. Then I drizzle the whole thing with a little dressing. This presentation is surprisingly elegant for such an easy meal.

Baked Fish Sticks

The only time I ate fish sticks growing up was at my grandmother's home in Vermont. When we'd visit, she'd make them for lunch and I loved them. Lots of gluten-free kids love fish sticks, too. This recipe is for them. Like the fish sticks I enjoyed as a kid, these are delicately flavored. But unlike the fish sticks I ate, these are baked, not fried.

▶ *For a how-to on making dried bread crumbs, see page 32.*

Gluten-free nonstick cooking spray

1^1/2 pounds skinless cod fillets, or other white fish such as tilapia

2 large eggs

^{1}/4 cup milk

1 cup gluten-free dried bread crumbs

^{1}/2 teaspoon garlic powder

^{1}/2 teaspoon onion powder

^{1}/2 teaspoon paprika

^{1}/2 teaspoon dried basil

^{1}/4 teaspoon salt

1. Adjust oven rack to the middle position and preheat the oven to 425ºF. Lightly spray a rimmed baking sheet with nonstick cooking spray.

2. Cut the fish into strips about ^{1}/2 by 3 inches long.

3. Set up two large dinner plates or pie pans in a line on your counter. At the end of the line, place the prepared baking sheet. In the first plate, whisk together the eggs and milk. In the second plate, combine the bread crumbs, garlic powder, onion powder, paprika, basil, and salt. Stir with a fork.

4. One at a time, dip the fish strips in the egg mixture, turning to coat them thoroughly, then coat with the bread crumb mixture. Be sure to coat them thoroughly both times. You don't want to leave any bare spots on the sticks. Place the breaded fish on the baking sheet.

5. Spray the fish sticks lightly with cooking spray. Bake for 10 to 12 minutes, until the fish flakes apart and breading is crisp. Serve hot.

Serves 4 to 6

SERVING SUGGESTION
Tartar sauce, lemon juice, or salsa all taste great with fish sticks.

Salmon with Dill Sauce

All you need to prepare this quick supper is a hot pan and oil for the salmon and a small bowl for the dill sauce. The next time you are really squeezed for time, pick up some salmon on the way home. You can have dinner on the table in less than 20 minutes.

1 pound salmon fillet, pin bones removed, skin on or off

1 teaspoon olive oil

$1/4$ cup nonfat Greek-style yogurt

$1/4$ cup mayonnaise

1 teaspoon freshly squeezed lemon juice

$1/2$ teaspoon dried dill

Salt and freshly ground black pepper

1. Cut salmon into 2-inch-wide pieces with a sharp knife. Heat the olive oil in a large (12-inch) nonstick frying pan over medium-high heat until the oil is hot and shimmering but not smoking. Place the salmon in the hot frying pan. If skin is present, place it skin side down. Cook for 6 minutes. Flip with a spatula or pancake flipper. Cook for an additional 5 minutes, or until fish is almost cooked through (still moist and slightly undercooked in the center). Remove from the pan and place on plates. Allow to sit while you make the sauce.

2. In a small bowl, combine the yogurt, mayonnaise, lemon juice, and dill. Stir. Season with salt and pepper to taste. Serve the sauce alongside the salmon.

Serves 4

Oven-Roasted Shrimp

Few seafood meals are easier than roasted shrimp. You simply toss shrimp together with olive oil, garlic, and herbs and bake.

Depending on my mood, some nights I make "garlicky" shrimp and use three cloves. Other nights? One will do. And I like to add a pinch of chives, tarragon, and a smidge of dill. But use any dried herbs you love.

1^1/2 pounds shrimp, peeled and deveined

1 to 2 tablespoons olive oil

^{1}/2 teaspoon kosher salt

^{1}/2 teaspoon freshly ground black pepper

1 to 3 cloves garlic, minced or put through a garlic press

Dried herbs (optional)

---

1. Adjust oven rack to the middle position and preheat the oven to 400°F.

2. On a rimmed baking sheet, toss together the shrimp and olive oil. You want the shrimp lightly coated in oil. Add the salt, pepper, garlic and, if using, herbs. Stir together well. Take care that the garlic doesn't clump. Once coated, spread shrimp on the baking sheet in one layer. I usually line the shrimp up in rows. It doesn't take too long.

3. Bake for 10 minutes, or until shrimp are firm and no longer opaque. Serve hot.

Serves 4

SERVING SUGGESTIONS

Serve with Cheddar Cheesy Grits (page 243) or Polenta (page 234).

Serve with rice and a vegetable (in the spring I serve this with roasted asparagus).

Eggs for Supper
(aka Egg and Potato Skillet)

Quick egg dishes have been around forever. This particular recipe was created by my husband who uses canned potatoes to speed up preparation. If you don't like canned potatoes, use cold, boiled potatoes instead. You'll need about $1^1/2$ cups to replace each can of potatoes.

1 can (15 ounces) no-salt-added sliced potatoes, drained

1 can (15 ounces) no-salt-added whole potatoes, drained and quartered

12 large eggs

$^1/4$ cup water

2 tablespoons unsalted butter

1 tablespoon olive oil

$^1/2$ green or red bell pepper, cored and cut into bite-size pieces

1 small onion, finely diced

$^1/2$ pound reduced-sodium smoked ham, cut into bite-size cubes

2 ounces cheddar cheese, grated ($^1/2$ cup)

1. Pat the potatoes dry on several layers of paper towels. This will prevent them from splattering too much when cooked. Whisk together the eggs and water in a medium bowl.

2. In a large (12-inch) cast-iron skillet, heat the butter and olive oil over medium-high heat until the butter is melted and the oil shimmers. Add the potatoes. Cook until the potatoes begin to brown, stirring occasionally with a wooden spoon. Add the bell pepper and onion and cook until soft, stirring frequently, 4 to 5 minutes. Add the ham and cook for 3 minutes, stirring occasionally, until the ham is heated.

3. Switch to a heatproof spatula. Pour in the eggs. Working quickly, stir the eggs into the potato mixture. As soon as the eggs set, stop stirring. Working in quarters, turn the mixture over. It will break apart as you do this. That's fine!

4. Turn off the heat. Sprinkle the cheese evenly over the top. Cover and allow to sit for 3 to 5 minutes, until cheese is lightly melted. Serve immediately.

5. If there are leftovers, transfer to a covered container and store in the refrigerator for up to 2 days. Reheat in the microwave.

Serves 4 to 6

NOTE

This dish works well even with modifications. Try adding some cooked drained spinach, swapping the potatoes for one cup of halved grape tomatoes, or omitting the cheese.

Easy Veggie Chili

At first glance, this recipe might look complicated thanks to the long list of ingredients. Once you look at the list, though, you will notice most of the ingredients come from cans. All you need to do is chop some veggies and throw everything in a pot. Try this recipe on a cold March night. It's so good, no one will miss the meat.

Depending on your preference, use more or less chili powder for a kick.

3 tablespoons olive oil

1 medium onion, finely diced

2 carrots, peeled and thinly sliced

1 green bell pepper, cored and finely diced

3 stalks celery, thinly sliced

2 cloves garlic, minced or put through a garlic press

3 cups water

1 can (28 ounces) crushed tomatoes

1 can (15 ounces) garbanzo beans, drained and rinsed

1 can (15 ounces) black beans, drained and rinsed

1 can (15 ounces) corn kernels, undrained

1 can (4 to 4.5 ounces) chopped green chiles, undrained

3 tablespoons chili powder

$^1/_2$ tablespoon ground cumin

1 teaspoon salt

1 teaspoon freshly ground black pepper

2 ounces cheddar cheese, grated ($^1/_2$ cup), for topping

1. In a large (8-quart) Dutch oven or heavy pot, heat the olive oil over medium-high heat. Add the onion, carrots, green pepper, and celery. Cook, stirring frequently with a wooden spoon, until tender, about 6 minutes. Add the garlic and cook for an additional minute.

2. Add the water, tomatoes, garbanzo beans, black beans, corn, green chiles, chili powder, cumin, salt, and pepper. Bring to a boil. Taste and add more chili powder, if desired. Lower the heat to low and simmer for 1$^1/_2$ hours (look for occasional gentle bubbles), stirring occasionally to prevent it from scorching on the bottom of the pot.

3. Serve hot in soup bowls. Top with cheese.

Serves 6, with leftovers

NOTE

This recipe makes a lot of chili. Consider using leftovers to make the Cornbread Chili Bake on page 143.

Pictured at right with Easy Veggie Chili: Cornbread, recipe on page 210.

Versatile Vegetable Frittata

I usually have leftover cooked vegetables kicking around the refrigerator. This recipe makes use of them. If you don't have leftover vegetables, simply cook whatever you like before making the frittata.

---

2 tablespoons plus 1 teaspoon olive oil

1 large onion, halved and thinly sliced

1 clove garlic, minced or put through a garlic press

8 large eggs

$1/2$ cup freshly grated Parmesan cheese

$1^1/2$ cups diced cooked vegetables (see Note)

Salt and freshly ground black pepper

---

1. Adjust oven rack to the middle position and preheat the oven to 400°F.

2. In a large (12-inch) cast-iron skillet, heat 2 tablespoons of the olive oil over medium heat. Add the onion and cook until soft, stirring occasionally, about 3 minutes. Remove the onion from the skillet and place on a plate. Allow the onion to cool for 5 minutes.

3. Whisk the eggs and cheese in a medium bowl until smooth. Add vegetables and cooked onions. Stir to combine. Season with salt and pepper. (The amount of salt and pepper will vary depending on how you've seasoned your vegetables. Use whatever you think is required.)

4. Heat the remaining oil in the skillet until hot and shimmering but not smoking. Pour in the egg mixture. Cook, undisturbed, for 10 minutes, or until the eggs aren't runny anymore. Transfer pan to the oven and bake for an additional 10 minutes, or until the top is set. Cut into wedges and serve immediately.

Serves 4

VARIATIONS

Mostly Egg White Vegetable Frittata: Using all eggs whites doesn't really work and isn't very tasty. But you can reduce the amount of whole eggs by using 6 egg whites and 4 whole eggs.

Quinoa Frittata: Replace $1/2$ cup of the vegetables with 1 cup cooked quinoa (see page 240). I especially like a quinoa frittata with red bell peppers, asparagus, and onions.

NOTE

Don't have leftover vegetables? Here's how to cook vegetables for this frittata.

- **Asparagus**: Cut stalks into quarters and steam or boil
- **Bell peppers, green or red**: Dice and sauté
- **Broccoli**: Chop coarsely and steam
- **Mushrooms**: Slice or dice and sauté
- **Spinach, kale, or Swiss chard**: Chop leaves and sauté
- **Tomatoes, fresh**: Seed and dice

8.
Burgers and Sandwiches

How to:

Shape Hamburger Patties

When shaping a burger, don't press or pack the meat together too firmly. You want to use enough force that the burger holds together but not so much that you are squishing the meat.

2. Gently form the meat into balls (it helps if you cup your hands slightly when you first start working with the meat).

1. Divide the meat into equal portions.

3. Once the meat is rounded, flatten into patties.

How to:
Cook Hamburgers

▲ 1. Lightly oil the grill or pan and heat until smoking. (Do not heat nonstick pans until smoking.) Place as many burgers as will comfortably fit in the pan (do not overcrowd). Let the burgers cook without moving them. Do not press them down with a spatula.

▲ 2. Flip the burgers once.

▲ 3. Continue cooking until the desired level of doneness is reached, about 3 minutes per side for rare, about 4 minutes per side for medium, and about 5 minutes per side for well done.

How to:
Freeze Hamburgers

Raw hamburger patties freeze well. Here's how to prepare them for the freezer:

▶ Shape burgers as directed. Place a square of parchment paper between each burger patty. Wrap with plastic wrap or place in freezer bag and freeze. If you're only freezing a few burgers, you can also place them in individual sealable plastic bags. Label and date the bags before freezing. Thaw the burgers overnight in the refrigerator before cooking. Frozen burger patties can be kept for up to 4 months.

Fall Turkey Burgers

This burger takes all my favorite flavors of fall and puts them between two pieces of bread. For ease, the recipe uses canned cranberry sauce. If I have some fresh cranberry sauce around, I'll use that on the burger. Use whichever sauce, canned or homemade, that you prefer.

Do not use extra-lean 99% fat-free turkey in this recipe. Burgers need some fat to be juicy!

2 tablespoons olive oil

1/2 cup finely chopped celery

1/2 small onion, finely diced

1 large green apple, peeled, cored, and shredded

1 pound lean ground turkey

1/2 teaspoon salt

1/4 teaspoon freshly ground black pepper

1/2 bunch parsley, finely chopped (about 2 tablespoons)

1/2 cup whole berry cranberry sauce

4 gluten-free hamburger buns, homemade (page 207) or store-bought, or 8 slices gluten-free bread, toasted

1. In a large (12-inch) cast-iron skillet, heat the oil over medium-high heat until hot and shimmering but not smoking. Add the celery and onion. Cook, stirring frequently, until soft, 4 to 5 minutes. Add the apple and cook until the apple is soft, another 3 minutes. Remove the vegetables and apple from the skillet and place on a plate. Wipe out the skillet and set aside. (If you have a grill pan and would rather use that to cook your burgers, don't bother wiping out the skillet. You are done with it.)

2. In a medium bowl, combine the ground turkey, salt, pepper, parsley, and 2 tablespoons of the cranberry sauce. Mix to combine. Add the apple mixture and stir until all the ingredients are thoroughly combined.

3. Divide into 4 burgers. (For a how-to, see page 183.) Lightly oil the skillet or grill pan and heat over medium-high heat until the oil begins to smoke. Cook the burgers about 3 minutes per side for rare; about 4 minutes per side for medium; and about 5 minutes per side for well done. (For a how-to, see page 184.) Top the burgers with the remaining cranberry sauce and serve on gluten-free hamburger buns or toast.

Makes 4 burgers

Meatloaf
Burgers

The first time I made these burgers, I didn't tell my husband what they were. They made him exclaim, "These are the best burgers ever!" This is high praise from a man who is a self-described burger expert. I must say, I agree with him. These are my favorite burgers to make and to eat. They are really flavorful and really moist—like a good burger should be!

▶ *For a how-to on making dried bread crumbs, see page 32.*

---

1 pound ground round (85 to 90% lean) or ground sirloin (90 to 92% lean)

---

1 pound ground pork

$1/2$ cup gluten-free dried bread crumbs

---

1 large egg

---

1 medium onion, finely diced

---

1 clove garlic, minced or put through a garlic press

---

1 teaspoon salt

$1/2$ teaspoon freshly ground black pepper

---

1 cup tomato sauce, homemade (page 126) or store-bought

---

8 gluten-free hamburger buns, homemade (page 207) or store-bought, or 16 slices gluten-free bread, toasted

---

1. In a medium bowl, mix together the beef, pork, bread crumbs, egg, onion, garlic, salt, pepper, and tomato sauce. Shape into 8 burgers. (For a how-to, see page 183.)

3. Heat a large (12-inch) lightly oiled cast-iron skillet or grill pan over medium-high heat until hot and beginning to smoke. Place the burgers in the pan and cook undisturbed for 6 minutes. Flip and cook for an additional 5 minutes. Because of the inclusion of ground pork, it's important that the internal temperature reaches 165°F. (For a how-to, see page 184.)

4. Serve on gluten-free hamburger buns or toast.

Makes 8 burgers

NOTE

This recipe makes a lot of burgers—I like to freeze half of the burgers when I make a batch. For a how-to on freezing, see page 184.

Mustard and Ketchup Burgers

These burgers, with the simple addition of ketchup and mustard, have a really nice classic burger flavor. You don't really taste the ketchup and mustard. This is a good thing; they just serve to heighten the flavor of the burger. And not only are these burgers really good, they are really easy. Can't beat that on burger night, right?

1 pound ground round (85 to 90% lean) or ground sirloin (90 to 92% lean)

2 teaspoons Dijon mustard

2 tablespoons ketchup

1/4 teaspoon salt

1/2 teaspoon freshly ground black pepper

4 gluten-free hamburger buns, homemade (page 207) or store-bought, or 8 slices gluten-free bread, toasted

1. In a large bowl, combine the beef, mustard, ketchup, salt, and pepper. Shape into 4 burgers. (For a how-to, see page 183.)

2. Heat a large (12-inch) lightly oiled cast-iron skillet or grill pan over medium-high heat until hot and beginning to smoke. Place the burgers in the pan and cook about 3 minutes per side for rare; about 4 minutes per side for medium; and about 5 minutes per side for well done. (For a how-to, see page 184.) Serve on gluten-free hamburger buns or toast.

Makes 4 burgers

Bacon-and-Cheese Turkey Burgers

Each time I wanted to try a bacon cheeseburger, I couldn't bring myself to do it. I'm not a "light" eater, but the idea of a burger topped with cheese and bacon was too much even for me. Enter ground turkey. While these burgers are still an indulgence, they aren't quite as rich as a traditional bacon cheeseburger. And I love them. They have bacon *and* cheese! What's not to love?

Do not use extra-lean 99% fat-free turkey in this recipe. Burgers need some fat to be juicy!

▶ *For a how-to on cooking bacon, see page 43.*

1 pound lean ground turkey

$1/4$ teaspoon salt

Pinch of garlic powder

4 thin slices cheddar cheese

8 slices bacon, cooked until crisp

4 gluten-free hamburger buns, homemade (page 207) or store-bought, or 8 slices gluten-free bread, toasted

1. Combine the ground turkey, salt, and garlic powder. Shape into 4 burgers. (For a how-to, see page 183.)

2. Heat a large (12-inch) lightly oiled cast-iron skillet or grill pan over medium-high heat until hot and beginning to smoke. Place the burgers in the pan and cook about 3 minutes per side for rare; about 4 minutes per side for medium; and about 5 minutes per side for well done. (For a how-to, see page 184.)

3. Top each burger with 1 slice cheese and 2 slices bacon. Cover the pan, lower the heat to low, and cook for 2 minutes, or until the cheese is melted. Serve on gluten-free hamburger buns or toast.

Makes 4 burgers

Taco Burgers

It's funny how you can take the same ingredients, put them together in a different way and get a totally different result. Take the basic taco. It usually contains ground beef, cheddar cheese, lettuce, salsa, and guacamole. Although these burgers have the same ingredients, they don't taste like your standard taco. They taste like, well, a burger with taco-ish influences. (See, these burgers are so good they are causing me to make up words like "taco-ish." When a burger causes you to make up words, you know it is a good burger!)

---

1 pound ground round (85 to 90% lean) or ground sirloin (90 to 92% lean)

---

1 tablespoon chili powder

$^1/_2$ teaspoon salt

---

4 gluten-free hamburger buns, homemade (page 207) or store-bought, or 8 slices gluten-free bread, toasted

---

$^1/_3$ cup guacamole, homemade (page 66) or store-bought

Shredded lettuce, about 1 cup

$^1/_3$ cup salsa, homemade (page 64) or store-bought

Grated cheddar cheese (optional)

---

1. In a medium bowl, mix the ground beef with the chili powder and salt. Shape into 4 burgers. (For a how-to, see page 183.)

2. Heat a large (12 inch) lightly oiled cast iron skillet or grill pan over medium-high heat until hot and beginning to smoke. Place the burgers in the pan and cook about 3 minutes per side for rare; about 4 minutes per side for medium; and about 5 minutes per side for well done. (For a how-to, see page 184.)

3. Remove from the pan and place on gluten-free hamburger buns or toast. Top with guacamole, lettuce, and salsa. Add cheese, if desired, and serve.

Makes 4 burgers

California Club Burgers

I might cause a bit of an uproar when I say this but a burger is just a hot sandwich, right? Two pieces of bread, great filling, you get the point. So why not take a great sandwich, the California Club, and combine it with a burger? The results are, you guessed it, a great burger! As always with avocados be sure your avocado is ripe. It makes all the difference in the world to the flavor of this burger.

Do not use extra-lean 99% fat-free turkey in this recipe. Burgers need some fat to be juicy!

▶ *For a how-to on pitting and peeling avocados, see page 39.*

1 clove garlic, minced or put through a garlic press

1 pound lean ground turkey

Salt and freshly ground black pepper

4 gluten-free hamburger buns, homemade (page 207) or store-bought, or 8 slices gluten-free bread, toasted

1 large tomato, cut crosswise into 8 slices

1 Hass avocado, pitted, peeled, and thinly sliced

Baby greens (optional)

Mayonnaise (optional)

1. Gently mix the garlic into the ground turkey. Shape the ground turkey into 4 burgers. (For a how-to, see page 183.) Generously salt and pepper each burger.

2. Heat a large (12-inch) lightly oiled cast-iron skillet or grill pan over medium-high heat until hot and beginning to smoke. Place the burgers in the pan and cook about 3 minutes per side for rare; about 4 minutes per side for medium; and about 5 minutes per side for well done. (For a how-to, see page 184.)

3. Remove the burgers from the pan and place on gluten-free hamburger buns or toast. Top with tomato, avocado slices, baby greens, and mayonnaise, if desired, and serve.

Makes 4 burgers

Patty Melts

I love that the patty melt can't decide if it's a burger or a sandwich. I have some days when I can't decide what I want to be, either. Maybe on those days I should make myself a patty melt and head for the couch. Actually, that sounds like a great idea . . .

1 pound ground round (85 to 90% lean)
2 tablespoons unsalted butter
8 slices gluten-free Rye-ish Bread, homemade (page 209) or store-bought
8 slices Swiss cheese
$1/2$ cup caramelized onions (see page 38)

1. Shape the ground beef into 4 patties. (For a how-to, see page 183.)

2. Heat a large (12-inch) lightly oiled cast-iron skillet or grill pan over medium-high heat until hot and beginning to smoke. Place the burgers in the pan and cook about 3 minutes per side for rare; about 4 minutes per side for medium; and about 5 minutes per side for well done. (For a how-to, see page 184.)

3. In a separate large (12-inch) nonstick frying pan, melt 1 tablespoon of the butter over medium heat. Put 4 slices of bread in the pan and cook until the bread is lightly toasted and golden. Remove and set aside. Repeat with remaining butter and bread but this time leave the bread in the pan.

4. Place 1 slice of Swiss cheese on each slice of bread. Transfer the hot patties onto the bread in the frying pan. Top each patty with caramelized onions and another bread slice, cheese side down. Cook for 2 minutes to melt the cheese, then flip the sandwiches and cook for an additional minute. Serve immediately.

Makes 4 patty melts

VARIATIONS

Mushroom Melt: Replace the caramelized onions with sautéed mushrooms. Sauté $1^1/2$ cups sliced white button mushrooms in 2 tablespoons unsalted butter or olive oil until they are soft and light brown, 6 to 8 minutes. Top the patties with the mushrooms before adding the second slice of bread.

Onion and Mushroom Melt: Too much of a good thing is a very good thing, as this loaded burger proves. Use both caramelized onions and sautéed mushrooms on the patties.

Greek Salad Burgers

A burger topped with kalamata olives and feta? How could you go wrong?

Sauce

1 container (6 ounces) plain Greek-style yogurt

1 tablespoon olive oil

Juice of $1/2$ lemon

$1/2$ teaspoon dried dill

1 clove garlic, minced or put through a garlic press

Milk (optional)

Burgers

8 ounces ground lamb

8 ounces ground chuck (80 to 85% lean)

Salt and freshly ground black pepper

4 gluten-free hamburger buns, homemade (page 207) or store-bought, or 8 slices gluten-free bread, toasted

1 small cucumber, peeled and thinly sliced

$1/4$ cup kalamata olives, pitted and halved

$1/4$ red onion, cut into thin rings

6 ounces feta, sliced or crumbled

1. Make the sauce by combining the yogurt, olive oil, lemon juice, dill, and garlic in a small bowl. The sauce should have the consistency of a thick mayonnaise. If it seems too thick, stir in a little milk.

2. To make the burgers, combine the lamb and beef and shape into 4 burgers. Season lightly with salt and pepper. (For a how-to, see page 183.)

3. Heat a large (12-inch) lightly oiled cast-iron skillet or grill pan over medium-high heat until hot and beginning to smoke. Place the burgers in the pan and cook about 3 minutes per side for rare; about 4 minutes per side for medium; and about 5 minutes per side for well done, to an internal temperature of 165°F. (For a how-to, see page 184.)

4. Remove the burgers from the pan and place on gluten-free hamburger buns or toast. Top with the sauce, cucumber, olives, onion, and feta and serve.

Makes 4 burgers

NOTE

If you have leftover sauce, don't throw it away! Use it on the Greek Salad Pizza (page 219). The sauce will keep up to four days covered in the refrigerator.

Croque Monsieur

For years I avoided trying a croque monsieur because, honestly, the thought of a sandwich topped with a cheesy sauce didn't sound appealing to me. Let me tell you, I was wrong. Terribly wrong. After one bite, I knew why this sandwich was a classic. When served with a green salad, this sandwich has become one of my favorite go-to comfort food meals!

Be sure to use whole or 2% milk; 1% and fat-free don't work well in this recipe.

8 slices gluten-free white sandwich bread, homemade (page 206) or store-bought

2 tablespoons unsalted butter

3 tablespoons sweet rice flour

$2^1/2$ cups whole or 2% milk, warmed

$1/4$ teaspoon salt

$1/2$ teaspoon freshly ground black pepper

6 ounces Gruyère cheese, grated (about 2 cups)

$1/4$ cup freshly grated Parmesan cheese

Dijon mustard

8 ounces sliced ham

1. Adjust oven rack to the middle position and preheat the oven to 425°F.

2. Place the bread on a rimmed baking sheet. Toast, flipping once, until the slices begin to turn golden brown. Remove from the oven and set aside. Leave the oven on.

3. Prepare the sauce: In a small (2-quart) pot, melt the butter. Add the sweet rice flour. Cook for 3 minutes, whisking constantly. The paste will turn beige. In a slow and steady stream, add the milk. Cook, whisking constantly, until the sauce begins to bubble. Season with salt and pepper. (For a how-to on making white sauce, see page 46.) Stir in $1/2$ cup of the Gruyère and all of the Parmesan. Whisk until smooth.

4. Make the sandwiches on the baking sheet. Spread a thin coat of mustard on each piece of bread. Place a few slices of ham and a generous sprinkle of Gruyère on each of 4 bread slices. (Reserve about one-quarter of the cheese.) Top with a second slice of bread, mustard side down. Spoon a generous amount of white sauce onto each sandwich. Divide the remaining Gruyère over the top.

5. Return the sandwiches to the oven. Bake for 5 minutes to heat.

6. Turn on the broiler. Adjust the baking sheet so it is directly under the broiler. Broil until the cheese is melted, light brown, and bubbling. Serve immediately.

Makes 4 sandwiches

Black Bean Cheese Quesadillas

Cheese, salsa, and black beans. Simple, right? But when sandwiched together between two corn tortillas, they are just perfect!

12 (6-inch) corn tortillas

1 cup salsa, homemade (page 64) or store-bought

8 ounces cheddar or mozzarella cheese, or a combination of cheddar and pepper Jack, grated (2 cups)

$3/4$ cup canned black beans, drained and rinsed

Gluten-free nonstick cooking spray

1. Lay out 6 tortillas on a rimmed baking sheet. Divide the salsa, cheese, and beans evenly over the tortillas. Top each quesadilla with a second tortilla and press down lightly so they hold together.

2. Lightly spray a small (8-inch) nonstick skillet with nonstick cooking spray and place over medium-high heat. Cook the quesadillas, one at a time, for 3 to 4 minutes. Flip and cook for an additional 2 to 3 minutes. The tortillas should be golden brown and the cheese melted and beginning to ooze out of the sides. Serve immediately.

Makes 6 quesadillas

Reuben

I love a good Reuben. Before going gluten-free, I'd often order one when I was out for dinner. Now I make them at home. To be honest, I think the ones I make at home are better!

Unsalted butter, at room temperature

8 slices gluten-free Rye-ish Bread, homemade (page 209) or store-bought

8 slices Swiss cheese

$1/2$ cup sauerkraut, drained

1 pound gluten-free corned beef

Thousand Island dressing or Elizabeth's Reuben Dressing (recipe follows)

1. Lightly butter one side of each piece of bread.

2. Heat a large (12-inch) nonstick frying pan over medium heat. Put 4 slices of bread, buttered side down, in the pan. Place a slice of cheese on each piece of bread. Divide the sauerkraut and corned beef among the sandwiches. Top with another slice of cheese. Allow to cook for 4 minutes.

3. Spread a thin coat of dressing on the unbuttered side of the remaining slices of bread. Put the bread, dressing side down, onto the sandwiches. Press down lightly with a pancake flipper. Flip the sandwiches in the pan and cook for 3 to 4 minutes. Serve hot.

Makes 4 sandwiches

VARIATION

Red Reuben: Replace the corned beef with turkey and the sauerkraut with drained canned red cabbage.

Elizabeth's Reuben Dressing

$1/3$ cup mayonnaise

1 tablespoon ketchup

1 tablespoon dill pickle relish

Freshly ground black pepper

● In a small bowl, stir together the mayonnaise, ketchup, and relish. Season with pepper to taste.

Makes about $1/2$ cup

Cheesy Turkey and Artichoke Panini

Bread plus melted cheese is one of my favorite combinations. Obviously, I love panini! They celebrate this combination. By adding a few artichoke hearts, this sandwich goes from being a traditional turkey sandwich to something a little more special.

Unsalted butter, at room temperature

8 slices gluten-free bread, homemade (page 206) or store-bought

8 slices provolone

1 cup quartered canned artichoke hearts

8 ounces thinly sliced gluten-free deli roasted turkey

1. Lightly butter the bread. Flip 4 slices of bread so they are buttered side down. On each of these, place 1 slice provolone. You might have to break the cheese to get it to cover the bread without hanging over. Add 2 or 3 pieces of artichoke and top with 2 or 3 slices of turkey. Top with the remaining cheese and place the remaining bread on top, buttered side up.

2. Heat a panini grill. Cook the sandwiches until golden brown, 4 to 5 minutes. Serve hot.

Makes 4 sandwiches

Making a Panini without a Panini Grill?

Don't have a panini grill? No problem! You can still make great panini at home. Heat butter or olive oil in a skillet, frying pan, griddle, or grill pan over medium heat. Add sandwiches to the hot pan. Cook until the cheese begins to melt and the bread is golden brown, about three minutes. Flip the sandwich and cook for another three minutes, pressing the sandwich down firmly with a pancake flipper until bread is toasted. Cooking time will vary depending on the size of your bread.

ALT (Avocado, Lettuce, and Tomato)

I've replaced the bacon in a traditional BLT with slices of avocado. It totally changes the sandwich. Use whatever lettuce you have in the house.

▶ *For a how-to on pitting and peeling avocados, see page 39.*

2 slices gluten-free bread, homemade (page 206) or store-bought, toasted

Mayonnaise

$1/2$ avocado, pitted, peeled, and thinly sliced

Small handful of chopped lettuce

3 or 4 tomato slices

Salt and freshly ground pepper

• Spread each slice of bread lightly with mayonnaise. Top with avocado, lettuce, and tomato. Season with salt and pepper to taste. Cover with the remaining bread and serve.

Makes 1 sandwich

VARIATION

BLAT (Bacon, Lettuce, Avocado, and Tomato): Add 2 slices of crisply cooked bacon to the sandwich. For a how-to on cooking bacon, see page 43.

Gooey Grilled Cheese Sandwich

There is only one way to describe this sandwich: gooey. Well, maybe two ways: gooey and delicious.

Unsalted butter, at room temperature

2 slices gluten-free white sandwich bread, homemade (page 206) or store-bought

About $1/3$ cup grated mozzarella cheese

• Generously butter the bread on one side. This is not a time to be shy with butter. Sandwich the cheese between the unbuttered sides of the bread. Heat a small (8-inch) nonstick frying pan over medium heat. Cook the sandwich, about 2 minutes on each side, until the bread is toasted and the cheese is beginning to ooze out.

Makes 1 sandwich

Almost–Pan Bagnat

This sandwich was inspired by the classic French *pan bagnat*. In that sandwich, a crusty French baguette is filled with tuna, onion, hard-cooked egg, and other goodies. Sounds good, right? But when I am alone, there is no way I am making that big a sandwich for myself. I created this Almost–Pan Bagnat for times I want the flavors of a pan bagnat but don't have someone to share it with. It has the same flavors, just slightly different preparation.

▶ *For how-to's on cooking and peeling eggs, see page 41.*

$1/2$ can (5 to 6 ounces) solid tuna in water, drained

1 tablespoon finely diced red onion

1 tablespoon olive oil

1 teaspoon red wine vinegar

Dijon mustard

2 slices gluten-free bread, homemade (page 206) or store-bought

1 hard-cooked egg, peeled and sliced

A few thin slices cucumber

2 or 3 slices tomato

A few kalamata olives, pitted and chopped

• In a small bowl, mix the tuna, onion, olive oil, and vinegar. Lightly spread mustard on 1 of the bread slices. Layer egg, cucumber, and tomato slices on the bread. Top with the tuna mixture. Sprinkle chopped olives over the top. Cover with the remaining bread and serve immediately.

Makes 1 sandwich

Chipotle Chicken Sandwich

I love chicken sandwiches, but some days I want a little more oomph than just lettuce, mayo, salt, and pepper. On those days, I make this sandwich. I love it with bacon but it's good without it, too!

Leftover chicken and bacon work fine here, or you could cook them fresh for this sandwich.

▶ *For how-to's on cooking chicken and bacon, see pages 45 and 43.*

---

1 tablespoon mayonnaise

1/8 teaspoon ground chipotle chile

2 slices gluten-free bread, homemade (page 206) or store-bought

1/2 boneless, skinless chicken breast, cooked and sliced

2 slices bacon, cooked until crisp

2 or 3 tomato slices

- Stir together the mayonnaise and chipotle. Spread on each slice of bread. Top 1 slice with chicken, bacon, and tomato. Cover with the remaining slice of bread and serve.

Makes 1 sandwich

Summer Grilled Veggie Wraps with Provolone

I love veggie wraps. This wrap uses grilled summer vegetables and provolone. It's easy and delicious. If you want, add whatever else sounds good to you. More vegetables, more chicken, different cheeses. This wrap is endlessly versatile.

1 small yellow squash, thinly sliced

1 small zucchini, thinly sliced

1 medium onion, cut into thin rings

Olive oil

4 (6-inch) corn tortillas

Mayonnaise

8 slices provolone cheese

Salt and freshly ground black pepper

1. Lightly brush the squash, zucchini, and onion with olive oil. Lightly oil a grill pan over medium-high heat. Working with one vegetable at a time, grill the vegetables until golden brown. For the squash and zucchini, grill about 3 minutes per side. For the onion, grill about 4 minutes per side. Cooking time varies depending on the thickness of the vegetables, but you want them to be golden brown and tender. Transfer the grilled vegetables to a large plate.

2. Once all the vegetables are grilled, heat the corn tortillas in the grill pan. Cook for about 2 minutes per side.

3. Place the tortillas on a work surface. Spread a little mayonnaise on each tortilla. Top each tortilla with 2 slices provolone and one-quarter of the grilled vegetables. Season with salt and pepper to taste. Turn up the bottom third of the tortilla over the filling, then fold in each side to close. Serve immediately.

Makes 4 wraps

9.
Breads

Sandwich Bread and Hamburger Buns

In my first cookbook, I created recipes for wonderful gluten-free breads. Many readers told me in classes and online how much they enjoyed the ease of those recipes. I also began hearing from folks who couldn't enjoy the recipes because they all contained dairy. While I provided dairy-free folks with a substitute, I wanted to create a naturally gluten-free, dairy-free recipe for this book. I had no idea what a challenge that would turn out to be.

I feel strongly that my bread recipes should not include hard-to-find flours. My goal is to use as few flours and starches as possible while still getting an amazing loaf of gluten-free bread. Sure, I could have easily created a gluten-free, dairy-free sandwich bread with lots of ingredients but that's not what I wanted to do—I wanted to recapture the ease of my Easy Sandwich Bread, which is made with only brown rice flour and cornstarch. After many, many failed loaves of bread, I finally created an easy-to-put-together bread with a soft crumb and a wonderful flavor. What more could I ask for? And in addition to being gluten-free and dairy-free, it is also corn-free. I'm really proud of this.

Since this isn't a baking book, I've only included two sandwich-bread recipes. These recipes are, of course, perfect for sandwiches and hamburger buns, but they are also great for bread crumbs and croutons.

If you've never made gluten-free bread before, I promise these loaves are really easy to make. And if you have made gluten-free bread before and have been disappointed by heavy, crumbly loaves, these recipes will delight you.

How to:
Make Gluten-Free Sandwich Bread

▲ 1. In the bowl of a stand mixer, whisk together the dry ingredients. In a small bowl, whisk together the wet ingredients. Pour the wet ingredients over the dry ingredients.

▲ 2. Mix, using the paddle attachment, until the dough comes together.

▲ 3. The dough should be thick.

▲ 4. Spread the dough evenly into a prepared loaf pan and cover with plastic wrap.

▲ 5. Allow the dough to rise for 1 hour, or until it reaches the top of the pan. Remove the plastic wrap and, if desired, cut 3 slashes lightly across the top of the dough with a knife.

▲ 6. Bake until the internal temperature of the bread reaches 205°F. Remove the bread from the pan and transfer to a wire rack to cool. Allowing the bread to cool on a wire rack keeps the crust crisp and prevents the interior from getting gummy.

◀ 7. Slice the bread with a serrated knife when cool.

White Sandwich Bread

I like to use instant yeast in this recipe. If you're using active dry yeast, use water at 110° to 115°F and dissolve the yeast in the water before mixing.

Gluten-free nonstick cooking spray

Dry Ingredients

3 cups brown rice flour

1 cup potato starch

1 tablespoon xanthan gum

1 tablespoon granulated sugar

1 teaspoon salt

1 teaspoon baking powder

1 packet ($2^1/4$ teaspoons) instant yeast

Wet Ingredients

2 cups very warm water (120° to 130°F)

2 large eggs

2 tablespoons olive oil

1. Lightly grease a 9 by 5-inch loaf pan with nonstick cooking spray.

2. In the bowl of a stand mixer, whisk together the dry ingredients. In a small bowl, whisk together the wet ingredients.

3. Pour the wet ingredients over the dry and mix on medium speed, using the paddle attachment, until a dough forms, about 2 minutes. The dough will be thick and sticky. If it appears dry, add another 1 to 2 tablespoons water.

4. Using a rubber spatula, scrape the dough into the prepared pan. Smooth the dough evenly in the pan with the spatula. Cover with a lightly greased piece of plastic wrap.

5. Allow to rise at room temperature until dough reaches the top of the pan, about 1 hour.

6. Adjust oven rack to the middle position and preheat the oven to 350°F. Remove the plastic wrap from the dough and cut 3 slashes lightly across the top of the bread with a serrated knife. Bake the loaf for 1 hour, or until the internal temperature reaches 205° to 211°F. Use an instant-read thermometer to test bread's temperature.

7. Remove the bread from the oven. Allow to cool in the pan for 2 minutes then remove from the pan and place on a wire rack to cool. Slice with a serrated knife when completely cool.

8. Store the bread, wrapped well in plastic, at room temperature for up to 3 days or in the freezer for up to 1 month.

Makes 1 loaf

How to:
Make Hamburger Buns

The same sandwich bread dough makes wonderful buns. Here's how you make them:

▶ *1. Line a rimmed baking sheet with parchment paper. Mix the bread dough as you would for a loaf.*

▲ *2. Scoop mounds of dough about 3 inches apart onto the prepared baking sheet. (I use a large ice cream scoop for this, about three-quarters cup per bun.) The surface of the dough will be a little ragged. If you want a smoother surface, wet your fingers and smooth the dough.*

◀ *3. Cover the pan lightly with a greased piece of plastic wrap.*

◀ *4. Allow the dough mounds to rise at room temperature until puffy and doubled in size, about 1 hour.*

▶ *5. Preheat the oven to 350°F. Remove the plastic wrap and bake the buns until golden brown, 35 to 40 minutes. The internal temperature should reach between 205° and 211°F.*

▲ *6. Remove the buns from the pan and place on a wire rack to cool completely.*

▲ *7. Store the buns, wrapped well in plastic, at room temperature for 1 day or in the freezer for up to 1 month. If freezing, split the buns first.*

Makes 6 large hamburger buns

Multigrain Sandwich Bread

Multi-grain bread often suffers from a bit of a heaviness problem. While sometimes a dense, heavy bread is great, it's not what I want for sandwiches. This bread avoids heaviness by borrowing the flavors of a great multigrain loaf and combining it with the lightness of a sandwich bread.

Gluten-free nonstick cooking spray

Dry Ingredients

$1^1/2$ cups gluten-free buckwheat flour

$1^1/2$ cups brown rice flour

$1/2$ cup sorghum flour

$1/2$ cup potato starch

$1/4$ cup flaxseed meal

1 tablespoon xanthan gum

1 tablespoon granulated sugar

1 teaspoon salt

1 teaspoon baking powder

1 packet ($2^1/4$ teaspoons) instant yeast

Wet Ingredients

$2^1/4$ cups very warm water (120° to 130°F)

2 large eggs plus 1 egg white

2 tablespoons olive oil

1. Lightly grease a 9 by 5-inch loaf pan with nonstick cooking spray.

2. In the bowl of a stand mixer, whisk together the dry ingredients. In a small bowl, whisk together the wet ingredients.

3. Pour the wet ingredients over the dry and mix on medium speed, using the paddle attachment, until a dough forms, about 2 minutes. The dough will be thick and sticky. If it appears dry, add another 1 to 2 tablespoons water.

4. Using a rubber spatula, scrape the dough into the prepared pan. Smooth the dough evenly in the pan with the spatula. Cover with a lightly greased piece of plastic wrap.

5. Allow to rise at room temperature until the dough reaches the top of the pan, about 1 hour.

6. Adjust oven rack to the middle position and preheat the oven to 350°F. Remove the plastic wrap from the dough. Bake the loaf for 1 hour, or until the internal temperature reaches 205° to 211°F. Use an instant-read thermometer to test bread's temperature.

7. Remove the bread from the oven. Allow the bread to cool in the pan 2 minutes, then remove from the pan and place on a wire rack to cool. Slice with a serrated knife when completely cool.

8. Store the bread, wrapped well in plastic, at room temperature for up to 3 days or in the freezer for up to 1 month.

Makes 1 loaf

Although buckwheat is naturally gluten-free, not all brands are free from gluten contamination. Be sure the bag of flour you purchase is labeled gluten-free.

I like to use instant yeast in this recipe. If you're using active dry yeast, use water at 110° to 115°F and dissolve the yeast in the water before mixing.

Rye-ish Bread: Before going gluten-free, rye bread was one of my favorites. Not only is it great on it's own, I believe that a great Reuben sandwich needs great rye bread. And this recipe makes a great "rye-ish" bread. As with many classic rye breads, the recipe contains caraway seeds. If you don't love caraway, omit the seeds and if you really love caraway, add additional seeds! This loaf can handle as many caraway seeds as you want to add to it.

• Replace the water with coffee and add 2 tablespoons caraway seeds.

Cornbread

I love a piece of cornbread with chili or a salad or anything, really. This recipe comes together in minutes. I've made it right before dinner and served it warm. You can also make it in a cast-iron skillet—preheat the skillet in a 425ºF oven, then add the batter. The baking time will be slightly shorter, about 20 minutes.

Gluten-free nonstick cooking spray

Dry Ingredients

1 cup gluten-free cornmeal

$1/2$ cup white rice flour

$1/2$ cup sweet rice flour

$1/4$ cup granulated sugar

1 tablespoon baking powder

$1/2$ teaspoon salt

$1/4$ teaspoon xanthan gum

Wet Ingredients

2 large eggs

1 cup milk

2 tablespoons unsalted butter, melted

1. Adjust oven rack to the middle position and preheat the oven to 350ºF. Lightly grease an 8-inch square baking pan with cooking spray.

2. Whisk together the dry ingredients in a medium bowl. Add the wet ingredients and whisk together until the batter is smooth. Pour into the prepared pan.

3. Bake the cornbread for 30 to 35 minutes, until lightly golden brown. A cake tester inserted in the center of the cornbread should come out clean.

4. Remove the pan from the oven and place on a wire rack to cool. Cut into 9 pieces when cooled.

5. Cornbread is best the day it's made. If you need to store it, wrap the cornbread well in plastic and store on the counter for up to 2 days.

Makes one 8-inch square pan cornbread, 9 servings

See photo, page 181.

10.
Pizzas

When I went gluten-free, one of my first thoughts was, "Pizza?!" Thankfully, I'd already created two great recipes for my first book. For a long time, I made those crusts and didn't give much thought to creating a new crust recipe. Then one night, right before dinner, I was in the mood for pizza. But I didn't have an hour to let the crust rise. Hmm, what to do, what to do? I decided to try making a crust with baking powder instead of yeast. In the time it took to preheat the oven, my crust was mixed, rolled, and put in the pan. Was that first crust perfect? Ha! Far from it. The poor crust cracked when baked and was dry, even with a generous amount of sauce. But in spite of all that, the crust had potential. The best quality of that first crust was that it was really crisp, followed by the short prep time.

Over the next few months, I kept tinkering with the crust until I got it right. Now the crust rolls out easily, and no matter how much sauce or how many toppings you pile onto it, the crust does not get soft or gummy. Even with all my modifications, this crust comes together, using only a wooden spoon. Great, right? It gets better. For fun I decided to test the recipe with yeast, too, for those nights when time allows for the crust to rise with yeast. Guess what? It worked! If you want a quick crust, use the baking powder version. If you have the time and want a traditional pizza crust, use the yeast version. Either way, this crust is delicious and I am really happy my craving for pizza led to such a delicious recipe!

Make Pizza Crust

▲ 1. In a medium bowl, whisk together the dry ingredients.

▲ 2. Add the wet ingredients.

▲ 3. Stir the wet and dry ingredients together with a wooden spoon until a dough forms. If the dough seems dry and isn't coming together to form a dough or is leaving lots of dry ingredients in the bottom of the bowl, add a splash of water.

▲ 4. Generously sprinkle your counter with white rice flour. Turn the dough out onto the counter. Knead dough until it is smooth. Roll out the dough on a piece of parchment as directed.

Roll Pizza Crust

▲ 1. Center the dough on a 16$\frac{1}{2}$ by 12$\frac{1}{2}$-inch piece of parchment paper. Dust the dough generously with white rice flour.

▲ 2. Roll the crust until it completely covers the parchment. If you don't want a really thin crust, roll it to cover two-thirds of the paper.

▲ 3. Slide the crust onto a rimmed baking sheet. Put the pan close to the crust, grab the corners of one of the long ends of the paper and pull it quickly over the lip of the pan.

▲ 4. Bake until the crust is lightly golden brown. Small cracks may appear all over the surface of the crust. This is normal.

◀ 5. Top the pizza as directed and return to the oven. Remove the pizza from the oven when the cheese is bubbling or as recipe directs.

How to:
Make Individual Pizzas

Personal pizzas are always fun to eat! Here's how to make them:

▶ *1. Adjust 2 oven racks to the upper-middle and lower-middle positions and preheat oven as directed in recipe. (Wait to preheat oven until after yeast-risen crust has risen.)*

▶ *2. Prepare either the no-rise dough (page 215) or yeast-raised dough (page 216) through step two. Divide the dough into 4 equal portions.*

▶ *3. Place 2 portions of dough on one $16^1/2$ by $12^1/2$-inch piece of parchment paper. (Place each portion on the short end of the parchment, about 3 inches from the edge.) Dust the dough generously with white rice flour. Roll the dough out to desired thickness. Pizzas will be about 8-inches each.*

▶ *4. Set a rimmed baking sheet very close to the rolled-out crust. Grab the corners of 1 of the long sides of the parchment paper and slide the crust into the pan. Do this quickly. Repeat with remaining dough, using a second pan.*

▶ *5. Bake crusts, one pan on each rack, until lightly golden brown, about 12-15 minutes, switching the baking sheets about halfway through baking.*

▶ *6. Use as directed in recipe.*

How to:
Reheat Pizza

Pizza fresh from the oven is great. Reheated pizza can sometimes leave much to be desired. Now, I know some people don't reheat their leftover pizza, preferring to eat it cold. That's all right, and if you love cold pizza, skip this how-to.

Okay, now that the cold-pizza lovers have left, I can say this: I don't like cold pizza. At all. Not even a little. It must be a family thing because my mom dislikes cold pizza, too. Years ago, she came up with a brilliant way to reheat pizza. Since heating it in the microwave leaves you with hot toppings but a soggy crust, she started to microwave it briefly, to take the chill off, and then she pops the slice into the toaster oven to crisp the crust. It works every time!

▶ *1. Microwave the pizza on HIGH for 15 to 20 seconds to warm it slightly. The time will vary depending on your pizza topping, the size of the slice, and so on. Heat it until it gets a little warm.*

▶ *2. Transfer the pizza slice to a toaster oven tray and toast until crust is crisp and pizza is hot. Again, cooking time will vary.*

No-Rise Pizza Crust

▷ *For a how-to on making pizza crust, see page 213.*

Dry Ingredients

2 cups white rice flour

$^3/4$ cup tapioca starch

1 tablespoon granulated sugar

1 teaspoon baking powder

$^1/2$ teaspoon salt

1 teaspoon xanthan gum

Wet Ingredients

$^1/2$ cup water

2 large eggs

2 tablespoons olive oil

1. In a medium bowl, whisk together the dry ingredients. In a small bowl, mix together the wet ingredients with a fork or small whisk until combined. Pour the wet ingredients over the dry. Using a wooden spoon, stir to combine until a dough forms. The dough will be on the dry side. This is normal.

2. Generously sprinkle your counter with white rice flour. Turn the dough out onto the counter. Knead the dough until it is smooth. If, after kneading for a minute, the dough is still dry and doesn't hold together, add a tablespoon more water.

3. Center the dough on a $16^1/2$ by $12^1/2$-inch piece of parchment paper. Dust the dough generously with white rice flour. Roll out the dough until it covers the parchment paper.

4. Set a rimmed baking sheet very close to the rolled-out crust. Grab the corners of one of the long sides of the parchment paper and slide the crust into the pan. Do this quickly.

5. Top and bake as directed in the recipe.

Makes 1 pizza crust, about $16^1/2$ by $12^1/2$ inches

Yeast-Raised Pizza Crust

I like to use instant yeast in this recipe. If you're using active dry yeast, use water at 110° to 115°F and dissolve the yeast in the water before mixing.

▶ *For a how-to on making pizza crust, see page 213.*

Dry Ingredients

2 cups white rice flour

$^3/_4$ cup tapioca starch

1 tablespoon granulated sugar

$^1/_2$ teaspoon baking powder

$^1/_2$ teaspoon salt

1 teaspoon xanthan gum

1 packet ($2^1/_4$ teaspoons) instant yeast

Wet Ingredients

$^1/_2$ cup very warm water (120° to 130°F)

2 large eggs

2 tablespoons olive oil, plus more for brushing

1. In a large bowl, whisk together the dry ingredients. In a small bowl, mix together the wet ingredients with a fork or small whisk until combined. Pour the wet ingredients over the dry. Using a wooden spoon, stir to combine until a dough forms. The dough will be on the dry side. This is normal.

2. Generously sprinkle your counter with white rice flour. Turn the dough out onto the counter. Knead the dough until it is smooth. If, after kneading for a minute, the dough is still dry and doesn't hold together, add a tablespoon more water.

3. Center the dough on a $16^1/_2$ by $12^1/_2$-inch piece of parchment paper. Dust the dough generously with white rice flour. Roll out the dough until it covers the parchment paper.

4. Set a rimmed baking sheet very close to the rolled-out crust. Grab the corners of one of the long sides of the parchment paper and slide the crust into the pan. Do this quickly.

5. Lightly brush olive oil over the top of the crust with a pastry brush. Cover the dough completely with plastic wrap. Allow to rise at room temperature for 45 minutes, or until dough is light and slightly puffy.

6. Top and bake as directed. If recipe calls for brushing the crust with olive oil, you can skip that step because the crust is already brushed with oil.

Makes 1 pizza crust, about $16^1/_2$ by $12^1/_2$ inches

Elizabeth's
Favorite Pizza

While writing this book, I kept debating whether or not to call this pizza my "favorite" because having a favorite pizza is tough for me. I love all pizzas, whether topped with pepperoni and cheese or loaded with vegetables. I do have to admit that I love this one a smidgen more than I love the others. It hits all my pizza buttons: crisp crust, sweet caramelized onions, chunky tomato sauce, fresh mozzarella, and anchovies! If I lost you at anchovies, I understand. Not everyone loves them. If you don't, replace them with chopped kalamata olives. You'll still get a salty-briny flavor. (But I do encourage you to at least give anchovies a try. They are pretty awesome, especially on this pizza!)

Olive oil

1 pizza crust (page 215 or 216), rolled out and placed on a rimmed baking sheet

Fresh Tomato Sauce (page 218)

3/4 cup caramelized onions (see page 38)

8 ounces fresh mozzarella, thinly sliced

1 or 2 cans (2 ounces each) flat anchovies, drained, or 1/4 cup pitted, chopped kalamata olives

8 to 10 fresh basil leaves

1. Adjust oven rack to the middle position and preheat the oven to 450°F. If you didn't brush the dough with olive oil before letting it rise, do so now.

2. Bake the crust for 12 to 15 minutes, until it begins to turn a light golden brown. Remove from the oven and place the pan on a wire rack. Leave the oven on.

3. Spoon the sauce and caramelized onions evenly over the crust. Top with mozzarella. There will be space between the slices of mozzarella. Place the anchovies between the slices of mozzarella.

4. Bake for 10 minutes, or until cheese begins to soften. Fresh mozzarella keeps it shape. Don't worry when you see that the slices haven't melted to cover the pizza.

5. Remove the pizza from the oven, return it to the wire rack, and allow to cool for 5 minutes before cutting. While the pizza cools, chop the basil. Sprinkle over the pizza and serve.

Serves 4 to 6

Fresh Tomato Sauce

This is one of my favorite pizza sauces. Made with lightly cooked grape tomatoes, its fresh flavor and chunky texture go with almost any pizza. If you like a saucier sauce, you have two options. The first is to use my Classic Pizza Sauce on page 225. The second is to mix this recipe with a half batch of Classic Pizza Sauce. This combination will give you the chunkiness of the grape tomatoes with enough extra sauce to coat the pizza.

2 tablespoons olive oil

$1/2$ small onion, finely diced

2 cloves garlic, minced or put through a garlic press

$1/2$ teaspoon kosher salt

1 pint grape tomatoes

$1/4$ cup freshly grated Parmesan cheese

$1/2$ teaspoon dried basil

1. In a small (2 quart) pot, heat the oil over medium-high heat until hot and shimmering but not smoking. Add the onion and cook for 2 minutes, stirring occasionally with a wooden spoon. Add the garlic and salt. Cook, stirring occasionally, until the garlic is soft and aromatic, about 2 minutes. Add the tomatoes and cook for 3 to 4 minutes, until the sauce begins to bubble. Lower the heat to low.

2. Cover and cook until all the tomatoes burst and a slight sauce develops. Remove from the heat, add the cheese and basil, stir to combine, and spoon over crust.

Makes enough sauce for one $16^1/2$ by $12^1/2$-inch pizza or 4 individual pizzas

Greek Salad Pizza

This pizza is remarkably easy to make. The crust is fully baked, then topped with all the good things that make up a Greek salad—feta, cucumbers, a dill sauce, you get the point, good stuff. Instead of serving a salad with a pizza, you serve a salad on a pizza!

▶ *See page 214 for a how-to on dividing a crust for individual pizzas.*

Dill Sauce

1 container (6 ounces) Greek-style yogurt

1 tablespoon olive oil

Juice of $1/2$ lemon (about 2 tablespoons)

$1/2$ teaspoon dried dill

1 clove garlic, minced or put through a garlic press

1 to 2 tablespoons milk

Pizza

Olive oil

1 pizza crust (page 215 or 216), divided into individual crusts

2 cups baby greens (I like baby romaine)

1 medium cucumber, peeled and cubed

About 1 cup halved grape tomatoes

$1/4$ cup pitted, halved kalamata olives

$1/4$ red onion, thinly sliced

6 ounces feta cheese, cubed

1. To make the sauce, in a small bowl, combine the yogurt, oil, lemon juice, dill, and garlic. Stir until smooth. Add about 2 teaspoons of the milk to thin the sauce to a "drizzle" consistency. If the sauce is still thick, add more milk, a few teaspoons at a time. Cover and refrigerate until needed.

2. For the pizza, adjust oven racks to the upper-middle and lower-middle positions and preheat the oven to 450°F. If you didn't brush the dough with olive oil before letting it rise, do so now.

3. Bake the crusts, one pan on each rack, for 12 to 15 minutes, until golden brown, switching the baking sheets about halfway through. Remove from the oven and place the pans on wire racks to cool. Turn off the oven.

2. Place about $1/2$ cup greens onto each cooled pizza crust. (Be sure the crusts are cool or the greens will wilt.)

3. Sprinkle the cucumber, tomatoes, olives, onion, and feta evenly over each crust. Drizzle dill sauce over each pizza. Serve and enjoy.

Makes 4 individual pizzas

Classic Veggie Pizza

This is the gluten-free version of the classic veggie pizza that pizzerias serve. Are the vegetables that top the pizza imaginative or cutting edge? No—but they are mighty tasty!

Olive oil

1 pizza crust (page 215 or 216), rolled out and placed on a rimmed baking sheet

1 red or green bell pepper, cored and diced small

1/2 medium onion, diced

1 cup sliced fresh mushrooms, or 1 can (4 ounces) sliced mushrooms, drained

Classic Pizza Sauce (page 225)

8 ounces mozzarella cheese, grated (2 cups)

1 can (2.25 ounces) sliced black olives, drained

Freshly grated Parmesan cheese, for topping (optional)

1. Adjust oven rack to the middle position and preheat the oven to 475°F. If you didn't brush the dough with olive oil before letting it rise, do so now.

2. Bake the crust for 10 to 12 minutes, until it begins to turn a light golden brown. Remove from the oven and place on a wire rack. Leave the oven on.

3. In a medium (10-inch) nonstick frying pan, heat 1 tablespoon olive oil over medium-high heat until hot and shimmering but not smoking. Add the red pepper. Cook, stirring occasionally with a wooden spoon, for 2 minutes, or until the pepper begins to soften. Add the onion and cook, stirring occasionally, until the onion is soft and translucent, 3 to 4 minutes. Transfer the pepper and onion to a small bowl.

4. Wipe out the frying pan with paper towels. Heat 2 tablespoons olive oil over medium-high heat until hot and shimmering but not smoking. Add the mushrooms. Cook, stirring frequently, until soft, 6 to 8 minutes. Transfer the mushrooms to the bowl with the pepper and onion and stir to combine.

5. Spread the sauce over the crust. Sprinkle mozzarella evenly over the crust. Top with the vegetable mixture and the olives. Sprinkle lightly with Parmesan, if using.

6. Return the pizza to the oven. Bake until the cheese is melted and golden brown, 10 to 12 minutes.

7. Remove the pizza from the oven. Return it to the wire rack and allow to cool for 5 minutes before slicing and serving.

Serves 4

Garlicky Spinach and Cheese Pizza

It doesn't get much easier than this pizza. Spinach is cooked with a generous amount of garlic and then added to a pizza crust along with some provolone cheese. For such simple ingredients, this pizza packs a flavorful punch.

Olive oil

1 pizza crust (page 215 or 216), rolled out and placed on a rimmed baking sheet

4 cloves garlic, minced or put through a garlic press

$^1/_2$ teaspoon kosher salt

1 bag (10 ounces) baby spinach

8 ounces provolone cheese, sliced

1. Adjust oven rack to the middle position and preheat the oven to 425°F. Place two layers of paper towels in a medium bowl and place the bowl near the stove. If you didn't brush the dough with olive oil before letting it rise, do so now.

2. Bake the crust for 12 to 15 minutes, until it begins to turn a light brown.

3. While the crust is baking, cook the spinach. Heat 1 tablespoon olive oil in a large (5$^1/_2$-quart) pot over high heat. Add the garlic and salt. Cook, stirring frequently, until garlic is golden brown. (This will happen very fast, so keep your eye on the pot.) Add the spinach and cook, stirring constantly, until tender, about 2 minutes. Using a slotted spoon, transfer the spinach to the paper towel-lined bowl. Gather the paper towels around spinach like a little purse. Squeeze the bundle to drain spinach. Transfer the spinach to a plate.

4. When the crust is golden, remove it from the oven and place on a wire rack. Leave the oven on.

5. Top the crust with the spinach and provolone. Bake until cheese is melted, 5 to 8 minutes. (The baking time varies depending on the provolone that you use. Check it after 5 minutes and then keep an eye on it.)

6. Return the pizza to the wire rack and allow it to cool for 5 minute before cutting.

Serves 4

Roasted Tomato Pizza

This pizza is sauce-free but not tomato-free. Rather, the tomatoes are oven-roasted for a deep, rich tomato flavor. I usually use grape tomatoes because they are easy to find and roast really well. In the summer use whatever great tomatoes you find at the farmers' market. I've used Sun Gold tomatoes, which are super sweet little yellow tomatoes, with fabulous results.

▶ *See page 214 for a how-to on dividing a crust for individual pizzas.*

2 pints grape tomatoes, halved

Olive oil

Kosher salt

1 pizza crust (page 215 or 216), rolled out and placed on a rimmed baking sheet or divided into individual crusts

3/4 cup caramelized onions (see page 38)

1 can (14 ounces) artichoke hearts, drained and halved (or quartered if large)

8 ounces fresh mozzarella, sliced

1. Adjust oven rack to the middle position and preheat the oven to 425°F. Line a rimmed baking sheet with parchment paper.

2. In a large bowl, toss the tomatoes with a generous drizzle of olive oil. You want the tomatoes to be glistening with olive oil but not drenched. Sprinkle lightly with kosher salt and toss to coat.

3. Spread the tomatoes on the prepared baking sheet. Roast until the tomatoes are soft; the edges should be a dark golden brown with some black spots. (Roasting time will vary depending on tomatoes. Check them after 20 minutes.)

4. Remove the tomatoes from the oven. Leave the oven on. Using a large spatula, scrape tomatoes into a small bowl.

5. If you didn't brush the dough with olive oil before letting it rise, do so now.

6. Bake the crust for 15 to 18 minutes, until lightly golden brown. Remove from the oven and place on a wire rack. Leave the oven on.

7. Top the crust with caramelized onions, tomatoes, artichoke hearts, and mozzarella.

8. Return the pizza to the oven. Bake until the cheese is melted and bubbly. Fresh mozzarella does not really brown; after 5 minutes check the pizza. If the cheese is melted, it is done. If not, bake for a little longer. Remove from the oven and return to wire rack. Allow to cool for 5 minutes before serving.

Serves 4

Classic Pepperoni Pizza

This isn't a recipe as much as a guide to making a really great gluten-free version of the beloved American classic: pepperoni pizza.

Olive oil

1 pizza crust (page 215 or 216), rolled out and placed on a rimmed baking sheet

Classic Pizza Sauce (page 225)

8 ounces mozzarella cheese, grated (2 cups)

Generous handful of pepperoni slices, as much or as little as you like

Freshly grated Parmesan cheese, for topping (optional)

1. Adjust oven rack to the middle position and preheat the oven to 475°F. If you didn't brush the dough with olive oil before letting it rise, do so now.

2. Bake the crust for 10 to 12 minutes, until it begins to turn a light golden brown. Remove from the oven and place on a wire rack. Leave the oven on.

3. Spread the sauce evenly over the crust. Top with mozzarella and pepperoni. Sprinkle lightly with Parmesan, if using.

4. Bake for 15 to 18 minutes, until cheese is melted and golden brown.

5. Remove the pizza from the oven. Return it to the wire rack and allow to cool for 5 minutes before slicing and serving.

Serves 4

Classic Pizza Sauce

This thick and flavorful sauce is perfect for pizza!

1 tablespoon olive oil

1 tablespoon unsalted butter

1 small onion, finely diced

2 cloves garlic, minced or put through a garlic press

1 teaspoon dried basil

$1/2$ teaspoon kosher salt

$1/2$ teaspoon dried oregano

$1/4$ teaspoon granulated sugar

3 tablespoons tomato paste

1 can (15 ounce) crushed tomatoes or petite diced tomatoes (see Note)

1. In small (2-quart) pot, heat the olive oil and butter over medium-high heat until butter melts and oil shimmers. Add the onions. Cook until soft, stirring frequently, about 3 minutes. Add the garlic and cook until aromatic, about 1 minute. Add the basil, salt, oregano, and sugar and stir to combine. Cook, stirring frequently, for 2 minutes. The mixture will thicken and turn light brown. Stir in the tomato paste, then the tomatoes.

2. Reduce heat to medium-low and cook for 10 minutes, stirring occasionally to prevent the sauce from scorching on the bottom. Spread on pizza crust.

Makes enough sauce for one $16^{1}/2$ by $12^{1}/2$-inch pizza or four individual pizzas

NOTE

For a smooth pizza sauce, use crushed tomatoes; for a chunky sauce, use petite diced tomatoes.

Summer Tomato and Basil Pizza

This pizza celebrates summer. You want to make it with garden-fresh tomatoes. Any other tomatoes and this pizza will fall flat, not sing. I like to use a combination of red and yellow heirloom tomatoes.

Olive oil

1 pizza crust (page 215 or 216), rolled out and placed on a rimmed baking sheet

3 cloves garlic, minced or put through a garlic press

$1/4$ teaspoon kosher salt

2 or 3 large tomatoes, sliced $1/4$-inch thick

8 ounces fresh mozzarella, sliced thin

8 to 10 fresh basil leaves

1. Adjust oven rack to the middle position and preheat the oven to 475°F. If you didn't brush the dough with olive oil before letting it rise, do so now.

2. Bake the crust for 10 to 12 minutes, until it begins to turn a light golden brown. Remove from the oven and place on a wire rack. Leave the oven on.

3. While the crust bakes, whisk together 3 tablespoons olive oil, the garlic, and salt.

4. Brush the crust with the garlic oil. Arrange slices of tomatoes all over the crust and top with mozzarella. Bake until the cheese begins to soften, 5 to 7 minutes.

5. Remove the pizza from the oven and return it to the wire rack. Allow the pizza to cool for 5 minutes. While the pizza cools, chop the basil and sprinkle it over the top. Slice and serve.

Serves 4

Cheddar-Chicken Pizza

This pizza is sort of new to me. I saw it on the menu of a restaurant but couldn't order it—because of the gluten, of course. Since the pizza sounded enticing, I went home and made my own version. The chicken and cheddar work really well on a pizza. I'm glad I stumbled across the pizza on a menu that I couldn't eat from!

▶ *For a how-to on cooking chicken, see page 45.*

Olive oil

1 pizza crust (page 215 or 216), rolled out and placed on a rimmed baking sheet

1 can (15 ounces) petite diced tomatoes

2 tablespoons tomato paste

1 clove garlic, minced or put through a garlic press

$1/2$ teaspoon dried basil

$1/2$ teaspoon dried oregano

Salt and freshly ground black pepper

2 cooked boneless, skinless chicken breasts, cut into strips

8 ounces cheddar cheese, grated (2 cups)

1. Adjust oven rack to the middle position and preheat the oven to 475°F. If you didn't brush the dough with olive oil before letting it rise, do so now.

2. Bake the crust for 10 to 12 minutes, until it begins to turn a light golden brown. Remove from the oven and place on a wire rack. Leave the oven on.

3. While the crust bakes, prepare the sauce. Drain the liquid from the tomatoes into a small bowl. Add the tomato paste to the liquid and stir to combine. Add the garlic, basil, oregano, and 2 teaspoons olive oil. Season with salt and pepper to taste. Add the reserved tomatoes and stir to combine.

4. Spread the sauce evenly over the crust. Scatter the chicken over the crust and top with cheddar. Bake until the cheese is melted, about 10 minutes.

5. Remove the pizza from the oven and return it to the wire rack. Allow to cool for 5 minutes before slicing and serving.

Serves 4

French Onion Soup Pizza

Soup pizza? Sounds soggy, right? Thankfully, this pizza isn't topped with soup. Rather, it's inspired by the flavors of French onion soup: caramelized onions and Gruyère cheese. Since this is a hearty pizza, I save it for the winter.

Olive oil

1 pizza crust (page 215 or 216), rolled out and placed on a rimmed baking sheet

3/4 cup caramelized onions (see page 38)

8 ounces Gruyère cheese, grated (2 cups)

1. Adjust oven rack to the middle position and preheat the oven to 475°F. If you didn't brush the dough with olive oil before letting it rise, do so now.

2. Bake the crust for 10 to 12 minutes, until it begins to turn a light golden brown. Remove from the oven and place on a wire rack. Leave the oven on.

3. Spread the onions evenly over the crust. Top with the cheese and return to the oven. Bake for about 10 minutes, or until cheese is melted and slightly golden brown.

4. Remove from the oven. Return to the wire rack and allow to cool for 5 minutes before slicing and serving.

Serves 4

Taco Pizza

This pizza for is perfect for nights when you can't decide if you want pizza or tacos. Why not have both?

▶ *For a how-to on pitting and peeling avocados, see page 39.*

Olive oil

1 pizza crust (page 215 or 216), rolled out and placed on a rimmed baking sheet

1 small onion, finely diced

2 cloves garlic, minced or put through a garlic press

8 ounces ground sirloin (90 to 92% lean)

$1^1/2$ cups salsa, homemade (page 64) or store-bought

8 ounces cheddar cheese, grated (2 cups)

1 cup canned pinto beans, drained and rinsed

1 can (2.25 ounces) sliced black olives, drained

1 can (4 to 4.5 ounces) chopped green chiles, drained (optional)

1 Hass avocado, pitted, peeled, and thinly sliced

Small bunch of cilantro, stems removed, leaves chopped

1. Adjust oven rack to the middle position and preheat the oven to 475°F. If you didn't brush the dough with olive oil before letting it rise, do so now.

2. Bake the crust for 10 to 12 minutes, until it begins to turn a light golden brown. Remove from the oven and place on a wire rack. Leave the oven on.

3. While the crust bakes, cook the ground beef. Heat 2 tablespoons olive oil in a medium (10-inch) nonstick frying pan over medium-high heat. Add the onion. Cook, stirring frequently with a wooden spoon, until soft. Add the garlic and cook for 1 minute, stirring frequently. Add the ground beef and cook, breaking up the clumps with the spoon, until thoroughly cooked and browned. If desired, remove and discard any excess fat. (For a how-to on cooking ground meat, see page 44.) Remove the pan from the heat.

4. Spread the salsa over the crust. Sprinkle with half the grated cheese. Top with ground beef, beans, black olives, and chiles, if using. Sprinkle the remaining cheese over everything.

5. Return the pizza to the oven and bake until cheese is golden brown and bubbling, 8 to 10 minutes.

6. Remove the pizza from the oven and return it to the wire rack. Allow to cool for 5 minutes. Right before slicing, top with the avocado slices and chopped cilantro.

Serves 4

Make Your Own Pizza

It's easy to be creative with pizza. Start with a crust that's been baked until lightly golden brown and use this chart to get started creating your favorite pizza.

Sauce	Vegetables	Meats	Cheese
Classic Pizza Sauce (page 225)	Artichoke hearts, sliced or diced	Chicken breast, cooked and diced or cut into thin strips	Mozzarella (traditional, fresh, or smoked)
Fresh Tomato Sauce (page 218)	Olives (black, kalamata, green)	Ham, cubed	Fontina
Roasted Grape Tomatoes (see page 223)	Caramelized Onions (page 38)	Chouriço/chorizo, cooked and sliced	Gruyère
Garlic oil (Not really a sauce per se, but mix a few tablespoons of olive oil with a clove or two of minced garlic. Brush over crust. Yum!)	Roasted Vegetables (page 250) Garlicky Baby Spinach (page 245) (Squeeze excess water out of the spinach to prevent the crust from getting soggy.) Zucchini, Tomatoes, and Parmesan (page 246)	Pepperoni, sliced	Feta (Top pizza with feta after it comes out of the oven.)

11.
Side Dishes

Red Potatoes with Olive Oil and Vinegar

Red potatoes, with their thin skin and creamy interior, are a delight with just splash of olive oil and red wine vinegar. Their delicate flavor is highlighted with this simple preparation. In the summer I make these potatoes with fresh basil from my garden; in the winter I use dried basil. Both taste great. Use whichever you have on hand or whatever herb you enjoy.

1 pound red potatoes, washed and quartered

Kosher salt

1 tablespoon olive oil

1 tablespoon red wine vinegar

4 to 6 fresh basil leaves, chopped, or $1^1/2$ tea-spoons dried basil

Freshly ground black pepper

1. Place the potatoes in a medium (4-quart) pot. Fill the pot three-quarters with cold water and add 1 teaspoon salt. Bring to a boil over medium-high heat and cook, uncovered, until the potatoes are fork-tender, about 20 minutes.

2. Drain the potatoes in a colander and return them to the pot. Toss the potatoes with the olive oil, vinegar, and basil. The potatoes should break down a little. If they seem dry, add a little more oil and vinegar. Season with salt and pepper to taste. Serve immediately.

Serves 4

See photo, page 147.

Salt Potatoes

About three years ago, I read Kim Severson's piece in the *New York Times* about salt potatoes. I remember thinking, "Those sound interesting. I should try them." Two years later, I finally did! (I am never one to rush.)

To be honest, I was surprised to learn salt potatoes are a central New York dish. I'd never heard of the practice of boiling new potatoes with copious amounts of salt. Somehow this dish didn't make the 150-mile jump from Syracuse to Albany. I'm sorry it didn't—these potatoes are fantastic.

What makes these potatoes unique? The texture! The interior is really tender—almost as if boiled potatoes, baked potatoes, and mashed potatoes got together and created a baby. A tender, delicious, salt potato baby.

If you are worried, as I was, that these potatoes will be too salty, fear not. The salt is just right. And they are nowhere as salty as potato chips. To finish them, I toss the potatoes in melted butter and herbs. Salt, potatoes, butter, and herbs? Sounds great, right?

10 cups water

$1^1/2$ cups kosher salt

2 pounds well-scrubbed small red or white potatoes

$^1/4$ cup (4 tablespoons) unsalted butter, melted

About $^1/4$ cup chopped fresh herbs

- In a large ($5^1/2$-quart) pot, bring the water and salt to a boil. Once it reaches a boil, add the potatoes. Boil for 20 minutes or until the potatoes are fork-tender. Drain the potatoes in a colander and return them to the pot. Toss with the butter and herbs. Serve immediately.

Serves 6

Potato Latkes

Latkes fresh from the frying pan are one of my favorite treats. Everyone thinks their latke recipe is "the best." I'm no exception! This is the recipe I make and, I'm happy to report, it always wins rave reviews.

I fry no more than three latkes at a time. This ensures that oil doesn't get cold. Cold oil equals greasy latkes.

1 medium onion, peeled

2^1/$_2$ pounds russet potatoes (about 5 large potatoes), peeled

^{1}/$_3$ cup plus 2 tablespoons white rice flour

2 teaspoons salt

1 teaspoon freshly ground black pepper

3 large eggs, beaten

Vegetable oil, for frying

1. Adjust oven rack to the middle position and preheat the oven to 200°F.

2. Grate the onion and potatoes. (I use a food processor fitted with the medium grating disk attachment. If you don't have a food processor, use a box grater.) Combine them in a medium bowl.

3. Place half of the onion and potato mixture on a clean kitchen towel. Roll the towel around the mixture and wring the towel to draw out excess moisture. Unroll the towel and transfer the mixture to a large bowl. Repeat with the remaining onion and potatoes.

4. In a small bowl, whisk together the white rice flour, salt, and pepper. Add to the potato mixture and stir to combine. Add the eggs and stir to combine.

5. Line a large plate with several layers of paper towels and set it near the stove but safely away from the burner. In a medium (10-inch) cast-iron skillet, heat ^{1}/$_8$-inch oil over medium-high heat until shimmering but not smoking.

6. Working in batches, drop the potato mixture into the hot oil by scant ^{1}/$_4$-cups. (The mixture should sizzle when it hits the oil.) Using a fork or spatula, flatten each latke a little in the pan. (Gently pull the latkes apart with a fork to flatten.)

7. Fry for 2 to 3 minutes. Flip with a pancake flipper or spatula and fry an additional 2 to 3 minutes, until deeply golden brown. Drain the latkes on the paper towel, then transfer to a rimmed baking sheet and keep warm in oven until ready to serve.

8. Repeat with the remaining latke mixture. Serve as soon as the last batch is cooked.

Serves 4 to 6

SERVING SUGGESTION
Try these with sour cream or applesauce.

Polenta

Polenta, that gorgeous porridge of cooked cornmeal, is one of my favorite winter dishes. Topped with tomato sauce, roasted vegetables, or on its own with a generous sprinkle of Parmesan cheese, it's a perennial favorite in my house.

This recipe can be doubled for a main course. For a main course, I sometimes like to serve it with meatballs. It's an easy twist on spaghetti and meatballs.

3 cups homemade chicken stock (page 69) or store-bought reduced-sodium broth

1 cup water

1 cup gluten-free cornmeal

$^1/_4$ cup freshly grated Parmesan cheese

2 tablespoons unsalted butter, at room temperature

- In a medium (4-quart) pot, bring the chicken stock to a boil over medium-high heat. In a small bowl, whisk together the water and cornmeal. Whisk water-cornmeal mixture into the boiling stock in a slow and steady stream. (If you add the cornmeal mixture too fast, it can clump.) Lower the heat to medium-low. Whisking constantly, cook the polenta for 10 minutes. Add the cheese and butter and stir until they are melted. Serve immediately.

Serves 4

STORING/REHEATING POLENTA

If you have leftover polenta, you'll notice that cooled polenta becomes very firm. Honestly, it's not worth trying to recapture its original creamy consistency. This doesn't mean it can't be reheated. Cut the cooled polenta into squares and pan-fry it. The texture is different but the flavor is still excellent!

1. Pour leftover polenta into a plastic wrap-lined baking pan. (Allow the plastic wrap to hang over the sides of the pan.) The size of your baking pan will vary depending on how much polenta you have leftover. You want the polenta to be about $^3/_4$-inch thick. Press another piece of plastic wrap onto the surface of the polenta and chill.

2. Remove polenta from pan by lifting the plastic wrap. Cut into squares. Add about 1 teaspoon of olive oil to a medium (10-inch) skillet and heat until shimmering. Brush the polenta squares on each side with a little olive oil. Place the squares in the hot pan. Cook until brown, about two minutes. Turn and repeat.

Zucchini Pancakes

Like latkes, these zucchini pancakes are crisp and best when eaten right out of the frying pan.

Use the shredding disk of a food processor, or a box grater if you don't have one.

3 medium zucchini, shredded (6 cups)

1 medium onion, shredded

$1/2$ teaspoon salt

1 large egg

$1/3$ cup white rice flour

Vegetable oil, for frying

1. Adjust oven rack to middle position and preheat the oven to 200°F. Line a large plate with paper towel.

2. Combine the zucchini and onion in a large bowl. Stir in the salt and allow to sit for 15 minutes.

3. Tilt the bowl to drain out excess liquid. Turn the vegetables out onto a clean kitchen towel. Roll up the towel, twist the ends, and squeeze excess liquid out of the zucchini and onions.

4. Before putting the zucchini mixture back in the bowl, wipe the bowl dry with a clean towel. Return the zucchini to the dry bowl and fluff it a little with a fork. Add the egg and white rice flour. Stir to combine.

5. Heat about $1/4$-inch of oil in a large (12-inch) cast-iron skillet. Using two forks, drop the zucchini mixture, about 3 tablespoons for each pancake, into the skillet. Working quickly, "pull" the mixture into a flat pancake using the two forks. Cook 3 to 4 minutes. Flip with a pancake flipper or spatula, and cook for an additional 3 minutes, or until crisp. Depending on the size of your skillet, you can cook 4 or 5 pancakes at a time. Drain the pancakes on the paper towel then transfer to a rimmed baking sheet and keep warm in the oven until ready to serve.

6. Repeat with remaining mixture. Serve hot.

Serves 4

Oven-Roasted Potatoes with Basil and Parmesan

I grow a lot of basil in the summer. One night while making a pan of oven-roasted potatoes, I thought it would be fun to purée basil, almost like a pesto, and toss it with potatoes. The resulting potatoes were delicious and now this is one of my favorite ways to use extra basil.

$1/4$ cup plus 2 teaspoons olive oil

$1^1/2$ pounds red or white potatoes, unpeeled, cut into bite-size pieces

1 cup packed fresh basil leaves

2 cloves garlic, coarsely chopped

2 tablespoons freshly grated Parmesan cheese

Salt

1. Adjust oven rack to the middle position and preheat the oven to 425°F.

2. Place the potatoes on a rimmed baking sheet and drizzle with about 2 teaspoons olive oil. Spread the potatoes out in a single layer; you don't want to pile the potatoes on top of each other. Bake for 25 to 30 minutes, or until golden brown.

3. While the potatoes are roasting, make the sauce. In a food processor, combine the basil and garlic. Pulse a few times until the basil is roughly chopped. Add $1/4$ cup of oil and pulse to combine. Add the cheese. Pulse a few times to combine.

4. Remove the potatoes from the oven and transfer to a large bowl. Toss with basil sauce. Season with salt to taste. Serve immediately.

Serves 4

Mashed Potatoes

What has happened to mashed potatoes lately? It seems as if every recipe I see is loaded with heavy cream, butter, cream cheese, sour cream, or cheese, or a little (or a lot!) of each. While rich mashed potatoes sound good, they aren't really what I want. Now, mine aren't lean but they aren't super-rich, either. I use a handheld mixer to make my mashed potatoes fluffy. If you prefer more dense mashed potatoes, use a potato masher.

5 large russet potatoes (about 2 pounds), peeled and cut into bite-size pieces

Salt

1 cup milk, warmed

2 tablespoons unsalted butter, at room temperature

Freshly ground black pepper

1. Place the potatoes in a large ($5^1/2$-quart) pot. Fill the pot three-quarters full with cold water and add 1 teaspoon salt. Bring to a boil over medium-high heat, then lower the heat to medium and cook the potatoes until fork-tender, about 25 minutes.

2. Set a colander in the sink. Drain the potatoes and return them to the pot. Add the milk and, using a handheld mixer, whip the potatoes until fluffy. Add the butter and stir to combine. Season with salt and pepper to taste. Serve immediately.

Serves 4 to 6

See photo, page 171.

Rice Pilaf

This recipe has a charming bit of history. It was one of the first dishes my husband made for me while we were dating. I can still picture him standing at the tiny stove in my really tiny apartment making this rice. At some point, he told me this was his mom's recipe. I think I loved it even more after learning that.

1 tablespoon olive oil

$^1/_2$ small green pepper, cored and cut into bite-size pieces

1 small onion, finely diced

1 teaspoon unsalted butter

1 cup long-grain rice

2 cups gluten-free beef stock, homemade chicken stock (page 69), or store-bought reduced-sodium chicken broth

1. In a medium (4-quart) pot over medium-high heat, heat the oil until shimmering but not smoking. Add the green pepper and cook, stirring constantly until the pepper begins to soften, about 3 minutes. Add the onion and cook, stirring constantly, until soft and translucent, about 3 minutes. Add the butter and stir until melted. Add the rice, stirring constantly, until the rice is brown and toasted, about 7 minutes.

2. Add the stock to the rice: the stock may steam and boil vigorously when you do this. If any rice clings to the side of the pot, push it into the liquid. Bring the stock to a boil, then lower the heat to low. Cover and cook for 30 minutes, or until the rice is tender and all the liquid has been absorbed.

4. Fluff with a fork and serve.

Serves 4

Rice Salad

Rice salad, like potato salad, for me is a summer side dish. It doesn't have to be, of course, but I don't tend to eat cold salads in the winter. This salad, made with cool cucumbers and a sweet-tart dressing, is a great accompaniment to a barbecue.

Use any beans you love, sometimes I use black beans, sometimes navy beans, sometimes red.

▶ *For a how-to on cooking rice, see page 42.*

Salad

1¹/2 cups cold cooked rice (white, brown, and red all work well)

1/2 red or yellow bell pepper, cored and diced

1 medium cucumber, peeled, seeded, and chopped

2 scallions (green onions), thinly sliced (white and green parts)

1 cup canned beans, drained and rinsed

4 fresh basil leaves, chopped

Dressing

2 tablespoons rice wine vinegar

2 tablespoons lime juice

1/4 cup olive oil

Salt and freshly ground black pepper

1. In a medium bowl, stir together all the ingredients for the salad with a fork.

2. In a small bowl, whisk together the vinegar, lime juice, and oil for the dressing. Season with salt and black pepper to taste. Pour the dressing over the salad. Stir together with a fork. Chill for 2 hours or overnight. Before serving, taste and adjust seasoning with salt and pepper.

Serves 4

Quinoa

Poor quinoa. Some people think it's bland. Not me! I think of quinoa as a blank canvas waiting for other flavors to make it come alive. Note that some brands are prerinsed, others are not. Check the package. If yours is not, put the quinoa in a very fine strainer and rinse until the water runs clear. Otherwise the quinoa will be very bitter.

2 cups water

1 cup quinoa grains

$1/4$ teaspoon salt

- In a medium (4-quart) pot, combine the water, quinoa, and salt. Bring to a boil over medium-high heat. Lower the heat to low, cover, and cook for 15 minutes, or until all the water is absorbed. The quinoa should "unfurl" and turn from solid white to almost clear. Serve immediately or use in one of the recipes that follow.

Serves 4, makes $2^1/2$ to 3 cups

Quinoa, Spinach, and Black Beans

Garlicky spinach and black beans turn quinoa into a hearty, flavorful side dish. I like black beans in this recipe, but if you'd like to use another bean, go for it!

2 teaspoons olive oil

2 cloves garlic, minced or put through a garlic press

Salt

1 bag (10 ounces) baby spinach

$1/2$ cup cooked quinoa (page 240)

1 can (15 ounces) black beans, drained and rinsed

$1/2$ teaspoon ground cumin

Freshly ground black pepper

1. In a large ($5^{1}/_{2}$-quart) pot, heat the olive oil over medium-high heat until hot and shimmering but not smoking. Add the garlic and cook, stirring constantly with a wooden spoon, until aromatic, about 45 seconds. Add a pinch of salt. Add the spinach and cook, stirring frequently, until it is wilted and tender, 2 to 3 minutes. Turn off the heat.

2. Stir in the quinoa, beans, and cumin. Season with salt and pepper. Serve immediately.

Serves 4

Quinoa with Corn, Tomatoes, and Cucumbers

Delicate quinoa paired with sweet corn and tomatoes makes for a nice summer salad. I like to serve this with a spicy main course. The coolness of the cucumbers always tastes right against something spicy and hot.

1 cup cooked quinoa (page 240)

1 cup frozen corn kernels, thawed

1 small cucumber, peeled, seeded, and diced small

1 cup grape tomatoes, halved

3 tablespoons rice wine vinegar

3 tablespoons olive oil

Kosher salt and freshly ground black pepper

1. In a medium bowl, toss together the quinoa, corn, cucumbers, and grape tomatoes.

2. In a small bowl, whisk together the rice wine vinegar and olive oil. Pour over the salad. Toss to combine. Season with salt and pepper to taste. Serve immediately.

Serves 4

Cheddar Cheesy Grits

If you love macaroni and cheese, you will love cheddar grits. They are creamy and loaded with cheddar—what's not to love?

4 cups homemade chicken stock (page 69) or store-bought reduced-sodium broth

1 cup gluten-free grits

4 ounces cheddar cheese, grated (1 cup)

2 tablespoons unsalted butter, at room temperature

1. Bring 3 cups of the chicken stock to a boil in a medium (4-quart) pot over medium-high heat. Whisk together the remaining 1 cup stock and the grits. In a slow and steady stream, add the grits to the boiling stock. (If you add the grits too quickly, lumps can form.) Cook, whisking constantly, until the grits bubble and start to thicken. (You may have to stop whisking for a second to see if they are bubbling.) As soon as the grits bubble, lower the heat to medium-low and cook for 15 minutes, stirring constantly.

2. Turn off the heat. Add the cheese and butter and stir just until just combined. (You don't want to stir too much because this can cause the cheese to separate and become oily.) Serve immediately.

Serves 4

Corn, Peas, and Bacon

While frozen vegetables are easy to make, they get a little boring. Four slices of bacon solves this problem! If you can find cob-smoked bacon, try it in this recipe. The smokiness of the bacon works really well with the sweetness of the corn and peas.

1 teaspoon olive oil

4 slices bacon

2 cups frozen corn kernels, thawed

1 cup frozen peas, thawed

Salt and freshly ground black pepper

1. Heat the oil in a large (12-inch) nonstick frying pan or cast-iron skillet over medium-high heat until hot and shimmering but not smoking. Cook the bacon until crisp, turning once during cooking. Remove the bacon from the pan, drain briefly on paper towels, and crumble. (For a how-to on cooking bacon, see page 43.)

2. Drain all but 1 tablespoon of fat from the pan. Add the corn and peas. Cook, stirring occasionally, until warmed through. Stir in the crumbled bacon. Season with salt and pepper to taste.

Serves 4

See photo, page 156.

Garlicky
Baby Spinach

I use something similar to this recipe a lot throughout this cookbook, with varying amounts of garlic. Whether I use this in another dish like pasta or pizza or eat it on its own, garlicky spinach is my favorite way to enjoy spinach. And I like it *really* garlicky; feel free to use less according to your family's tastes.

Spinach starts out really voluminous but then cooks down tremendously. Ten ounces of spinach fits into my large pasta pot. If your pot isn't large enough, simply make the spinach in two batches, dividing the oil and garlic evenly between the batches. Spinach cooks so quickly, even making two batches takes very little time.

1 tablespoon olive oil

5 cloves garlic, minced or put through a garlic press

$^1/_2$ teaspoon kosher salt

1 bag (10 ounces) baby spinach

- In a large (5$^1/_2$-quart) pot, heat the olive oil over medium-high heat until hot and shimmering but not smoking. Add the garlic and salt. Stir with a wooden spoon until the garlic is aromatic and begins to brown slightly, about 45 seconds. Add the spinach and cook, stirring constantly, until the spinach is wilted and tender, 2 to 3 minutes. Serve immediately.

Serves 4

Zucchini, Tomatoes, and Parmesan

This was one of the first vegetables dishes I learned to make. The combination of zucchini and tomatoes is still one of my favorites.

The zucchini is cooked until it is very tender. If you prefer your zucchini with a firmer bite, reduce the cooking time.

1 tablespoon olive oil

1 small onion, finely diced

1 medium zucchini, quartered lengthwise and sliced $1/4$-inch thick

1 pint grape tomatoes, halved

Kosher salt and freshly ground black pepper

$1/4$ cup freshly grated Parmesan cheese

1. In a large (12-inch) nonstick frying pan, heat the oil over medium-high heat until the oil is hot and shimmering but not smoking. Add the onion. Cook, stirring occasionally, for 2 minutes, or until soft. Add the zucchini. Cook for 5 minutes, or until zucchini begins to soften. Add the tomatoes and stir to combine. Season with salt and pepper. Cook for 5 to 7 minutes, until the tomatoes are soft and the juices are running.

2. Stir in the cheese and cover. Lower the heat to low. Cook until cheese is melted and juices begin to bubble, 3 to 5 minutes. Stir and adjust the seasoning with salt and pepper. Serve immediately.

Serves 4

Tomatoes and Green Beans

If zucchini and tomatoes are my first loves of summer, green beans and tomatoes are my second.

1 tablespoon olive oil

1 medium onion, finely diced

2 cloves garlic, minced or put through a garlic press

1 pint grape tomatoes, halved, or 2 large tomatoes, chopped

1 pound green beans, trimmed

Salt and freshly ground black pepper

1. In a large (12-inch) nonstick frying pan over medium-high, heat the oil until hot and shimmering but not smoking. Add the onion and cook, stirring often, for 2 minutes. Add the garlic. Cook until the onion and garlic are aromatic, about 3 minutes.

2. Add the tomatoes and stir. Cook for 4 to 5 minutes, until tomatoes begin to soften and release their juices. Stir occasionally.

3. Add the green beans. Stir to combine. Cover, lower the heat to medium-low, and cook 5 to 10 minutes, until the beans are bright green and tender. Season with salt and pepper. Serve immediately.

Serves 4

See photo, page 170.

Kale

For some reason I think of kale as "grown-up" spinach. Probably because the adults in my family would eat it on Christmas Eve. Back then I turned my nose up at kale because I thought it was too bitter. Now I love its bitter kick. Whenever I have leftover cooked kale in the house, I stir it into scrambled eggs the next morning for breakfast. Try it sometime; the combination is really wonderful.

1 pound kale

1 tablespoon olive oil

4 or 5 cloves garlic, minced or put through a garlic press

1/2 teaspoon kosher salt

1. Wash the kale. Remove and discard the stems. Chop the leaves into 2-inch pieces.

2. In a large (8-quart) pot, heat the olive oil over medium-high until hot and slightly smoking. Add the garlic and salt. Cook, stirring constantly with a wooden spoon, until garlic is soft, about 45 seconds.

3. Add the kale. Cook, stirring, until the leaves wilt a little. Cover, lower the heat to medium-low, and cook 25 to 30 minutes, until the leaves are tender.

Serves 4

NOTE

Chopping kale takes a bit of time. I usually buy a bag of kale leaves. The stems have already been removed and the kale is already chopped. It makes this side dish really quick to make.

Swiss Chard

Did you know that Swiss chard is from the same family as beets? Often Swiss chard can be bitter or tough but when just picked at the height of freshness, it can be delicate and gently sweet. I always buy my Swiss chard at the farmers' market to ensure I get delicate, not bitter, Swiss chard. This recipe is so easy and uses both the stalks and leaves.

$1^1/2$ pounds Swiss chard

2 tablespoons olive oil

2 teaspoons granulated sugar

Salt and freshly ground black pepper

1. Wash the chard thoroughly. Chop off about $^1/2$ inch at the end of the stems and discard. (You want to get rid of the tough end of the stems.)

2. Set out two large bowls. Cut the leaves and stems apart. Chop the stems into $^1/2$-inch pieces and put in one bowl. Slice the leaves crosswise into 1-inch shreds, or tear them into pieces with your hands.

3. In a large ($5^1/2$-quart) pot, heat the olive oil over medium-high heat until hot and shimmering but not smoking. Add the stems. Cook, stirring occasionally, for 5 to 7 minutes, until they begin to soften. Add the leaves, stir, and cover. Cook for 10 minutes, or until the stems are tender. Stir in the sugar and salt and pepper to taste. Serve warm or cold.

Serves 4

Roasted Vegetables

I love roasting vegetables. This cooking method, no matter which vegetables you use, brings out the vegetables' sweetness and seems to concentrate their flavor. Below are some of my favorite vegetables to roast. Pick one and roast following the directions.

Roasted Summer Vegetables

1 large zucchini, halved lengthwise and sliced $1/4$-inch thick

$1/2$ pint grape tomatoes, halved

1 large onion, halved and thickly sliced

Olive oil

Salt and freshly ground black pepper

Roasted Asparagus

1 bunch asparagus (or enough for your family), tough ends trimmed off

Olive oil

Salt and freshly ground black pepper

Roasted Carrots and Squash

1 butternut squash (about 1 pound), peeled, seeded, and cut into bite-size chunks

$1/2$ pound carrots, peeled and cut into bite-size chunks

Olive oil

Salt and freshly ground black pepper

Roasted Tomatoes and Onions

1 pint grape tomatoes, halved

1 medium onion, halved and thickly sliced

Olive oil

Salt and freshly ground black pepper

4 or 5 basil leaves

Roasted Potatoes

3 or 4 medium russet potatoes, peeled and cut into bite-size pieces

Olive oil

Salt and freshly ground black pepper

$1/2$ teaspoon chopped fresh rosemary (optional)

Roasted Sweet Potatoes

2 large sweet potatoes peeled and cut into bite-size pieces

Olive oil

Salt and freshly ground black pepper

Roasted Potatoes and Sweet Potatoes

1 large sweet potato, peeled and cut into bite-size pieces

2 large russet potatoes, peeled and cut into bite-size pieces

Olive oil

Salt and freshly ground black pepper

1. Adjust oven rack to the middle position and preheat the oven to 425°F. Place the vegetable(s) in a large bowl. Drizzle lightly with olive oil and sprinkle with salt and pepper. No matter which vegetable you are roasting, it should just shimmer lightly with olive oil. You don't want it to be dry or swimming in oil.

2. Spread the vegetable(s) on a rimmed baking sheet in a single layer. Bake for 20 minutes. Remove from the oven and using a spatula, stir and turn the vegetables. Return to the oven and roast until lightly brown and tender. (Baking time will vary depending on the vegetables you select. Hard vegetables such as squash and carrots take the longest.)

3. Remove from the oven and sprinkle with herbs, if using. With basil, chop it right before using or it will turn black. Serve immediately.

Serves 4

Grilled Corn

This is one recipe just for the summer, when fresh corn is at its best and you can fire up the grill in the backyard!

Fresh ears of corn—1, 2, or more ears per person

$1^1/_2$ tablespoons salt, plus more for serving

Unsalted butter, for serving

1. Pull the husks away from the corn but don't remove. Pull all the silk off corn. Pull husks back up to cover the corn.

2. Put the corn in a container large enough to hold it all, sprinkle with the salt, and cover completely with cold water. Soak for 30 minutes.

3. Meanwhile, preheat the grill to medium.

4. Drain the corn. Grill for 25 to 30 minutes, turning with tongs every 5 minutes or so. The husks may char, but this is okay.

5. Remove from the grill and serve immediately with butter, salt, and lots of napkins.

12.
Desserts

Cupcakes

Kids of all ages love cupcakes. Here are my recipes for vanilla and chocolate cupcakes.

Vanilla Cupcakes

Dry Ingredients

2 cups granulated sugar

$1^1/_2$ cups white rice flour

$^3/_4$ cup cornstarch

$^1/_2$ cup sweet rice flour

$1^1/_2$ teaspoons baking powder

$1^1/_2$ teaspoons baking soda

1 teaspoon salt

1 teaspoon xanthan gum

Wet Ingredients

2 large eggs

$1^1/_2$ cups buttermilk

$^1/_2$ cup vegetable oil

2 teaspoons pure vanilla extract

1. Adjust oven rack to the middle position and preheat the oven to 350°F. Line the cavities of two regular muffin pans (24 cavities) with paper liners.

2. In a large bowl, whisk together the dry ingredients. Add the wet ingredients and mix until a smooth batter forms. (Use medium speed on a stand mixer or medium-high on a handheld mixer.)

(continued)

3. Spoon or ladle the batter evenly into the prepared pans, filling each cavity about half full.

4. Bake for 20 to 25 minutes, until a tester inserted into the center of the cupcakes comes out clean.

5. Remove from the oven. Allow the cupcakes to cool for 5 minutes in the pans. After 5 minutes, transfer the cupcakes to a wire rack to cool completely.

6. Once cupcakes are cool, ice as desired. Covered with plastic wrap, these cupcakes keep for about 3 days at room temperature but are best 1 or 2 days after baking. Wrapped well in plastic wrap, they can be frozen, either plain or iced, for up to 1 month.

Makes 24 cupcakes

Chocolate Cupcakes

Dry Ingredients

2 cups granulated sugar

1 cup white rice flour

$1/2$ cup sweet rice flour

$1/2$ cup cornstarch

$1/2$ cup cocoa powder (natural or Dutch-process)

2 teaspoons baking powder

1 teaspoon salt

$1/2$ teaspoon xanthan gum

$1/4$ teaspoon baking soda

Wet Ingredients

2 large eggs

1 cup milk

$1/2$ cup vegetable oil

2 teaspoons pure vanilla extract

1. Adjust oven rack to the middle position and preheat the oven to 350°F. Line the cavities of two regular muffin pans (24 cavities) with paper liners.

2. In a large bowl, whisk together the dry ingredients. Add the wet ingredients and mix until a smooth batter forms. (Use medium speed on a stand mixer and medium-high on a handheld mixer.)

3. Spoon or ladle the batter evenly into the prepared pans, filling each cavity about half full.

4. Bake for 30 to 35 minutes, until a cake tester inserted into the center of the cupcake comes out clean.

5. Remove from the oven. Allow the cupcakes to cool for 5 minutes in the pan. After 5 minutes, transfer the cupcakes to a wire rack to cool completely.

6. Once cupcakes are cool, ice as desired. Covered with plastic wrap, these cupcakes keep for about 3 days at room temperature but are best 1 or 2 days after baking. Wrapped well in plastic wrap, they can be frozen, either plain or iced, for up to 1 month.

Makes 24 cupcakes

Vanilla Buttercream

1 cup (2 sticks) unsalted butter, at room temperature

1 pound (4 cups) powdered sugar

$1/2$ cup milk

2 teaspoons vanilla extract

Food coloring, if desired

1. In a medium bowl, cream together the butter and powdered sugar until light and fluffy (use medium speed on a handheld or stand mixer). Mixture will be thick.

2. Turn off the mixer. Add the milk, vanilla extract, and food coloring, if using. Turn the mixer to low and blend until smooth. Use at once or cover with plastic wrap and store in the refrigerator. Bring buttercream to room temperature before using.

Make 3 cups of icing

Chocolate Buttercream

Add $3/4$ cup cocoa powder along with powdered sugar. Follow recipe as directed.

NOTE

If the buttercream is too thick, don't panic; just add more milk until it reaches the consistency you desire.

Crunchy Chocolate Chip Cookies

This recipe was a complete accident. I was attempting to make a chewy chocolate chip cookie and failed miserably. The resulting cookies were not chewy, they were totally crispy . . . crispy and delicious! A good chocolate chip cookie is never a failure.

Dry Ingredients

$1^1/4$ cups white rice flour

$^1/2$ cup sweet rice flour

$^1/2$ cup cornstarch

$^1/2$ teaspoon baking soda

$^1/2$ teaspoon salt

Wet Ingredients

$^3/4$ cup (12 tablespoons) unsalted butter, melted

1 cup dark brown sugar, packed

$^1/2$ cup granulated sugar

1 large egg

1 egg yolk

2 teaspoons pure vanilla extract

1 bag (12 ounces) chocolate chips

1. Adjust oven rack to the middle position and preheat the oven to 325°F. Line 2 rimmed baking sheets with parchment paper.

2. In a small bowl, whisk together the dry ingredients. In a large bowl with a handheld mixer or in the bowl of a stand mixer, mix together the wet ingredients on low speed until smooth.

3. Turn off the mixer and add the dry ingredients. Turn mixer on to medium speed and blend until a dough forms. Turn off mixer and add the chocolate chips. Turn mixer to low and blend until just combined.

4. Drop the dough onto the prepared baking sheet, about 2 teaspoons for each cookie. Space cookies about 2 inches apart.

5. Bake for 15 to 18 minutes, until golden brown. Remove the pan from the oven and allow the cookies to cool on the pan for 2 minutes, then transfer cookies to a wire rack to cool completely.

6. Repeat with remaining dough. Placed in an airtight container, these cookies will keep for about 5 days. Wrapped tightly in plastic, they can be frozen for up to 1 month.

Makes about 3 dozen cookies

Peanut Butter Cookies

Since this recipe is a gluten-free adaptation of the classic, crispy peanut butter cookies my mom made when I was little, I anxiously awaited her review. Thankfully, she loved them!

You can use either white or brown rice flour for these cookies. Brown rice flour gives them a nuttier flavor.

Dry Ingredients

$1^1/4$ cups white or brown rice flour

$3/4$ cup cornstarch

2 teaspoons baking powder

$1/2$ teaspoon salt

$1/4$ teaspoon xanthan gum

Wet Ingredients

1 cup dark brown sugar

$1/2$ cup (8 tablespoons) unsalted butter, at room temperature

$1/2$ cup creamy peanut butter

2 large eggs

2 teaspoons pure vanilla extract

Granulated sugar, for rolling

1. Adjust oven rack to the middle position and preheat the oven to 350°F. Line 2 rimmed baking sheets with parchment paper.

2. In a small bowl, whisk together the dry ingredients. In a large bowl with a handheld mixer or in the bowl of a stand mixer, cream together the brown sugar, butter, and peanut butter until a thick paste forms, about 45 seconds. Use medium speed on a stand mixer; medium-high speed on a handheld mixer.

3. Add the eggs one at a time, mixing well between each addition. Once eggs are fully incorporated, turn off the mixer and scrape down the sides and bottom of the bowl. Add the vanilla extract and mix for an additional 30 seconds.

4. Turn off the mixer and add the dry ingredients. Turn the mixer on to medium speed. Blend until the dough comes together.

5. Shape the dough into balls of about 1 tablespoon each. Roll the dough in granulated sugar and place on prepared baking sheet, spacing the cookies about 2 inches apart. Flatten the dough with a fork. If you want, make a crisscross pattern on the top of the cookie with the tines of the fork.

6. Bake for 10 to 12 minutes, until golden brown. Remove the pan from the oven and allow the cookies to cool on the pan for 2 minutes, then transfer cookies to a wire rack to cool completely.

7. Repeat with the remaining dough. Placed in an airtight container, these cookies will keep for about 5 days. Wrapped tightly in plastic, they can be frozen for up to 1 month.

Makes about 3 dozen cookies

Sugar Cookies

Don't ask me to choose between sugar cookies and chocolate chip cookies! I can't decide which cookie I like more. I guess it depends on my mood and the time I have to make the cookies. This dough needs to be chilled before you roll and cut the cookies; chilling helps them keep their shape.

Also helping them keep their shape is the shortening. If you prefer, you can replace the shortening with butter. But when made with butter, these cookies will spread.

Dry Ingredients

$1^1/4$ cups white rice flour, plus more for rolling

$1/2$ cup cornstarch

$1/4$ cup sweet rice flour

$1^1/2$ teaspoons baking powder

$1/4$ teaspoon salt

$1/4$ teaspoon xanthan gum

Wet Ingredients

$2/3$ cup vegetable shortening

$3/4$ cup granulated sugar

1 large egg

4 teaspoons milk

1 teaspoon pure vanilla extract

1. In a medium bowl, whisk together the dry ingredients.

2. In a large bowl with a handheld mixer or in the bowl of a stand mixer, cream together the shortening and sugar on medium-high speed until a thick, fluffy paste forms. Add the egg and blend until the egg is thoroughly incorporated.

3. Turn off the mixer and add the dry ingredients. Turn the mixer on at medium speed and blend to combine. The dough will look dry. Add the milk and vanilla extract. Mix until the dough comes together, about 1 minute.

4. Turn the dough out onto the counter. Pat into a circle. Cut dough in half with a sharp knife. Wrap each half in plastic wrap and refrigerate for at least 1 hour or up to 12 hours.

5. Adjust oven rack to the middle position and preheat the oven to 350°F. Line 2 rimmed baking sheets with parchment paper.

6. Sprinkle the counter lightly with white rice flour. Roll out one of the dough pieces to $1/4$-inch thick. Cut the dough into shapes with a cutter. Place cookies on prepared baking sheet. Gather the scraps together, reroll, and cut more cookies.

7. Bake the cookies until the edges are lightly golden brown. The baking time will vary depending on the size of your cookies. My 3-inch cookies took about 12 minutes. Keep your eye on the first batch of cookies to help

you with the timing. Remove the pan from the oven and allow the cookies to cool on the pan for 2 minutes, then transfer cookies to a wire rack to cool completely.

8. Repeat with the other half of the dough. Placed in an airtight container, these cookies will keep for about 5 days. Wrapped tightly in plastic, they can be frozen for up to 1 month.

Makes about 2 dozen cookies, 3 inches across; the yield will vary depending on the size of the cutter you use.

NOTE

This recipe makes a small batch of cookies, about 2 dozen. If you want to make more cookies, double or triple the recipe. (If you are going to triple the recipe, make it in a stand mixer. A triple recipe will be too big for a handheld mixer to chug through!)

Baking Cookies

Although I like to bake one pan of cookies at a time, I always line two pans with parchment paper. As soon as one pan comes out of the oven, the second pan is loaded with cookie dough and ready to go into the oven. You don't want to put dough onto a hot pan. Allow hot pans to cool before putting dough on them.

Oatmeal-Raisin Cookies

Chocolate chip, sugar, and oatmeal-raisin cookies make up my cookie trinity. They have a special place in my cookie-loving heart. No other cookie, no matter how delicious, can compete with them. This oatmeal-raisin cookie, made with brown sugar and ground cinnamon, tastes like an oatmeal cookie should: delicious.

Dry Ingredients

1 cup white rice flour

$1/2$ cup sweet rice flour

$1/4$ cup cornstarch

1 teaspoon baking powder

$1/2$ teaspoon ground cinnamon

$1/4$ teaspoon baking soda

Wet Ingredients

$3/4$ cup (12 tablespoons) unsalted butter, at room temperature

$1^1/4$ cups dark brown sugar

1 large egg

1 teaspoon pure vanilla extract

2 cups gluten-free rolled oats

1 cup raisins

1. Adjust oven rack to the middle position and preheat the oven to 375ºF. Line 2 rimmed baking sheets with parchment paper.

2. In a small bowl, whisk together the dry ingredients. In a large bowl, beat the butter and brown sugar together until a thick, fluffy paste forms, about 1 minute. (Use medium speed on a stand mixer; medium-high on a handheld mixer.) Add the egg and vanilla extract. Mix until the egg is thoroughly incorporated.

3. Turn off the mixer. Add the dry ingredients. Turn the mixer back on to medium speed and mix until a dough forms. Turn off the mixer again. Add the oats and raisins. Mix on low speed until thoroughly incorporated.

4. Drop the dough onto the prepared baking sheet, about 2 teaspoons for each cookie. Space the cookies about 2 inches apart.

5. Bake for 10 to 12 minutes, until edges are brown. Remove the pan from the oven and allow the cookies to cool on the pan for 2 minutes, then transfer cookies to a wire rack to cool completely.

6. Repeat with the remaing dough. Placed in an airtight container, these cookies will keep for about 1 week. Wrapped tightly in plastic, they can be frozen for up to 1 month.

Makes about 3 dozen cookies

Brownies

Sometimes there is nothing better than a brownie. In addition to eating them out of hand, I also like to cut brownies into little cubes and freeze them. Then, when I feel like being decadent but lazy, I tumble the brownie cubes over vanilla ice cream. If I am feeling really decadent, I'll pour some caramel or chocolate sauce over the whole affair for a brownie sundae.

Gluten-free nonstick cooking spray

Dry Ingredients

1 cup cocoa powder (natural or Dutch-process)

$^3/4$ cup white rice flour

$^1/2$ cup sweet rice flour

1 teaspoon salt

$^1/2$ teaspoon baking powder

Wet Ingredients

$^1/2$ cup (8 tablespoons) unsalted butter, melted

$1^3/4$ cups granulated sugar

4 large eggs

1. Adjust oven rack to the middle position and preheat the oven to 325°F. Grease a 13 by 9-inch baking pan with nonstick cooking spray.

2. In a medium bowl, whisk together the dry ingredients. You can do this by hand or with an electric mixer.

3. In a small bowl, whisk together the butter and sugar until smooth (mixture will still be grainy). Add the eggs, whisking until smooth. Pour the wet ingredients over the dry and mix until a batter forms. Pour the batter into the prepared pan. Spread the batter evenly with the back of the spoon.

4. Bake for 35 minutes, or until brownies are set and a knife inserted into the center comes out clean.

5. Place the pan on a wire rack to cool to room temperature. When cool, cut brownies into rectangles. Wrapped tightly with plastic wrap, these brownies will keep for about 4 days at room temperature or about 1 month frozen.

Makes 15 brownies

Rustic Pies

I love pie. And these pretty rustic pies are one of the easiest ways to make one. Once you've let your crust chill for several hours, simply roll it out, pile a seasonal filing in the center, and fold the crust over the center. That's it!

Crust

Dry Ingredients

1 cup white rice flour, plus more for rolling

$1/4$ cup sweet rice flour

$1/4$ cup tapioca starch

2 tablespoons granulated sugar

$3/4$ teaspoon salt

Wet Ingredients

$1/2$ cup (8 tablespoons) unsalted butter, chilled and diced small

3 tablespoons vegetable shortening, chilled

$1/4$ cup ice water

Sugar, for sprinkling

Fruit filling (see next page)

1. To make the crust, in a food processor, combine dry ingredients. Pulse to combine. (If you don't have a food processor, whisk ingredients together in a large bowl.) Add the butter and shortening. Pulse to combine until no large pieces of butter or shortening remain and mixture looks coarse. (If making by hand, cut in the butter or shortening with a pastry cutter.) Add water. Run food processor until the dough comes together. (Stir together with a wooden spoon.)

2. Sprinkle the counter lightly with white rice flour. Turn the dough out onto the counter and pat it into a disk. Wrap tightly in plastic wrap. Chill at least 2 hours or up to 12 hours.

3. When you are ready to assemble and bake the pie, adjust oven rack to the middle position and preheat the oven to 425°F. Remove dough from refrigerator. Allow it to sit at room temperature for 10 minutes.

4. Place the dough on a $16^1/2$ by $12^1/2$-inch piece of parchment paper. Generously sprinkle the dough with white rice flour. Roll the dough into a 13-inch circle. Carefully slide parchment and dough onto a rimmed baking sheet.

(continued)

5. To prepare your choice of filling, in a large bowl, stir the fruit and cornstarch together with a wooden spoon. Be sure fruit is lightly dusted with cornstarch. Add the sugar, lemon juice or vanilla extract, and ground cinnamon, if using. Stir to combine.

6. Pile the filling onto the center of crust, leaving a 4-inch border around the filling. Fold the dough border up and over the filling; the dough will pleat as you do this. Slide your hand under the paper and lift it to fold the dough onto the filling. The center of the pie remains uncovered. Generously sprinkle sugar on the folded-over top of crust.

7. Bake for 35 minutes, or until the crust is golden brown and the filling is bubbling. Remove pie from the oven and allow to cool slightly in the pan before serving. This pie is best served the day it's made, but wrapped well in plastic wrap, it can be stored overnight at room temperature.

Makes one 9-inch pie

Blueberry Filling

1 pint blueberries, washed and picked over to remove stems

2 teaspoons cornstarch

3 tablespoons granulated sugar, more or less depending on the sweetness of your berries

Apple Filling

2 medium Granny Smith apples, peeled, cored, and cut into thin slices

1 tablespoon cornstarch

3 tablespoons granulated sugar, more or less depending on the sweetness of your fruit

2 tablespoons freshly squeezed lemon juice

$1/2$ teaspoon ground cinnamon

Peach Filling

4 ripe medium peaches, peeled and thinly sliced

2 tablespoons cornstarch

3 tablespoons granulated sugar

1 teaspoon pure vanilla extract

Peach-Blueberry Filling

2 ripe medium peaches, peeled and thinly sliced

$1/2$ pint blueberries, washed and picked over to remove stems

3 tablespoons cornstarch

3 tablespoons granulated sugar

1 tablespoon freshly squeezed lemon juice

Cheesecake Cups

I love cheesecake but making it can be a bit of a pain. Not this one! I can throw a batch of these together before friends join me for dinner. Made with cottage cheese and cream cheese, these cups aren't as heavy as ordinary cheesecake.

8 ounces full-fat cream cheese, at room temperature

1 cup full-fat small curd cottage cheese, at room temperature

$3/4$ cup granulated sugar

2 large eggs

1 teaspoon freshly squeezed lemon juice

1 teaspoon pure vanilla extract

Fresh berries or jam, for serving (optional)

1. Adjust oven rack to the middle position and preheat the oven to 350°F.

2. In a food processor, combine the cream cheese and cottage cheese. Process until smooth. Add the sugar, eggs, lemon juice, and vanilla extract. Blend until smooth. Divide the batter evenly among six ovenproof 6-ounce dessert (custard) cups.

3. Bake for 30 minutes, or until mixture is puffy and does not jiggle.

4. Remove from the oven and place on a wire rack to cool. The custard will collapse as it cools; this is normal.

5. Serve warm or chilled. In the center of the cup, you could put a few berries or a dollop of jam. Wrapped well with plastic wrap, these will keep in the refrigerator for up to 3 days.

Makes 6 servings

Whoopie Pies

My memory of whoopie pies stretches back a long way. When I was in the first grade, I was invited to a friend's house for a play date. (Only I don't think we called them "play dates" then.) Her mom had made a batch of whoopie pies. In my mind's eye, I remember them as the perfect whoopie pie: two dark chocolate cakes sandwiched together with a white, fluffy cream. The thing was, I couldn't eat one! My mom wasn't home and, in the time before cell phones, there was no way to reach her to find out whether or not the treat was safe for my allergies. I remember sitting there as my friend munched through her whoopie pie. My allergy-safe snack, to state the obvious, paled in comparison. With this recipe, I can now safely enjoy whoopie pies whenever I want.

If you only have natural (nonalkalized) cocoa, that will work. The finished cakes just won't be as dark.

Dry Ingredients

1 cup white rice flour

$1/2$ cup sweet rice flour

$1/2$ cup Dutch-process cocoa powder

$1/2$ cup tapioca starch

$1^1/4$ teaspoons baking soda

1 teaspoon salt

$1/2$ teaspoon xanthan gum

Wet Ingredients

$1/2$ cup (8 tablespoons) unsalted butter, at room temperature

1 cup packed dark brown sugar

1 large egg

1 teaspoon pure vanilla extract

1 cup buttermilk

Cream Filling (recipe follows)

1. Adjust oven rack to the middle position and preheat the oven to 350°F. Line 2 rimmed baking sheets with parchment paper.

2. In a small bowl, whisk together the dry ingredients.

3. In a large bowl, beat together the butter and brown sugar until the butter-sugar paste lightens slightly, about 1 minute on medium-high speed in a stand mixer or high speed with a handheld mixer. Add the egg and vanilla extract and mix for 1 minute. Turn off the mixer and scrape sides and bottom of bowl.

4. Add half of the dry ingredients. Mix until combined. Add half of the buttermilk. Mix until smooth. Add the remaining dry ingredients. Mix until combined. Add the remaining buttermilk. Mix the batter for 30 seconds.

(continued)

5. Scoop six $^1/_4$-cup mounds of batter onto the baking sheet. Be sure to space batter several inches apart, as the cakes will spread during baking.

6. Bake for 15 to 18 minutes, until the cakes are set and spring back to the touch.

7. Remove from the oven and place on a wire rack. Allow the cakes to cool on the pan for 2 minutes. Transfer the warm cakes to the wire rack to cool completely.

8. Repeat with the remaining batter. As the cakes cool, make the cream filling.

9. When the cakes are all completely cooled, sandwich them together with the filling. (If the cakes are too warm, the filling will melt. Be sure to wait until the cakes are completely cool.) Wrap tightly with plastic wrap and store at room temperature for up to 3 days. These pies don't freeze well.

Makes 6 large whoopie pies

NOTE

Classic whoopie pies are large. If you'd prefer a smaller treat, simply reduce the size of the scoop of batter and reduce the baking time.

Cream Filling

$^1/_2$ cup (8 tablespoons) unsalted butter, at room temperature

$^1/_4$ cup vegetable shortening

$^3/_4$ cup powdered sugar

1 jar ($7^1/_2$ ounces) marshmallow creme

1 teaspoon pure vanilla extract

• In a medium bowl, cream together the butter and vegetable shortening until light and fluffy. (Use high speed on a handheld mixer or medium-high speed on a stand mixer.) Add the powdered sugar and beat until combined. Add the marshmallow creme and vanilla extract. Mix until fluffy.

Makes enough filling for 6 large whoopie pies

Summer and Fall Fruit Cobblers

In the summer, I make this cobbler with blueberries; in the fall, with apples. I still can't decide which I like best! Usually it's the one I am eating at the time.

Butter, for the baking dish

Blueberry Filling

4 pints blueberries, washed and picked over to remove stems

$3/4$ cup granulated sugar

1 tablespoon cornstarch

2 teaspoons ground cinnamon (optional)

Apple Filling

6 cups peeled, sliced Granny Smith apples (about 5 large apples)

$1/2$ cup granulated sugar

1 tablespoon cornstarch

1 teaspoon ground cinnamon

2 tablespoons freshly squeezed lemon juice

Biscuit Topping

Dry Ingredients

1 cup tapioca starch

$2/3$ cup white rice flour

$1/3$ cup cornstarch

$1/4$ cup granulated sugar

1 tablespoon baking powder

$1/2$ teaspoon salt

Wet Ingredients

6 tablespoons unsalted butter, chilled and diced

$3/4$ cup plus 1 to 2 tablespoons heavy cream, chilled

1. Adjust oven rack to the middle position and preheat the oven to 425°F. Butter a 13 by 9-inch baking dish.

2. To make the filling, in a large bowl, toss together the fruit of your choosing, sugar, cornstarch, ground cinnamon, if using, and lemon juice, if called for. Stir until well combined. Pour the fruit mixture into the prepared dish.

3. To make the biscuit topping, in a large bowl, whisk together the dry ingredients. Add the butter. Using your fingers or a pastry cutter, work the butter into the dry ingredients until no large pieces of butter remain. The mixture

should be coarse, with tiny pebbles of butter distributed throughout. Add the cream. Stir with a wooden spoon until the dough comes together. If the mixture is too crumbly, add additional cream, 1 tablespoon at a time, until the dough can form a ball.

4. Pinch off golf ball-size portions of dough and place on top of the fruit, leaving a little space between the biscuits. (This recipe makes a generous amount of biscuit topping. There won't be much room between biscuit pieces.)

5. Bake for 35 minutes, or until biscuits are golden brown and the filling is bubbling. (Thanks to the cornstarch, the filling will thicken when it boils.) Remove from the oven and place on a wire rack to cool. Cobblers are best served the day they are made. However, they can be covered with plastic wrap and stored in the refrigerator for 1 or 2 days. If stored in the fridge, rewarm slightly in the microwave before eating.

Serves 6

Sources

Gluten-Free Flours and Starches

Arrowhead Mills
Gluten-free buckwheat flour and rice flours
ArrowheadMills.com

Bob's Red Mill
Rice flours, potato starch, tapioca starch, and
xanthan gum.
BobsRedMill.com

Koda Farms
Sweet Rice Flour
KodaFarms.com

Gluten-Free Pasta

Jovial Pasta
Spaghetti and capellini
JovialFoods.com

Tinkyada Pasta
Wide assortment of gluten-free rice pasta,
including penne, elbows, and mini-shells
Tinkyada.com

Spices

Penzey's Spices
Ground chipotle and assorted dried herbs
and spices
Penzeys.com

Pots, Pans, and Other Good Stuff for the Kitchen

All-Clad
Assortment of pots and pans
All-clad.com

Chicago Metallic
Half-sheet (rimmed) pans, loaf pans, and
cake pans
ChicagoMetallicBakeware.com

Confectionery House
Cake pans, baking sheets, cupcake liners, gluten-
free sprinkles, parchment paper, and other fun
stuff for baking
ConfectioneryHouse.com

Cuisinart
Blenders and food processors
Cuisinart.com

Kitchen Aid
Stand and handheld mixers
KitchenAid.com

Le Crueset
Dutch ovens
LeCreuset.com

Lodge Cast Iron
Skillets, Dutch ovens, and grill pans
Lodgemfg.com

Williams-Sonoma

High quality handheld tools, including spatulas, box graters, and knives. Food processors, stand mixers, and handheld mixers.

williams-sonoma.com

Zojirushi

Two pound bread machine

Zojirushi.com

Index

Elizabeth Barbone is the founder of GlutenFreeBaking.com. A graduate of the Culinary Institute of America, she teaches classes on gluten-free baking throughout the country, writes a weekly gluten-free cooking column for SeriousEats.com, and has regular television appearances. She is the author of *Easy Gluten-Free Baking*, a well-loved staple in many gluten-free kitchens. She lives in Troy, NY.

Praise for Easy Gluten-Free Baking and GlutenFreeBaking.com:

"My family just loves your cookbook. I have three celiac children and am always looking for new ideas. No one could even tell that the chocolate cake I made was gluten free!!!"

—Joy B., Minnesota

"Every recipe we have tried has been wonderful. Your cookbook and website have made living gluten free so much easier. Thanks for all your experimenting to make everyday recipes safe for someone who is gluten free. Everything is so yummy."

—Barbara H., New York

"Using your recipes has helped me to never feel deprived. Even my gluten eating kids prefer your recipes over the regular choice most of the time!"

—Jessica P., Pennsylvania

"Love your cookbook and recipes. I make them to share at work and for bake sales and they are always gone quickly. Many are surprised they're gluten free and those of my coworkers who have celiac or are wheat allergic are thrilled to have something they can eat. I always send them to your website and recommend your book to my patients."

—Judith S., New York

"I love your site, thanks so much for all the information and the help living gluten free! Your recipes are the best!"

—Nicole L., Ohio